D1612496

# The Madness of Alexander the Great

Also by Richard A. Gabriel:

*Between Flesh and Steel: Military Medicine From The Middle Ages to the War in Afghanistan* (2013)
*Man and Wound in the Ancient World* (2012)
*Hannibal: The Military Biography of Rome's Greatest Enemy* (2011)
*Philip II of Macedonia: Greater Than Alexander* (2010)
*Thutmose III: Egypt's Greatest Warrior King* (2009)
*Scipio Africanus: Rome's Greatest General* (2008)
*Muhammad: Islam's First Great General* (2007)
*The Warrior's Way: A Treatise on Military Ethics* (2006)
*Soldiers' Lives: Military Life and War in Antiquity: 4,000 BCE to 1453 CE* (2006)
*Jesus The Egyptian: The Origins of Christianity and the Psychology of Christ* (2005)
*Ancient Empires at War*, 3 vols (2005)
*Subotai The Valiant: Genghis Khan's Greatest General* (2004)
*Lion of the Sun* (2003)
*The Military History of Ancient Israel* (2003)
*Great Armies of Antiquity* (2002)
*Sebastian's Cross* (2002)
*Gods Of Our Fathers: The Memory of Egypt in Judaism and Christianity* (2001)
*Warrior Pharaoh* (2001)
*Great Captains of Antiquity* (2000)
*Great Battles of Antiquity* (1994)
*A Short History of War: Evolution of Warfare and Weapons* (1994)
*History of Military Medicine: Ancient Times to the Middle Ages* (1992)
*History of Military Medicine: Renaissance to the Present* (1992)
*From Sumer To Rome: The Military Capabilities of Ancient Armies* (1991)
*The Culture of War: Invention and Early Development* (1990)
*The Painful Field: Psychiatric Dimensions of Modern War* (1988)
*No More Heroes: Madness and Psychiatry in War* (1987)
*The Last Centurion* (French, 1987)
*Military Psychiatry: A Comparative Perspective* (1986)
*Soviet Military Psychiatry* (1986)
*Military Incompetence: Why The US Military Doesn't Win* (1985)
*Operation Peace For Galilee: The Israeli-PLO War in Lebanon* (1985)
*The Antagonists: An Assessment of the Soviet and American Soldier* (1984)
*The Mind of the Soviet Fighting Man* (1984)
*Fighting Armies: NATO and the Warsaw Pact* (1983)
*Fighting Armies: Antagonists of the Middle East* (1983)
*Fighting Armies: Armies of the Third World* (1983)
*To Serve With Honour: A Treatise on Military Ethics* (1982)
*The New Red Legions: An Attitudinal Portrait of the Soviet Soldier* (1980)
*The New Red Legions: A Survey Data Sourcebook* (1980)
*Managers and Gladiators: Directions of Change in the Army* (1978)
*Crisis in Command: Mismanagement in the Army* (1978)
*Ethnic Groups in America* (1978)
*Programme Evaluation: A Social Science Approach* (1978)
*The Ethnic Factor in the Urban Polity* (1973)
*The Environment: Critical Factors in Strategy Development* (1973)

# The Madness of Alexander the Great

## and the Myth of Military Genius

Richard A. Gabriel

Pen & Sword
MILITARY

First published in Great Britain in 2015 by
**PEN & SWORD MILITARY**
an imprint of
Pen & Sword Books Ltd
47 Church Street
Barnsley
South Yorkshire
S70 2AS



ISBN 978-1-78346-197-4



A CIP catalogue record for this book is available from the British Library.



Typeset by Concept, Huddersfield, West Yorkshire, HD4 5JL.
Printed and bound in England by CPI Group (UK) Ltd, Croydon CR0 4YY.

Pen & Sword Books Ltd incorporates the imprints of Pen & Sword Archaeology, Atlas, Aviation, Battleground, Discovery, Family History, History, Maritime, Military, Naval, Politics, Railways, Select, Social History, Transport, True Crime, and Claymore Press, Frontline Books, Leo Cooper, Praetorian Press, Remember When, Seaforth Publishing and Wharncliffe.

For a complete list of Pen & Sword titles please contact
PEN & SWORD BOOKS LIMITED
47 Church Street, Barnsley, South Yorkshire, S70 2AS, England
E-mail: enquiries@pen-and-sword.co.uk
Website: www.pen-and-sword.co.uk

# Contents

## DEDICATION

For my beloved Susan,
who makes my heart sing

and for

Archie Frangoudis
Ray Grenier
Arnie Macalmont
Roger Pritchard
Frank Sousa
All old men now, but once young, when they
answered their country's call to service and war

Thank you

# Introduction

Of all the subjects that have occupied the study of ancient military history, none has done so more than Alexander the Great. An online bibliographic search reveals no fewer than 4,897 books about Alexander and another 16,000 or so published academic journal articles and popular magazine pieces.[1] What strikes one as remarkable is that this outpouring of Alexander scholarship is rooted in only five basic ancient sources, only one of which was written during Alexander's lifetime. There were some twenty other contemporary sources, but only one has survived.

The only source contemporary with Alexander is Nearchus' chronicle of the sea voyage from India to Persia, following Alexander's Indian campaign. It survived because it was incorporated into Arrian's later work. Nearchus was a boyhood friend of Alexander, and his appreciation of Alexander's psychology is worth more serious consideration than it has often been given. The other ancient sources are Diodorus Siculus (80–20 BC), a Sicilian Greek, who devoted one of the forty books of his universal history to the life of Alexander; Quintus Curtius Rufus; the dates of Curtius' life are unknown, and the subject of much debate. He wrote the only history of Alexander in Latin and some say he wrote during the reign of Emperor Claudius (41–54 AD), others attribute his writing to Vespasian's (69–71 AD) reign, and Plutarch (45–120 AD), perhaps the best known of the ancient sources, who provides much of the information about Alexander's youth available to us. Lucius Flavius Arrianus' (Arrian's) work is generally considered to be the more reliable of these 'vulgate' sources because the author drew upon accounts, now lost, written by two of Alexander's senior staff officers, Aristobulus and Ptolemy. As is often the case in studies of ancient history, everyone is dependent upon the same sources.[2]

What we are left with, then, are the *interpretations* of the sources that this or that historian chooses to emphasize. The result is literally thousands of books and articles that offer different perspectives on Alexander and his life. There is, of course, no good reason why this book ought to be different, and it isn't. However, I have been researching and writing books and articles on ancient history for more than forty years, and in the process have examined a good deal (but by no means all!) of the literature on Alexander. Despite the insightful analyses of many classicists, historians, linguists, and others whose works comprise the extant body of literature on Alexander, it strikes me that one of the most basic aspects of Alexander's life has gone largely unexamined.

The most basic and unavoidable fact of Alexander's life was that he spent some thirteen years at war, virtually all his adult life. His very existence was characterized by constant exposure to violence, death, the slaughter of women and children, the destruction of villages and towns, the loss of friends and comrades, and his own exposure to death and wounding. These experiences often left Alexander spattered with the blood, brains, and gore of his victims, for war in ancient times was conducted at very close quarters indeed, and Alexander was an enthusiastic participant in its waging. Alexander was a very different person at the end of his life than he was at the beginning, before he experienced the horrors of war, and was suffering from almost every symptom of what we now call post-traumatic stress disorder.

This book offers an examination of Alexander's personality and war experiences to answer the question of whether Alexander suffered from post-traumatic stress disorder and other psychiatric conditions that can reasonably be explained by his prolonged exposure to war, and to the injuries, physical and psychiatric, he received during that exposure. The focus arises out of my experience as a US Army officer assigned to the Department of Combat Psychiatry at the Walter Reed Army Institute of Research in Washington DC. in the mid-1980s. While there, I became interested in the problem of combat and war related stress of Vietnam veterans. This led to further research, some of it with the Israeli Defence Force, and the publication of two books and several articles on the subject.

While on the faculty of the US Army War College a few years later my research interests shifted to the field of ancient military history, particularly to the subject of military leadership and the great commanders of ancient armies. This emphasis led to the publication of a number of books, including several biographies of the great captains of the ancient world. In the last few years, however, my interests shifted again, this time to the history of military physical and psychiatric medicine as it developed from ancient times to the present. The result has been the publication of my two histories of the subject. I mention all this only to establish that I have some limited expertise in the subject areas that this book addresses.

When the opportunity arose from a British publisher to attempt a work on Alexander, my thinking naturally centred around my previous research. I have attempted to combine my previous areas of research interest in the present book by posing three questions about Alexander that, for the most part, have been largely ignored by other scholars of the subject. Firstly, did Alexander suffer from psychiatric symptoms due to his long exposure to war and, if he did, how did this affect his personality and behaviour? Secondly, were Alexander's wounds as serious as portrayed in the sources, or are they exaggerated accounts, some of which were impossible to have survived given the state of Greek military medicine at the time? An important aspect of the analysis of Alexander's wounds is an investigation of the severe head injury he suffered in 328 BC at Cyropolis. This head injury has gone largely unaddressed by Alexander scholarship even though it is crucial to explaining Alexander's behaviour. Thirdly, compared to other generals of antiquity, was Alexander really a great general as is often supposed, or something quite less? It should be obvious that this book does not purport to present a complete compendium of Alexander's life, but only offers some new perspectives on selected aspects of it, some new ways of thinking about one of military history's most famous subjects.

I wish to acknowledge my debt and appreciation to two researchers whose work rekindled my interest in the subject of combat stress, and serves as the underpinning of my efforts here. Jonathan Shay in his wonderful book, *Achilles in Vietnam: Combat Trauma and the Undoing of Character*, did much to bring the research on combat stress up to date and in greater detail than any work of which I am aware. Shay's comparisons and metaphors drawn from the *Iliad* with modern day psychiatric cases are brilliant, and forced me to reread that great work from a new perspective. I also owe a debt to the work of Lawrence A. Trittle, himself a Vietnam combat infantryman, whose personal experience in war and its attendant suffering are clearly illuminated in his book, *From Melos to My Lai: War and Survival*. Like Shay, Trittle compares the modern experience of combat stress with that reported in ancient texts. He deserves much credit for being the first scholar of whom I am aware to suggest that Alexander may have suffered from post-traumatic stress disorder. While both these fine writers have contributed much to this book, they cannot be held responsible for any errors that might appear in it.

Richard A. Gabriel

# Timeline

| | |
|---|---|
| **356 BC** | (20 July) Birth of Alexander. |
| **344/343** | Alexander tames Bucephalas. |
| **344/341** | Aristotle tutors Alexander. |
| **340/339** | Alexander appointed regent in Philip's absence. |
| **336** | Philip II of Macedonia assassinated. |
| **336–323** | Reign of Alexander the Great. |
| **336** | (summer) Alexander recognized as Philip's successor and head of the League of Corinth. |
| | (October): Alexander's first regnal year begins. |
| **335** | (spring–June) Campaigns in Thrace against Triballi and in Danube region. |
| | (June–August) Campaigns in Illyria. |
| | (early October) Destruction of Thebes. |
| **334** | (spring) Assumes command of Persian expedition; crosses into Asia. |
| | (May) Battle of the Granicus River. |
| | (May–August) Campaigns in Asia Minor; disbands the allied fleet. |
| | (August–September) Siege of Halicarnassus. |
| | (autumn–winter) Campaigns in Caria, Lycia, Pamphylia. |
| **333** | (spring) Phrygia and Gordian knot incident |
| | (summer) To Ancyra, through the Cilician Gates, to Tarsus and Soli. |
| | (November) Battle of Issus in Cilicia. |
| | (December) Parmenion captures Damascus. |
| **332** | (January–July) Siege of Tyre. |
| | (September–November) Siege of Gaza. |
| | (November) Crowned Pharaoh of Egypt. |

**331** (January–March) Founding of Alexandria; consults oracle at Siwan oasis.
(spring) Goes to Tyre.
(July–August) Goes to Thapsacus.
(autumn) Antipater puts down revolt in Greece; defeat Agis III at Megalopolis.
(October 1) Battle of Gaugamela.
(October–December) March through Babylonia and Sittacene to Susa and on to Persepolis.

**330** Campaign in the interior of Iran.
(April–May) Return to Persepolis; burning of royal palace; departure for Media.
(June) Greek allied contingents dismissed at Ecbatana; move to Rhagae (Teheran) and march to the Caspian Gates.
(July) Capture of Darius' body; advance to border of Hyrcania; advance to Zadracarta; begins to act like Persian king; adopts oriental dress.
(August) Moves toward Bactria; diverts to Artacoana (Herat); revolt of Satibarzanes.
(September) Murder of Parmenion; execution of Philotas; trial of Amyntas and his brothers.
(winter) Through land of the Drangaeans and Arimaspes; into Arachosia, through Paropamisadae to the foot of the Hindu Kush.

**330/329** (winter) founding of Alexandria by the Caucasus (near Bagram, Afghanistan).
(spring) Crossing of Hindu Kush, march to Drapsaca (Kunduz) and Bactra; older men and Thessalia volunteers sent home; crossing of Oxus River.
(summer) Capture of Bessus; advance to Marakanda (Samarkand, summer capital of Sogdiana), march to Jaxartes River; founding of Alexandria Eschate (Khodjend); revolt of local Scythian tribesmen and of Sogdians; campaign against Spitamenes.

**329–328** (winter) At Bactra, Alexander received embassies from Scythians and Chorasmians.
(spring) Pacification of Sogdians begins; guerilla war against Massagetae of Turkestan and against Spitamenes.

(late summer) Alexander wounded at Cyropolis. Returns to Marakanda.
(November) Alexander murders Cleitus at Marakanda; Spitamenes killed by Massagetae.

**328/327** Alexander winters at Nautaca.
(spring) Capture of Sogdian Rock and Rock of Chorienes; marries Roxanne, daughter of Oxyartes. Bactria, defeat of last opposition; *proskynesis* episode; pages' conspiracy; arrest and execution of Callisthenes.
(late spring) Departure from Bactria; re-crossing of Hindu Kush; invasion of India begins.

**327/326** Alexander quarters in Assacene (Swat); capture of Massaga and Rock of Aornus; advance to Indus River.

**326** March to Taxila.
(May) Battle of the Hydaspes River against Porus.
(May–June) Halt in Porus' kingdom.
(late June) Advance to the Acesines River and Hyphasis River; mutiny of the army; retreat from the Hyphasis and return to the Hydaspes River; death of Coenus; fleet built.
(November) Journey down the Hydaspes River to the Indian Ocean begins.

**325** Battle with Malli; Alexander wounded.
(July) Pattala (Hyderabad) reached.
(August–November) Approach to march through the Gedrosian desert.
(September) Alexander reaches Oreitae.
(September–October) Nearchus departs with fleet; Alexander marches through Gedrosian desert and reaches Pura.
(mid–December) Nearchus reaches Hormozeia (Hormuz).
(late December) Alexander and Nearchus link-up in Carmania.

**325/324** (winter) Executions of satraps and generals.
(January) Alexander reaches Pasargadae.
(March) Alexander and Nearchus reunite at Susa; mass weddings at Susa; Alexander voyages up the Tigris River.
(June) Mutiny at Opis (Baghdad); banquet of reconciliation.
(August) Nicanor promulgates Alexander's Exiles Decree at Olympic games.

(October) Hephaestion dies at Ecbatana.

**324/323** (winter) Extermination campaign against the Cossean nomads; Alexander in Babylon; Greek envoys acknowledge Alexander's divinity.

(June 10) Alexander dies at Babylon; age 33.

*Chapter 1*

# Alexander's World

The settlement of Macedonia began at the end of the Bronze Age when a people called West Greeks migrated south into Upper Macedonia. They spoke a form of Greek, but also possessed their own Macedonian dialect.[1] By Alexander's day, Macedonian had developed into its own unique language with Thracian influences, and was unintelligible to Greek speakers.[2] By 700 BC there were 'Macedonic' tribes living on the lower plains. Among these were the Arestai, a powerful clan that traced their ancestors to the Argeadai, a family claiming descent from Argead of the Teminid kings of Argos in the Peloponnese, and through them to Heracles himself.[3] By the eighth century BC, the Temenid family had become the royal house of the Macedonian kings. The Temenids sustained an unbroken dynastic lineage from the eighth century until the death of Alexander the Great's son in 312 BC. According to legend, the first of these Macedonian kings, Perdiccas I, followed a herd of wild goats through the mountains to the Macedonian plain where he founded the first city in Macedonia. Perdiccas named the city Aegae (modern Vergina) which means 'goat town'.[4] Aegae became the capital of the country and the sacred burial place of Macedonian kings.

Around 410 BC, King Archelaus transferred the capital to Pella. The new capital was located on the shores of Lake Loudias surrounded by low-lying swampy terrain that made it more defensible from invasion by sea, afforded it access to the Thermaic Gulf, and made communication with the interior easier.[5] Archelaus spent considerable sums on the new capital, and Pella was soon the largest city in Macedonia. Philip II, Alexander's father, converted the lake into a spacious harbour by connecting it to the Axius River by means of an artificial channel permitting direct access to the Thermaic Gulf. The flow of the channel was controlled by artificial gates. This was the first harbour constructed on a river estuary in Europe.[6]

The city was heavily fortified from the beginning, and in Alexander's day the walls were 8km long, longer than the circuit wall of Athens.[7] The walls were constructed of mud brick set upon bases of stone.[8] The city itself was laid out in a regular urban grid with buildings and houses running along its streets. Main roads, 30ft wide, ran east to West and north to south. Two roads connected the city to the artificial harbour. The city had a permanent water source that supplied its many fountains, reservoirs, baths, and sewers. The government compound and palace occupied 15 acres, and was the heart of the Macedonian government, with offices for all financial, military, economic, diplomatic, and administrative activities. The Greek complaint that Macedonians were a primitive people was hardly believable after a Greek diplomat had visited Pella.[9]

The society that the Teminids took over was a transhumant society of pastoralists who moved their herds each season in search of pasture. The social order was divided into pastoral groups, each led by a *tshelniku* or 'chief shepherd'.[10] All land and livestock were held in common, and the *tshelniku* had wide authority to look after the group's welfare. He alone directed the timing and seasonal movements of the group, conducted its internal affairs, and negotiated with outsiders as the only representative of the group. He controlled the group's economic life by decisions regarding when to cut timber, hunt, and slaughter livestock. To protect the group from attack and to enforce his decisions, the *tshelniku* surrounded himself with a group of warrior companions who carried out his orders. In these three elements of the first pastoralists – land owned in common, a powerful chief, and a group of companion warriors to protect the group – 'we see the seeds of the constitutional monarchy that was the mark of the later Macedonian state'.[11]

Another important legacy of Macedonia's pastoral past was the absence of slavery. Unlike the Greeks whose societies rested upon a sub-stratum of slave labour and whose wealthy households might contain as many as fifty slaves, slavery as a formal institution did not exist in Macedonia. Some parts of the population were serfs whose labour could be commandeered, however, and criminals and prisoners were forced to work in the mines. For the most part, however, Macedonian peasants and shepherds tilled their own fields and herded their own animals with their own hands and energy. Women cooked the meals, tended the children, and made the family's clothes. When Alexander the Great entered the Persian capital as conqueror, he was dressed in simple homespun clothes fashioned for him by his sister. There was no royal household to attend the Macedonian king. His wife and relatives performed all the chores of daily life. For most of the king's subjects, Macedonia was a relatively egalitarian society in which all enjoyed the same basic rights.

It was this sense of all subjects being part of the same society and one people and the absence of slavery that made Macedonian cities and towns relatively peaceful places to live. The political purges, executions, factionalism, expropriations of property, and forced exile which so often characterized the political life of the cities of the 'democracies' of the Greek states are noticeably absent from Macedonian history. Curtius says as much when he tells us, 'The Macedones were indeed accustomed to the rule of a king, but they lived in a greater semblance of liberty than any other who were subject to a king.'[12] Macedonian subjects enjoyed greater liberty and freedom from fear than could be found in most Greek city states.

Without a substructure of slaves or foreign peoples living in Macedonian cities or on its farms, Macedonians came to think of themselves as one people, *Macedones*. This sense of belonging to the same societal group had its origins in the pastoral past when everyone was part of the same pastoral group, where everything was held in common, where everyone contributed by working the land or tending animals, and where everyone shared in the life and defence of the society. Occasionally, some new person would be added to the group by marriage or other circumstance, in which case they would be considered a *Macedone*. Over time the Macedonians came to live in cities and towns as well as tending their herds in the mountain pastures. Regardless of where they lived or how they earned their living, the people of Macedonia considered themselves as one people and accepted the rule of the Teminid royal house and its king.

Thus it was that the Macedonians were the first Europeans to develop a sense of national identity defined as being members of a territorial state. To be a *Macedone* came to mean being anyone who lived within the territory over which the king exercised direct authority.[13] As Macedonia expanded, especially under Philip II, each newly acquired territory was regarded as being part of Macedonia itself, and its people regarded as Macedonians. In modern legal parlance, Macedonian 'citizenship' was defined by the doctrine of *ius territoriale* and not *ius sanguinis*. The Macedonian idea of who constituted a *Macedone* was different from the idea of citizenship common in the Greek states. The Greek states were 'citizen states', in that their fully enfranchised persons, whether residing in Attica or in Athenian possessions overseas, were regarded as citizens of their home state. Whenever a Greek state took over other territory by conquest, they planted some citizen-landholders (*klaroukhoi*) on the land, but did not regard the conquered peoples as citizens. Citizenship was limited to residents of the city-state, and no provision was made to accommodate large numbers of new inhabitants to full participation in the polity.

The Macedonian practice of extending the status of kings subject to newly conquered peoples made possible the establishment of the first national territorial state in Europe. When new peoples were absorbed into the realm, the full rights of all *Macedones* were extended to them. The towns and tribes were mostly left to govern themselves, often retaining their own kings or assemblies. Conquered peoples were permitted to practise their own religions, laws, and customs, to speak their own language, and raise their own taxes. Even the military forces of local chieftains were sometimes permitted to remain, but were retrained in the new weapons and doctrines of the Macedonian army, and redefined as the king's militia. Particularly powerful and talented local barons and warriors were invited to come to Pella where they became Companions of the king. Parmenio, Philip's most talented and trusted general and a Pelagonian by birth, was one of these.[14] The Macedonian king remained the ultimate authority on all matters unhindered by local representatives. One tenth of all produce or its cash equivalent was paid annually to the state, and the Macedonians demanded the personal service of segments of the population for use as soldiers or labourers.

Thinking of Macedonia and its acquired territories as one national unit is what permitted Philip II to develop his kingdom along national lines. To this end, he established new cities, transplanted populations to live in them, drained swamps, constructed roads, fortified key passes, and drew military units from specific geographical areas of the kingdom, permitting them to retain their local designations.[15] This is what Alexander meant when he reminded his troops that 'he [Philip] brought you down from the mountains to the plains, making you a match in battle for the neighbouring barbarians, trusting for your salvation no longer in the natural strength of places so much as in your courage. He made you dwellers in cities and graced your lives with good laws and customs.'[16] The effect of Philip's policy was to bring under his command manpower and economic resources greater than those of any Greek state or alliance of states. Philip of Macedonia created the first nation state in the West.

## The Land and Its People

In the fourth century BC, Macedonia was the largest and most fertile area of Greece.[17] Lower Macedonia comprised extensive alluvial plains at the mouths of its two great rivers, the Haliacmon and the Axius, that flowed into the Thermaic Gulf.[18] The Lower Macedonian plain was ringed by hills and mountains, except to the east where the Strymon River formed its natural boundary with Thrace. Along with Thessaly, Lower Macedonia comprised the largest area of alluvial plains on the Hellenic peninsula.[19] West and northwest of Lower Macedonia were the smaller plains and pastures that lay at higher altitudes between the mountain ranges that comprised the cantons of Upper Macedonia. Together, the territories of Upper and Lower Macedonia were able to support a population larger than any of the Greek states or combination of Greek states of the day.[20] Estimates of the country's population during Philip's reign range from 500,000 to 1,000,000 inhabitants.[21]

The plains of Lower Macedonia were well-watered by the country's perennial rivers and streams, producing rich pasture lands ideal for raising horses, cattle, goats, and sheep. The alluvial soil was fertile, and extensive farming produced large harvests of cereal grains that provided the staple diet of the inhabitants and sufficient surplus to serve as a major export crop. The population of peasant farmers lived in the towns, villages, and cities scattered upon the plain. The Macedonian plain was almost devoid of rock, so that the houses and town buildings were constructed of mud brick. Almost all cities and towns of Lower Macedonia were fortified with walls, a necessary means of defence against the frequent raids conducted by the neighbouring tribes and the military expeditions of the Greek city-states.[22]

Upper Macedonia was a very different place. Its population was smaller than on the plains, and life was harder. The economy centred upon the pastoralism of animal husbandry, mostly sheep and goats. The climatic severity of the area forced the transfer of livestock on a seasonal basis from winter to spring pastures. The mobility required by this mode of economic existence made it impossible to establish cities of any size, and the population lived mostly in small hamlets and a few trading towns when not on the move or living in tents with their animals.[23] Alexander described the hard life in Upper Macedonia when he scolded some mutinous army units that had been drawn from the Upper Cantons. 'When Philip took you over you were nomadic and poor, the majority of you clad in skins and grazing sparse herds on the mountains, and putting up a poor fight for them against Illyrians, Triballians, and the neighbouring Thracians. He gave you cloaks to wear instead of skins.'[24]

Not all Macedonians were shepherds or farmers, however. The country possessed large forests of pine and fir. Macedonia was a land of lumberjacks that produced much of the wood for the ships of the Athenian and other navies of the Greek city-states. Macedonia was also rich in metals. Hundreds of mines produced iron and copper, and some of the largest silver and gold mines were found there. It is not surprising that so rich a land became the target of frequent attacks by neighbouring tribes, states, and nomadic peoples seeking access to its resources. Macedonia was the wealthiest area of Greece.

Besides breeding large warhorses, Macedonians did so in larger numbers than anywhere else in Greece except, perhaps, for Thessaly. While elsewhere insufficient pasture and grain supply for horses forced cavalry to remain a secondary arm of Greek armies, cavalry in Macedonia became the primary combat arm of Philip's army. There were hundreds of stud farms in the country, and the nobility prided itself on its horseflesh and horsemanship. It was said that a Macedonian boy could ride before he could walk. Many Greek states had difficulty feeding even their small populations. Athens imported almost half its food, and malnutrition and sporadic famines were not uncommon throughout Greece. Macedonia had sufficient meat and grain for its people, with the result that Macedonians were a large, strong, and healthy people. They were probably the largest people in Greece. They made excellent soldiers, and their ability to endure the rigors of the campaign amazed the Greeks.

**The Macedonian State**

The king and the *Macedones* meeting in Assembly were the only official organs of Macedonian state government. The roots of the Macedonian monarchy reached back to Homeric times. The original kings brought with them a Homeric view of kingship and imposed it upon the native peoples. Over time, however, this concept was modified by elements incorporated from Macedonia's own pastoral past, when the original society of pastoral companies was ruled by the 'chief shepherd' or *tshelniku*, whose position seems to have been largely confined to members of the same family, confirmed from time to time by election of the warriors around him. The powers that the Macedonian king derived from both traditions, Homeric and pastoral, were extensive, although not absolute.

The Homeric idea that the king was descended from the gods and embodied their favour was central to the Macedonian king's legitimacy. This embodiment was seen to reside in the person of the king who passed it on to his male heirs. Macedonian kings were always chosen from within the same bloodline, if not from the same immediate family. By Alexander's time, the Teminid dynasty had ruled Macedonia for more than three centuries, and Alexander himself was its direct heir. In some instances, the infant son of the previous king was anointed while a regent ruled until the child was old enough to assume his rightful position. For a Macedonian king to be legitimate, however, required that the *Macedones* meeting in Assembly consent to his appointment by formal election, a practice rooted in the pastoral past when the warriors around the 'chief shepherd' were required to consent to a new chief. The central obligation of the Macedonian king, like that of the ancient *tshelniku*, was to attend to the religious and material welfare of his people.

As in the old pastoral system when the goods of the company were held in common, the Macedonian king claimed all the material goods of the country as his own. In practice, this meant that he disposed of all lands and products of the land, mines, and stands of timber for shipbuilding that were not already taken, with the obligation to use them for the good of his people. Any 'spear-won' land outside the country proper also fell to his ownership, and might be used as he saw fit. This arrangement made Philip the wealthiest king in all Greece, and he had few limits on how to use his wealth. The king awarded fiefs to important Companions and allies, and gave grants of land to captured populations who were resettled in Macedonia. In other cases, he settled Macedonians on conquered lands, turning once foreign lands and cities into Macedonian territories. The income from taxes, custom duties, the sale of horses, and the output of the gold and silver mines, was used to pay the army well, and military service became a full-time profession at which a man could earn a proper living. This transformed the former militia into a professional army. The king paid for the equipment of his infantry, but required the cavalry to purchase their own horses, often from his own stud farms. Philip's great wealth made it possible for him to maintain large numbers of men and animals under arms year-round, something no other Greek state could afford to do.

For all this, however, the Macedonian king was by no means an absolute monarch, and his authority was limited by the *Macedones* who met in Assembly to discuss and advise the king on important matters.[25] The Assembly of *Macedones* was the embodiment of the Macedonian people, and was comprised of serving soldiers and recent veterans of the king's Army, what Aristotle called 'the citizens in arms'. The military composition of the Assembly reveals its origins in the group of professional warriors that surrounded the *tshelniku* and protected the people during pastoral times. These two institutions, the monarchy and the Assembly, were the only formal organs of state government. It had been the king and his warriors who had created the Macedonian state, and it was they who remained responsible for protecting it.

The egalitarian atmosphere that commonly attends any assembly of warriors was evident in the meetings of the Assembly. Aristotle noted that the Assembly met 'under arms'; that is with its members in full military kit with their weapons handy. Each *Macedone* was entitled to speak, and the Macedonians prided themselves on what Curtius calls their 'equal rights of speech'. If a speaker addressed the king, he removed his helmet as a sign of respect, but spoke freely and without fear. The king had only his single vote in a debate, the same as any other *Macedone*. While Greek was the official administrative language of Macedonia, the proceedings of the Assembly were conducted in Macedonian, as a sign of military camaraderie and informality. The Assembly was a gathering of soldiers, of comrades in arms, of equals bearing the same risks and hardships in defence and protection of their people. One's standing therein was assigned not by birth or wealth, but by one's demonstrated courage on the battlefield. It was with his comrades' help and advice that the king governed Macedonia.

The Assembly did not sit permanently or even regularly as in other Greek states, but was convened by the king or his representative if the king was on campaign whenever important issues had to be discussed and decided.[26] These included questions dealing with relations with other states, treaties, requests made by foreign governments, religious matters, payments of debts, and reports regarding finances. The Assembly had the responsibility of electing a new king and, if necessary, choosing a guardian for him. It also heard trials in cases of treason, and could sentence a person to death. Sometimes the sentence was carried out on the spot by members of the Assembly themselves, executing the condemned with javelins and spears.

Governing the Macedonian state and fighting its wars required more than an Assembly of warriors that met only when important issues arose, however. To govern effectively, the king needed advice and expertise on a more regular basis. For this he turned to his Companions. The Companions were a group of the king's most trusted advisors and military commanders upon whom he relied for frank advice and expertise. The institution had its earliest roots in Homeric times when Achilles was said to have had his most trusted companions around him. But the institution also had roots in the Macedonian pastoral past when a smaller group of advisors (*parea*) was selected from the warriors to advise the *tshelniku* in carrying out the affairs of the group.[27] During Alexander's day, there were three types of Companions: the *hetairoi* or companions, the *philoi* or friends, and the *hegemones* or military commanders. This latter comprised the unit commanders of the field army. The Companions were not comprised of only military men, but included others that the king thought valuable to have around him. When Philip incorporated the Upper Cantons into Macedonia proper he disbanded their local aristocracies, but made their most important nobles Companions. Others included a number of renowned mercenary officers.

Although the Companions were an important part of the government, they had no constitutional or formal status. They were chosen by the king from among those he thought could best serve him in time of war or in administering the state, and there were no restrictions upon whom he might choose. The position did not pass from father to son, and the favour of the king could be withdrawn at any time, and with it a person's status as a Companion. There had never been a feudal landed nobility in Macedonia, and the Companions did not constitute a landed feudal class like that found in Medieval Europe. They had no institutional, property or independent power base from which to resist the king, and were not in command of any element of the polity like militia troops or independent cavalry units raised by their own efforts.[28] They were a military nobility, and on the field of battle the Companions were the king's best combat commanders, his elite cavalry, and his bodyguards whom he relied upon for his life.

In most important respects Macedonia was a military state. Its army was larger than any in Greece, and its complexity approached that of a modern military force. The country itself was far-flung and economically diverse, conditions that required competent administration to function effectively and to provide the resources needed by the army. There was, too, the need to provide the army with competent combat leaders and generals to fight the battles and win the wars. The Macedonians turned to a traditional institution, the Royal Page School, to identify, train, and develop new leaders.

The Royal Page School existed long before Alexander, perhaps from as early as the fifth century BC.[29] In earlier times it had been the primary means for educating the royal princes, the sons of allied tribal chiefs, and Macedonian nobles. The school still served these purposes in Alexander's day, but was expanded to become the primary educational and military training school for the sons of the king's Companions, other important friends, and foreign allied nobles.

Located in Pella, the school served as the Macedonian West Point. It was a boarding school and required a four year demanding curriculum of study and military training for successful graduation. Cadets entered at age 14, and moved through the curriculum in class years as in modern military schools, finally graduating at age 18. Each class was comprised of about 50 students, so that there were some 200 enrolled at any one time.[30] The usual Greek liberal educational curriculum was taught, and we might suspect some emphasis was placed upon reading the many treatises of Greek military history that had appeared since the end of the Peloponnesian war. It was expected that the sons of the nobility and the royal princes attend the school. Part of their education was military socialization and bonding, learning to associate with the sons of the other Companions who, when their time came, would be their own Companions in the service of the country.

Besides the formal liberal Greek education, the students were put through rigorous military training. Rough living, hunger, endurance training, hunting wild animals with spears, riding, weapons drill, and other experiences central to Macedonian military training were required of all, including the royal princes. Senior cadets were permitted access to the king. They served as night guards when he slept, were allowed to sit at his table, and looked after the king's horses. Discipline was strict, and breaches were punished by caning, which the king himself sometimes administered. It was said that Philip once beat a student to death for failing to carry out a military order.[31]

Senior cadets, those aged 18 in their last year at the academy, accompanied the king on campaign as his bodyguard, where some of them fell in battle protecting their sovereign. If we are to believe Justin, some of Philip's 'many sons' had been killed in battle this way. The Page School was the training ground for Macedonia's future combat officers and administrators, and Aristotle called it 'a school for generals'. These leaders made Macedonia a large, wealthy, and well-managed state that remained a major economic and political force in Greece and the Eastern Mediterranean until it was dismantled by the Romans after the battle of Pydna in 168 BC.[32]

To organize and staff his infantry forces, Philip established the universal training of all suitable boys in the cities of Macedonia, where they entered the local militia to be trained as light infantry. The best of these militia were selected for advanced training in the heavy-armed phalanx infantry. Given that Philip went to great pains to put the infantry on equal footing with the elite cavalry, it is likely that the period of infantry training from militia to phalanx infantryman may well have lasted for four years, the same as the Page School cadets who went on to join the Companion cavalry.

## A Homeric Culture

To understand Alexander, it is necessary to understand the culture that shaped him. In almost all aspects of cultural life, Macedonia was regarded by the Greeks as a geographic backwater, inhabited by semi-savage barbarians who spoke an uncouth form of language, were governed by primitive political institutions, whose customs, social values, and sexual practices bordered on the unspeakably depraved, who were untrustworthy, dressed in bear pelts, drank their wine without mixing it with water, and were given to regular bouts of incest, murder, and regicide. To the degree that Greeks thought about Macedonia at all, it was from the perspective of snobbish and self-satisfied contempt. Neither Greeks nor Macedonians considered Macedonians to be Greek at all.

Most Alexander historians have treated Alexander as a Greek, so much so that it is commonly assumed by many that Alexander *was* a Greek. In fact, Alexander was not a Greek, and nothing in the accounts of his life suggest that he was fond of Greek culture, values, or habits. Alexander's father was Macedonian and his mother was Illyrian. Neither the Macedonian nor Illyrian people nor their languages were Hellenic in origin, and the languages they spoke were mutually unintelligible with Greek. The language of the Macedonian court, Assembly, and the army was Macedonian, not Greek.

Alexander's famous tutor, Aristotle, although a Greek, was raised from childhood in the Macedonian court where his father was physician to King Amyntas. It was here that he became a boyhood friend of Philip. Aristotle surely spoke Macedonian as well as Greek, and there is no reason to suspect that when he tutored young Alexander he did not do so in Macedonian. As for Alexander's supposed love of Greek culture, he did not import Greek culture to Persia, but instead 'went native' and adopted Persian dress and customs. Alexander massacred Greeks with the same abandon with which he massacred Persians, Afghans, and Indians, including the wholesale extermination of a Greek colony in Persia that welcomed him with open arms as a fellow Greek. The Greeks certainly did not consider Alexander a Greek, and more Greeks fought against him as mercenaries than with him.[33]

Owing to Macedonia's geographic and linguistic isolation from mainland Greece and the peculiar circumstances of its historical development, Macedonian society retained a number of practices and values that were Homeric in origin, form, and function. Where the Greeks regarded the city-state as an expression of advanced political culture, Macedonia remained a land of powerful clans and tribes held together by the bonds of warrior-hood, dynastic bloodlines, and a powerful monarchy. In many ways the Macedonia of Alexander's day very much resembled the society of the Mycenaean age, a male-dominated warrior society that had long since died out in Greece proper. Alexander's world was a world of clan warrior barons where the *Iliad* was not just an ancient heroic tale, but reflected how men lived. Their king was akin to Agamemnon, first among equals, the bravest and most able warrior, chieftain and protector of his people, the Mycenaean *wanax*, maintaining his authority over powerful and fierce warriors by personal example and a lineage of royal blood derived from the gods.

A Macedonian king ruled only so long as his barons respected and feared him, his position legitimized by his dynastic lineage and his reputation for bravery. The king sat among his barons as first among equals, the fiercest of them all, and could be removed by the will of the Assembly. The Macedonian king wore the same clothes, the purple cloak and broad brimmed hat of the Macedonian aristocrat, and wore no royal insignia upon his person to set him apart. Philip dressed in clothes of simple homespun fashioned by his wife. The king ate the same food as his troops. There were no household slaves to wait upon him at table as in the households of the Greek democracies.

Among themselves, and especially when the king addressed his soldiers and officers or in the Assembly, they spoke Macedonian.[34] When hearing cases brought by common subjects or in discussions with his barons in the

Assembly, the king was called like anyone else only by his name, his patronymic, and his ethnic, without any honourific or title. Philip was called Philippos Amyntou Makedonios or simply Philippos Makedonios, but not king.[35] In all his years, Philip never described himself as king in any of his official documents or public statements.[36] In the ancient sources, Alexander is always addressed by Macedonians by name, never his title. The only requirement when addressing the king in the Assembly was that the speaker remove his helmet. Among his troops the king was addressed as 'fellow soldier'.[37] In every cultural sense, the king was a Macedonian Agamemnon.

A warrior culture requires values, rituals, and ceremonies to define it, and the values of Alexander's Macedonia were starkly similar to those of the *Iliad*, in particular the value placed on the cult of the heroic personality. The highest social values were power, glory (*kydos*), and excellence (*arete*), and warriors were expected to demonstrate their bravery for the sake of honour (*time*) and reputation among fellow warriors. The noblest of all soldiers was the warrior king fighting in the defence of his people, and the appropriate arena of competition for reputation and honour was war, conquest, and performance on the field of battle.[38]

A number of rituals and practices in Alexander's Macedonia lend some credence to the Greek slur of barbarism, however. War dances were a common Macedonian ritual. Alexander's uncle, Alexander II, was murdered during one of these performances. Witches, too, abounded. Alexander's mother, Olympias, was said to be a witch who worshipped snakes, and to have had the quaint habit of taking the reptiles to her bed! One of the more ancient Homeric practices was the Macedonian ritual of purifying the army as it set out for war. Priests cleaved a female dog in two, and the army marched between the severed halves to bless the soldiers.[39] The king was the chief priest of the Macedonians, and sacrificed daily for the protection of his people.

The all-male, violent, warrior culture of Philip's Macedonia required men to prove their bravery at a young age. A man who had not yet killed a wild boar single-handedly with a spear and without a net was not permitted to recline at table and eat meat with fellow warriors. He had to sit upright for all to notice.[40] The boar hunt had its origins in Greek mythology when one of Heracles' Twelve Labours required him to slay the Erymanthian Boar as punishment for killing his wife in a fit of rage. The Macedonians considered themselves descendants of Hercules, and the single-handed killing of a boar became a rite of passage for all young warriors to prove their manhood. The wild north European boar is a very dangerous and aggressive animal, averaging 50–72 inches in length, 36–40 inches at the shoulder, weighing 160–300 pounds, and armed with long sharp tusks. To kill a boar without a net tossed over the animal to immobilize it, and to do so with only a spear was not a task for the fainthearted.

In yet another Homeric ritual, a young man was not considered a warrior until he had slain an adversary in battle. Macedonian youths who had not yet killed a man were required to wear a cord around their waists to mark them as un-blooded. Only when he had slain his first victim was the cord removed, and the young warrior permitted to join the ranks of other warriors. This, then, was the world of Alexander's youth, a loud clamorous male world of rough soldiers who rode, drank, fought, fornicated, and did battle with the same rude energy and enthusiasm. It was not a place for the timid.

As a royal prince Alexander attended the *symposia*, the all-male eating and drinking bouts where tales of bravery, war, killing, and one's sexual exploits were expounded by drunken storytellers. Macedonian kings frequently entertained their friends and officers at these gatherings in much the same way a modern colonel might entertain his officers at the mess in wartime. Macedonians were prodigious drinkers, and the Greeks thought them barbarians because they did not follow the Greek custom of diluting their wine with water. This, of course, made it easier for the *symposia* to degenerate into drunken brawls. It was at just such an event that Alexander almost got himself killed when he got into a violent argument with his father at Philip's wedding to a new wife. Philip drew his sword and attacked his son. Fortunately for Alexander, Philip was so drunk that he fell down before he could reach his target, and Alexander escaped unharmed. Unlike Greek *symposia* that were seen as intellectual meetings where women were not permitted, the Macedonians regularly were entertained by female courtesans, dancers, musicians and other entertainers of various talents.[41] Not surprisingly in a warrior culture, the sexual conquest of women and the procreative powers of the males were held in high regard and, no doubt, the subject of much male braggadocio.

The Homeric nature of Alexander's Macedonia was nowhere more evident than in the manner in which his father was interred. Philip's funeral ceremonies were strongly similar to those of Patroclus and other heroes portrayed in the *Iliad*. Philip's body was cremated in a wood fire, hot enough to destroy the flesh but not the bones.[42] The bones were retrieved from the ashes and carefully washed in wine before being wrapped in purple cloth and laid in a gold box (*larnax*), then placed in a vault covered with a mound of earth (*tumulus*). As in Patroclos' funeral, horses were sacrificed and their remains left atop the grave mound to decay. The body of Philip's assassin was hung on a cross above the grave for all to see, before it was cut down and cast into the sea, the traditional punishment for those who had committed the sacrilege of killing a king. Two others implicated in the crime, Heromenes and Arrhabaeus, were executed at the site of the grave, and their corpses allowed to rot on top of it.[43] Philip's funeral rites were those of the kings of the Homeric Age as Alexander's would have been had his body not been hijacked by Ptolemy and taken to Egypt.

Of all the ancient Greek accounts disparaging Macedonians, none are more distorted and propagandistic than those dealing with the wives of the royal family. These accounts accused Macedonian wives of being common prostitutes, practitioners of incest, murderers of their husbands, adulteresses, conspirators in assassination plots, and roasting babies alive. And these are the outrages claimed to have been committed by only *one* of Philip's wives, Olympias! The disrepute in which Greeks held Macedonian royal women was rooted in the Greek cultural prejudice that the polygamy practiced from ancient times by Macedonian kings was little more than promiscuity, and that their wives were but royal prostitutes.[44]

The nature and purpose of marriage in antiquity and in Macedonia in particular was not the amorous or sexual satisfaction of the bride and groom. Its primary purpose was the production of children, especially so in a royal family where producing an heir was of paramount importance. Beyond this, Macedonian kings married for political reasons, that is, as a means of forging alliances or guaranteeing treaties.[45] Alexander's father had at least seven and, most likely, eight wives, all of them a consequence of state policy that required assurances of alliances or treaties. If diplomatic marriages were to serve as an effective means of conducting international diplomacy, it was obvious to Macedonians that a king would require more than one wife.

The most important reason for polygamy in the Macedonian royal house, however, was the need for heirs. The ancient world was a lethal place, and having enough children to ensure that at least one of the males survived to occupy the throne was the surest way to increase the odds that a king could pass on his realm to his son. In Alexander's time, the average life span was only thirty-eight years, and 49–50 per cent of the children died before five years of age.[46] Of a hundred children born, half died before age five. Of the fifty survivors, twenty-seven died before age twenty-five; of the twenty-two survivors, nine died by age thirty-five; of the eleven remaining, only six lived to age fifty. Beyond that, only three of the original hundred births lived to see the age of sixty.[47] Under these circumstances, polygamy was almost a statistical necessity if a Macedonian king was to have a realistic chance of producing a surviving heir.

Polygamy permitted a king to marry younger women, giving him access to women of child-bearing age throughout his lifetime. The king increased his chances further by taking concubines and occasional lovers, a custom, no doubt, to the liking of Alexander's father who was an unrepentant womanizer. Unlike the Pharaohs who designated one of their wives as Chief Wife, thus signifying that her son would be the likely heir, Macedonian royal wives possessed no such status. All of the king's children, whether by his wives or lovers, were regarded as legitimate heirs, but only children born of royal wives were officially recorded.[48] Justin tells us that 'Philip had many sons, all recognized by royal tradition'.[49] All sons of the king had an equal claim on the throne until the king himself designated an heir from among them and the selection was approved by the Assembly. The Assembly usually approved the king's choice of the oldest male heir, but there was no fixed rule to this effect. There were a number of instances in Macedonian history where the Assembly chose another heir. Philip himself was chosen in this manner, replacing the 5-year-old Amyntas IV who had succeeded his father, Perdiccas III, after he was killed in battle.

This, then, was the world into which Alexander was born, raised, and expected to live as an adult. One would expect, *ab initio*, the strong cultural influences of Homeric Macedonia to exert a profound influence on Alexander's psychology and actions, that he would be a man of his times, deeply rooted in the ethos of Macedonian society, especially its warrior ethos. It comes as a bit of surprise to discover that this was not the case, and that Alexander, from his earliest days, was a man outside his culture in many respects and, in other respects, marginalized by it. It was not the Homeric culture of Macedonia that shaped Alexander's psychology as much as it was his inability to adjust to it.

*Chapter 2*

# The Young Alexander

It is curious that we should know so little about the youth and upbringing of someone as famous as Alexander. Except for a few lines in Diodorus and Justin, only Plutarch's few pages about Alexander's youth have come down to us. Even Plutarch says little about Alexander's crucial teenage years, when Alexander would have been expected to demonstrate the personal qualities and achievements required of a young Macedonian warrior, especially one who was heir to the throne. The near silence on Alexander's education, military training, combat experience, and his relations with the Macedonian elite that commanded the army is suspicious.

It is surprising that ancient historians found it appropriate to include events that occurred when Alexander was a mere child, and yet not include events in the years from then until Alexander's temporary regency when he was 17, or his performance at the battle of Chaeronea when he was 18, or the years after that until Philip was assassinated. The years when we would have expected the historians to record and emphasize Alexander's manly pursuits as a Macedonian warrior are strangely silent. One reason may be that Alexander was not raised as a typical Macedonian warrior prince, but may have grown up somewhat removed from the usual Macedonian warrior culture in a number of important respects.

What is intriguing about Alexander's early life is that he seems not to have accomplished some of the things required of every young Macedonian warrior. There is no evidence of his having hunted and killed a wild boar, for example, the most basic rite of passage of the young warrior, and one that we would surely expect to have been celebrated had it occurred. Nor do we hear anything about Alexander's 'first kill' in combat, another very important achievement for every young Macedonian warrior. Indeed, until he had done so, no warrior could 'sit at meat' with other warriors, and had to wear a conspicuous coloured cord around his waist.[1] There is no evidence of Alexander having been to war until he led a minor expedition against a rebellious Thracian tribe when serving as temporary regent at age 17 while his father was away engaged in his Thracian campaign. Even here, we hear nothing of Alexander's first kill, and there is no evidence that there was even a battle.

The historians' silence on such important events raises the suspicion that Alexander might not have accomplished the tests of a warrior at the usual age, although he might have done so later, perhaps after becoming king. Macedonians expected their kings to be physically capable, competent warriors, and leaders in war. That is why they expected an heir to slay a wild boar early in life, and to slay a man in battle before he became an adult. In the Macedonian view, preparing for leadership entailed participation in real and dangerous events, not set-piece exercises, as tests of one's ability.[2] These tests entailed the heir's exposure to genuine battle, as was the norm for Royal Page School cadets who served as the king's bodyguard on the battlefield. Alexander seems not to have met any of these tests as a young man.

Alexander's education was also atypical for a Macedonian noble, especially for a warrior prince. When Alexander was 14, the age at which he would normally have been enrolled in the Royal Page School for military training, he was sent from the court at Pella to Mieza, a small settlement three miles from the capital, to a school that had been established by Aristotle for Alexander's tutoring. Much is often made of the fact that Alexander was educated by the famous philosopher. But Aristotle was not then the famous person he was to become in the eyes of medieval and modern scholars. He had just been denied appointment to head Plato's academy, and had not yet written any of the philosophical treatises that would later define his fame. Aristotle was a boyhood friend of Philip's, the son of King Amyntas' court physician, who spent much of his childhood at the Macedonian court. Aristotle spent the next three years tutoring Alexander at Mieza.

Alexander's curriculum was typical of the education of the Greek, but not Macedonian, nobility. Alexander received his early boyhood education under the tutelage of Leonidas, a relative of Alexander's mother, Olympias. The gymnasium curriculum was supervised by *didaskalos*, instructors who taught javelineering, hand-to-hand combat, and bowman ship. But the Greek curriculum stressed listening to lectures, taking notes, reading, and writing on subjects offered by one's tutor. Music and drawing were taught, not to actually perform these arts, but to gain an appreciation for them.[3] Alexander read the plays of Euripides, Sophocles, and Aeschylus, and received the usual grounding in geometry, astronomy, and medicine. Alexander's best subject seems to have been eristics, that branch of rhetoric that taught arguing a point from either side with equal facility.[4] To ordinary Macedonians, however, 'a man ready to speak pro and con was clearly a false person who proved that he was a good liar,' and no less a person than Isocrates wrote Alexander warning him to this effect.[5]

Gymnastic exercise and physical conditioning were included in the curriculum, but even as a young man Alexander had little use for athletic competitions and exercises. Nor did he encourage them when he was king. Alexander learned to play the lyre and sing at Mieza, both common pursuits of the Athenians, but not Macedonians. Philip thought these talents effeminate, and criticized Alexander for doing both.[6] Aristotle's curriculum was Greek, not Macedonian, and neglected the teaching of military subjects like military history, tactics, and strategy that were emphasized at the Page School. Nor did it stress the development of Macedonian military values and habits like courage in battle, fearlessness, and endurance, subjects that the later Roman curriculum stressed. Alexander's education, then, was not typical for the sons of the Macedonian warrior nobility.

Little of Alexander's education at Mieza did much to prepare him to be a warrior king. It has been suggested that Alexander's love of the *Iliad* and his carrying the book with him on campaign was where Alexander obtained his education in military subjects. It is from the *Iliad* that Alexander is said to have acquired his thirst for glory and his imitation of Achilles as his role model.[7] Certainly the *Iliad* was Aristotle's favourite book, but not because it was a manual from which to learn war. Aristotle valued the book for its literary organization and narrow focus, as the perfect example of epic literary form, not for its treatment of war and heroics.[8]

Although it describes sixty ways in which a soldier might be slain on the battlefield, the *Iliad* is not primarily about the glory of war or individual heroism.[9] The *Iliad* is about the 'wrath of Achilles', who, in his own words, has become 'a nobody' when Agamemnon takes one of Achilles' captive girls (the beautiful Briseis whom Achilles came to genuinely love), for himself. Achilles fought at Troy not because he had a quarrel with the Trojans, but to soothe his wrath at the loss of his status and regain it in his own eyes.[10] Alexander would have learned little about the techniques and tactics of Macedonian warfare from the *Iliad*, whose narrative conveys a style of war that had been dead for more than 700 years before Alexander was born. With regard to Achilles, perhaps it was Alexander's own fear of becoming 'a nobody' that drew him to Achilles and, later, to try and redeem himself through military prowess.

It is often believed that it was at Mieza that Alexander formed a circle of close friends that later became his key advisors and generals. Depending upon which historian one consults, the friends who supposedly studied with Alexander include Ptolemy, Hephaestion, Cassander, Alexander Marysas, and Leonatus.[11] It is important to note that there is no direct evidence that *any* of these individuals were with Alexander at Mieza.[12] Alexander's stay at Mieza corresponds roughly to the time when Macedonian youths usually attended the Royal Page School. Some of Alexander's friends, notably Ptolemy, Alexander Marysas, and, perhaps, Hephaestion were a bit older than Alexander, and there is evidence that at least Ptolemy, Marsyas, and Hephaestion were at the Page School during the time that Alexander was at Mieza.[13] It is most likely that Cassander, the son of Antipater, one of Philip's two great cavalry generals, also attended the Page School. All these men were Alexander's *syntrophoi*, that is boyhood friends, probably thrown together at court because of their fathers' status and presence there. There is, however, no reason to believe that these boys were given an exclusive education at Mieza with Alexander as a consequence. Their demonstrated military talent and accomplishments later in Alexander's service suggest strongly that they acquired military training at the Royal Page School.

It is most interesting that Alexander does not appear to have attended the Royal Page School. An important function of the School was to afford young warriors, especially royal princes, the opportunity to form strong bonds of comradeship, trust, and loyalty among their fellow nobles who would later serve with them in war. This was singularly important for a royal prince since a lack of trust, respect, and confidence in a royal commander could quickly lead to mutiny in the field or, worse, the collapse of centralized control at home.[14] Military training also afforded the young prince the opportunity to demonstrate his military competence before his peers and, equally important, before the senior officers and staff who actually ran the Macedonian army. By not attending the academy, Alexander lost the opportunity to form a cadre of trusted military peers and friends.

His absence also removed him from interaction with the old generals who wielded considerable influence in the army. The consequence was that when Alexander assumed command of the Macedonian army after Philip's assassination, he was almost completely unknown as a soldier to his senior commanders, his peers, and his troops. The only senior officer who seems to have known Alexander well was Antipater, who mentored him when he was regent.

It was only after Philip's death that Alexander recalled the friends he had known since boyhood that Philip had exiled and who had military training, and whom he thought he could trust.[15] Alexander had only limited exposure to combat before becoming king. When Alexander was 17, his father appointed him temporary regent under the careful eye of Antipater. While Philip campaigned in Perinthus and Scythia (340–339 BC), Alexander mounted a small expedition against the Maedi, a tribe living on the upper Strymon River. Using Macedonian militia units, he put down the revolt, and established 'a city' (probably only a small fortified outpost) and named it after himself

(Alexandroupolis).[16] We have only Diodorus for Alexander's combat experience at Chaeronea. While it is often assumed that Alexander commanded 'the cavalry' in the battle, in fact no ancient source mentions Alexander as the cavalry commander, although Diodorus implies it, but does not expressly say so. He tells us that Philip placed Alexander on the left flank with the cavalry, but 'stationed alongside him his most important commanders,' i.e., Parmenio and Antipater, keeping the inexperienced Alexander on a short leash.[17]

Diodorus tells us that 'Alexander and his men were the first to force their way through' the enemy line.[18] But this may mean only that Alexander commanded one of the many wedge-shaped cavalry squadrons that struck all along the line, creating gaps for the remaining cavalry to burst through.[19] No source records that Alexander killed his first man in battle at Chaeronea, although he surely should have. Given the importance that Macedonians placed upon this rite of passage, its absence is startling. Many of Alexander's officers had served with Philip for more than twenty years, were veterans of numerous battles, had been wounded, and had killed men up close. When Alexander assumed command of the army, it is unlikely that his minimal combat experience would have impressed them.

But if, as seems likely, Alexander was not afforded the military training required of a royal prince, the question remains, why was this the case? One reason may have been that Philip intended to command the Persian expedition himself, and may have intended to leave Alexander behind as regent, again under the watchful eye of Antipater, who was not given a major command in the Persian expedition. This afforded the benefit of protecting the two heirs, Alexander and Philip's new son, Karanos, to the Argead dynasty if Philip were killed.[20] We have the list of commanders who comprised the invasion force. It is notable that they are all Philip's men, and there is no command reserved for Alexander.[21]

It may have been that Philip decided to continue with his plan to produce an heir with his new Macedonian wife, Cleopatra, carry out the Persian expedition, and return to Pella to live a long life, passing the throne eventually to his new fully Macedonian son.[22] At 46, Philip seemed to be in the prime of his life. He had just fathered a second child with Cleopatra, still possessed all his teeth, and his father had lived beyond the age of 80.[23] Philip might have seen little need to ensure that Alexander was trained in the military skills necessary to govern Macedonia because Philip intended to do it himself. Alexander may have been correct in his fear that Philip had decided to replace him as heir to the throne.

Alexander's education, military training, and combat experience stand in marked contrast to Philip's before he became king. Philip was sent to Thebes (*ca.*368 BC) at the age of 15 as part of a guarantee for a settlement imposed by Thebes upon the warring factions of a dynastic dispute in Macedonia. It is likely that Philip was regarded by the Thebans as another Macedonian in need of civilizing. Diodorus records, however, that Philip eagerly took to his learning. His tutor was Lysis of Tarentum, a Pythagorean. It would be difficult to imagine a much less willing convert to a creed requiring pacifism, vegetarianism, and total abstinence than young Philip![24]

Philip lived with Pammenes, a skilled general and close friend of the great Epaminondas, the victor of Leuctra and regarded as the best tactician in all Greece. Philip also made the acquaintance of Pelopidas, the commander of the famous Sacred Band and an excellent cavalry general as well. Philip was an eager student of war, and applied himself diligently to the lessons taught by his hosts. He had opportunity to observe the drills of the Sacred Band, where he learned the importance of disciplined infantry, unit cohesion, and *esprit de corps*. The Sacred Band became the model for his own elite corps of infantry. From watching the Theban cavalry in its practice drills Philip came to appreciate the need for cavalry to fight as units instead of as small tribal bands or as individuals, as was the common Macedonian method. He learned there was no substitute for a professional officer corps trained in common tactical drills. Only professionally skilled officers could carry out the coordination of cavalry and infantry that was characteristic of Theban tactics, and later became the hallmark of Philip's tactics. Philip learned, too, that meticulous staff planning supported by accurate intelligence lay behind tactical success.[25]

Greek education placed an emphasis upon reading, and in Thebes Philip had access to Pammenes' library that contained the classic military treatises of the Greek world. The Persian and Peloponnesian wars had led to the publication of a number of works on military training and tactics that were available to Philip. Of those, only a few have come down to us. It is likely that Philip read Thucydides' *History of the Peloponnesian Wars*, Herodotus' *Histories* and the accounts of the Persian wars, and possibly some of the works by Xenophon, including *On Horsemanship*, *The Cavalry Commander*, and the *Anabasis*. It would be difficult to imagine where Philip might have obtained a better military education than when he was a hostage at Thebes.[26]

Philip was 18 when he returned to Pella in 365 BC. His brother, King Perdiccas, appointed him provincial governor in the Amhaxitis region, an area of great strategic importance for defending the country from raids by Paeonians, Thracians, and Athenians landing troops on the Macedonian coast. Philip also had the responsibility to raise and train militia. The region's terrain lent itself more to cavalry than infantry, and it was here that Philip equipped his cavalry with the longer 9ft lance (*xyston*) to give it an advantage over the shorter 6ft spears and javelins used by Greek and tribal cavalry.[27] It is also likely that Philip fought a number of skirmishes with local invaders, although we cannot be certain. Four years later, Philip was a major troop commander in the battle with the Illyrians in which the Macedonian army was destroyed and his brother killed. Two years later, 357 BC, at the age of 23, Philip became king of Macedonia.

Even Alexander's physical appearance seemed to set him apart from the Macedonian warrior culture. The Macedonians were a big people, the result of good nutrition from the plentiful supplies of meat and grain their land produced. The men were tall, robust, dark-skinned, had thick cropped hair, and wore beards. Not so Alexander. Alexander stood only about 5ft 2in tall. His hair was blond and tousled, and it is said that he wore it long to 'resemble a lion's mane'. He was fair skinned and went about clean-shaven. Theopompus tells us that in Macedonia, men who 'continue to be close-shaven and smooth-skinned' were thought to be effeminate.[28] Alexander's eyes were odd, one being gray-blue and the other dark brown. His teeth were sharply pointed 'like little pegs'. Alexander's voice was high-pitched and 'tended toward harshness when he was excited'. He was given to scurrying about in a fast and nervous gait, and carried his head to the left, either out of some physical defect (torticolis) or mere affectation.[29] Plutarch says Alexander had a 'melting eye', probably implying a physical condition in which one eye was always partially closed due to some nervous disorder or childhood injury.[30] Peter Green suggests 'there was something almost girlish about his earlier portraits, a hint of leashed hysteria'.[31] Alexander's appearance and demeanour would have struck a Macedonian soldier as decidedly effeminate. When Hannibal replaced his slain father as commander of the Carthaginian army in Spain, Livy tells us that the troops could easily see Hamilcar in the son.[32] Alexander's appearance was so unlike that of Philip, that it was rumoured that he was not Philip's son at all, but the result of Olympias' infidelity, the precise charge that Philip levied against Olympias when Philip took his new Macedonian wife.

Then there is the subject of Alexander's homosexuality. The apologias of Tarn and others that Alexander's sexual habits were within the mainstream of Macedonian sexuality are not credible, and are based on the false equation of Athenian mores regarding homosexuality with the more conservative mores of the Macedonians.[33] In Athens, sexual contact between men and boys was accepted as a part of 'mentoring'. Even in Athens, however, long-term sexual relationships between adult men were frowned upon because they were thought to render the participants effeminate.[34] Athenians used the term *kinados* to mean homosexual, a term that translates as 'he who provides the shame'.

In Macedonia, man-boy sexual contacts were seen as more of an occasional fashion, and long-term sexual relationships between male adults were regarded negatively by a society that stressed manliness, bravery in war, the sexual conquest of women, and the fathering of children as indicators of manhood. Macedonian society was far less tolerant of homosexuality than Athens, although its practice, even among soldiers, was evident enough. Theopompus tells us that soldiers who were homosexuals 'might justly be supposed them to be not companions but whores, and one might not have called them soldiers but harlots. For although they were men-slayers, by nature they were men-sodomizers.'[35]

Alexander's sexual proclivities seem obvious enough to the modern eye. Philip and Olympias began to worry early on about their son's 'almost girlish' appearance and his apparent lack of heterosexual interests. Theophrastus says they feared that Alexander might be turning into a *gynnis* or a 'womanish-man', implying homosexuality and effeminacy. Olympias went so far as to procure a Thessalian courtesan named Callixeina to 'help develop his manly nature'.[36] The effort was not successful, however, and Plutarch tells us that Alexander 'did not know any woman before he married other than Barsine' (when he was 24), a Persian noblewoman with whom Alexander had a five-year relationship that supposedly resulted in the birth of his first son, Heracles.[37] One can only wonder if it was Alexander's sexual proclivities that caused Philip not to send him to the Royal Page School.

It is commonly assumed that Alexander may have begun his homosexual activities with his friend, Hephaestion, sometime in their teens, although there is no ancient source that directly charges that Hephaestion and Alexander were lovers.[38] Yet, Alexander seems to have continued an open sexual relationship with Hephaestion throughout his adult life. Athenaeus, a Greek anthologist (200 AD) claims that his reading of the sources in his day suggests that 'Alexander was insanely fond of boys'.[39] Plutarch tells us that two of Alexander's generals, Philoxenus and Hagnon, sent Alexander letters offering to purchase young boys for him. Although Plutarch reports that the offer angered Alexander, for two senior generals to suggest that they send Alexander young boys clearly implies that Alexander's sexual preferences were well known in the army.[40]

Alexander seems to have had sexual relationships with at least four males: Hephaestion; Bagoas, the notorious Persian male prostitute; Excipinos, a page who caught Alexander's eye; and Hector, a boy who may have been the son of someone at court named Parmenion, that Alexander acquired after Hephaestion's death, and who later drowned.[41] Alexander also had sexual relations with four wives: Barsine, the daughter of the Persian noble

Artabazus; Roxane, the captive Bactrian noblewoman who gave birth to his heir, Alexander IV; Stateira, the eldest daughter of the dead Persian king, Darius III; and Parysatis, the youngest daughter of the former Persian king, Artaxerxes III Ochus. It is generally conceded that all these marriages were pursued primarily for political purposes in much the same manner as Philip had done and a military-diplomatic purpose can be easily advanced in the case of each of the unions.[42]

Although Alexander had other male lovers over the years, he retained Hephaestion as his long-term lover to the end. When Hephaestion died at Ectabana in 324 BC, Arrian tells us that Alexander's grief was so great that 'he flung himself upon the body of his friend and lay there nearly all day long in tears, and refused to be parted from him until he was dragged away by force by his Companions; and again, that he lay stretched upon the corpse all day and the whole night too'.[43] After Alexander arranged for Hephaestion's funeral, he led the army against a people called the Cossaeans. He spent forty days attacking village after village in a murderous rage.[44]

In many respects, then, Alexander was not a typical Macedonian warrior, and shortly after he ascended the throne following Philip's murder, it is likely that everyone knew it, especially the senior officer corps of the army. Alexander may have thought that his senior officers regarded him as an untested adolescent which, indeed, he was. Even Alexander's claim to the throne was tenuous. He was only one of Philip's three surviving sons of which we are aware, and Justin tells us that there were others when he says that 'Philip had many sons ... all recognized by royal tradition ... but some of these died in war, by accident, or of natural causes'.[45] Alexander himself criticized Philip for having so many sons by so many women. In Macedonian practice, any son fathered by the king, legitimate or illegitimate, had an equal claim to the throne. At least one of Philip's other sons by a concubine, Karanos, was killed by Alexander as a rival for the throne.[46]

The sons of other branches of the royal family also had legitimate claims. Alexander's mother's status as one of Philip's wives conferred no special priority to Alexander's claim, and Alexander had no constituency at court or in the army to support his claim. It was Antipater, the only one of Philip's senior officers who had formed a close relationship with Alexander when Alexander was acting regent, who quickly called the Macedonian Assembly into session after Philip's death, and convinced them to proclaim Alexander king. In Macedonian tradition, it was the army as representatives of the people who conferred kingship by their vote. The successful vote was possible only because the proponents of more powerful branches of the royal family, Attalus and Parmenio, were not present, both being occupied with the advance invasion force in Ionia. Thus it was that the untested and little-known Alexander became king of the *Macedones*.

It is not difficult to imagine that Alexander lacked confidence in his ability to gain the respect of and lead an army of combat veterans. He had little personal military experience, and with little technical knowledge of military affairs, had no alternative but to rely upon his more experienced generals and their staffs for advice and guidance. There was also the question of how his manliness and sexual practices were perceived by his seniors and peers. Alexander took no trouble to conceal his homosexual activities. But it was not Alexander's homosexuality that may have produced his rage, but the rejection and isolation that it engendered in the minds of his officers and troops. Alexander may have spent much of his life thinking that his officers thought little of him as a warrior captain, and he may have desperately desired to be accepted as one of them by doing what warriors do, that is, fighting battles and killing people.[47] Perhaps this is why Alexander seemed later to delight in atrocity and slaughter.

The relationship between the Macedonian officer corps and the king was open and democratic in that a soldier's standing was based upon demonstrated courage on the battlefield and not upon birth or wealth. The king was first among equals, and every soldier had 'an equal right to speech', as Curtius tells us. Macedonian kings had no formal title, were called only by their first name, and wore no formal attire or special insignia of rank. One is struck by the lack of use of royal titles in the accounts of Alexander's conversations with his officers and men. One need not wonder, then, why, when Alexander appeared before his officers wearing the white robes, jewelled slippers, and upright tiara of the Persian king, his officers disapproved so strongly.

Macedonian officers were expected to speak openly and without fear, and criticism of Alexander's plans and his personal behaviour was frequent and frank. Eumenes, for example, had the temerity to criticize Alexander's inattention to affairs of state because Alexander 'was too fascinated by Hephaestion's thighs!'[48] The historical texts offer several accounts in which Alexander's officers criticized his military plans and his behaviour, criticism that Alexander took personally. These criticisms were often made publically in the drinking bouts that Alexander frequently attended. To compete with his officers, big men with years of experience at these drinking parties, Alexander often drank far more than his smaller frame could tolerate until, at last, he became an alcoholic.

Insecure adolescents do not take criticism lightly, and Alexander certainly did not. Alexander's desire to win his officers' confidence in his abilities and to be accepted by his warrior comrades seemed constantly thwarted, if only in his own mind, by the frequent disagreements and criticisms of his decisions by his staff and senior officers. He may also have suspected that they disapproved of his homosexual activities. His resentment grew into a suppressed rage that found explosive expression in massacre, murder, torture, and disfigurement whenever his will was thwarted. Alexander grew to hate his Macedonian critics, and eventually had them murdered.

Alexander's lack of military experience may have been what prompted the senior military staff to order a military expedition against the Thracian tribes only a year after Philip's death. The Macedonian army was a professional standing army, and its long experience in combat required no additional training or exercises to get it up to speed for the Persian expedition. Some units were already deployed forward for the invasion of Persia, and the rest were undergoing training and preparations for movement to the combat theatre. Moreover, Philip's plan always called for Antipater to remain behind in command of a large force to keep order in Greece and on the borders. It was Alexander, not the army, who needed practical experience in operational command, and to be introduced to the army. Above all, the senior commanders had to determine if they could place their confidence in the young and militarily inexperienced king. A small expedition against largely defenceless tribal opponents was just the thing to accomplish this.[49]

The notion that Alexander was securing Macedonia's borders with these raids before marching off to Persia is not credible. The tribes presented no such threat, and Alexander's 'Illyrian campaign' amounted to little more than a modest scale training exercise,[50] in which the army demonstrated stock manoeuvres and capabilities – battlefield marching manoeuvres, night marches, river crossings, coordinated infantry and cavalry attacks, logistic support, and long range strategic marches – all first introduced to the Macedonian army by Philip.[51] The 'campaign' was little more than a field exercise, in which Alexander's attack on the Getae was 'a gratuitous act of terrorism on a helpless people'.[52] Alexander's presence nonetheless allowed the new king, heretofore unknown to the army, to introduce himself to the troops and its commanders for the first time.[53]

A central fact of Alexander's life is that he grew up in the shadow of his father. If ever there was a father whose son would have difficulty emulating, it was Philip. Philip II of Macedonia (382–336 BC), dynastic heir to the Agead kings who traced their lineage to Heracles, son of the Temenid family from Argos that had ruled Macedonia since the eighth century BC, unifier of Greece, author of Greece's first federal constitution, creator of the first national state in Europe, the first general of the Greek imperial age, founder of Europe's first great land empire, and Greece's greatest general, was one of the preeminent statesmen of the ancient world. Philip saved Macedonia from disintegration, military occupation, and destruction by securing it against external enemies, bringing into existence an entirely new form of political organization in the West, Europe's first national territorial state. Having made Macedonia safe, Philip developed mining, agriculture, urbanization, trade, commerce, and Hellenic culture to transform a semi-feudal, tribal pastoral society into a centralized national state governed by a powerful monarchy and protected by a modern army.

Philip achieved this over a twenty-three year reign marked by a programme of territorial expansion and military conquest, in the process creating a Macedonian army that revolutionized warfare in Greece and became the most effective fighting force the Western world had yet seen. Through shrewd statecraft and military force, Philip doubled the size of Macedonia and incorporated most of the Balkans into the Macedonian state. He overpowered the Greek city states, uniting them for the first time in history in a federal constitutional order under his political leadership, and directing them toward the larger strategic vision of conquering Persia. He fought over twenty battles and sieges, winning all but one, was wounded five times, and was the greatest strategic and tactical mind in all Greece.[54] If ever there was a Macedonian warrior hero, it was Philip.

Only a few instances of conversations between Philip and Alexander have come down to us, and except for the obviously false story of Alexander taming Bucephalas at the age of 8, all of the conversations involve harsh criticisms by the father of his son.[55] Aeschines reports that when Alexander entertained an Athenian delegation by playing the lyre, Philip asked Alexander whether or not he was ashamed to play so well, 'for a king, it is surely enough if he can find time to hear others play.'[56] In what may be another version of the same incident, Philip is recorded as 'hearing in his son's sweet-toned voice a trace of effeminacy. Philip rebuked him, saying that he should be ashamed to sing so well. Alexander never sang again; the insult was too deep.'[57] It was no secret that Philip regarded the Athenian nobility's habit of playing the lyre as effeminate. When Alexander went to study with Aristotle, his father urged him to study hard and pay attention to his teachers. Alexander responded by criticizing Philip for 'having children by other women beside his wife'.[58] Here we see a young Alexander already worried that his father may have produced a future competitor for his claim to the throne. Philip did little to soothe the boy's fears. 'Well then, if you have many competitors for the kingdom, prove yourself honourable and good, so that you may obtain the kingdom not because of me, but because of yourself.'[59] Philip's criticisms of his young son were not designed to reduce Alexander's insecurity as to his own manliness or future.

In another incident, Philip had advised the teenage Alexander to cultivate friends among the Macedonian nobility.[60] When Philip received a report that Alexander was trying to secure the friendship of some Macedonians by bribes, he strongly rebuked the young man's naivety with the comment, 'What on earth gave you the deluded idea that you would ever make faithful friends out of those whose affections you had bought?'[61] In 336 BC, Alexander found himself caught up in what became known as the Pixodrus affair in which he foolishly offered to marry the daughter of a Carian king.[62] When Philip discovered Alexander's proposal, he was furious and exiled Alexander's close friends, Ptolemy, Nearchus, Erigyius of Mytilene, and Laomedon. Plutarch tells us that Philip 'bitterly reviled his son as ignoble and unworthy of his high estate, in that he desired to become the son-in-law of a barbarian king'.[63] Philip was astounded at his heir's lack of political skill.

Alexander's insecurity is further evident in Plutarch's tale about how Alexander, by now almost 18, reacted to news of his father's victories. Plutarch says that instead of rejoicing, 'he would tell his companions that his father would anticipate everything, and leave him and them no opportunities of performing great and illustrious actions ... he esteemed all that he should receive from his father as diminution and prevention of his own future achievements.'[64] When Philip took a new Macedonian wife, Alexander's worst fears that he would be replaced by one of his father's other sons seemed realized. The incident at Philip's wedding feast where Philip drew his sword and attacked Alexander in defence of Attalus' toast that the marriage would bring a son of truly Macedonian blood, was the final straw. Alexander and his mother fled into exile. Alexander was now completely isolated, with no friends at court, perhaps save Antipater, and no allies in the army.

Once he had assumed the throne after Philip's murder, Alexander had his cousin, his half-brothers, his step-sisters, and their entire families put to death. He ordered the execution of Philip's new wife and her young child, as well as her extended family, to include Attalus, her guardian and a well-known general. Justin records that 'when he (Alexander) set out to the Persian War, he put to death all his step-mother's relations whom Philip had advanced to any high dignity, or appointed to any command. Nor did he spare such of his own kinsmen as seemed qualified to fill the throne lest any occasion for rebellion should be left in Macedonia during his absence'.[65] This was murderous behaviour indeed for a young man who had not shown any propensity for violence at all during his young life and, perhaps, had not yet even slain a man in battle.

The victims were all important dynastic players, and the speed with which the murders were carried out suggests the work of an experienced hand, someone who understood the nature of the dynastic threats that might emerge against Alexander if left unchecked. Only two people possessed the ability to plan and carry out the executions: Eumenes of Cardia, Philip's long time trusted intelligence chief, who continued in his post under Alexander, and Antipater, the wily old general, Alexander's friend, and the only person who had influence in the army to secure its loyalty to Alexander. Alexander probably gave the order for the killings, but it is likely he did so at the urging of Eumenes and/or Antipater, who made Alexander aware of the necessity for the murders if he was to keep his throne.

Alexander had been mostly removed, and then politically isolated, from the life and conspiracies of the Macedonian court for most of his teenage years, and there is no evidence that he had yet developed the keen sense for murderous conspiracy that he would later demonstrate. His young life was not exposed to the dynastic violence and wars that had marked Philip's adolescence. But suddenly Alexander was given a crash course in violent dynastic politics at the hands of one or two experienced conspirators. Alexander now had blood on his hands, and seems never to have fully trusted anyone again.[66]

There are a number of studies that describe Alexander's personality, most of which are summed up in N.G.L. Hammond's description:

> The facets of Alexander's personality include his deep affections, his strong emotions, his reckless courage, his brilliance and quickness of mind, his intellectual curiosity, his love of glory, his competitive spirit, his acceptance of every challenge, his generosity and his compassion; and on the other hand his overweening ambition, his remorseless will, his passionate indulgence in unrestrained emotion, his inexorable persistence, and his readiness to kill in combat, in passion, and in cold blood, and to have rebellious communities destroyed.[67]

One might easily add paranoia, alcoholism, inability to trust, and megalomania to Hammond's list.[68] Hammond's description of Alexander's personality is generally correct, however, as far as it goes. What is intriguing is that few of these traits are evident in Alexander's early life. To be sure Alexander's early life was quite different from what we would have expected from a Macedonian warrior who was heir to the throne. But very little, if anything, of that life seems to have presaged the emergence of the traits suggested by Hammond. What he describes is *what Alexander became by the end of his life.*

It is not surprising that adolescents change as they become adults. Biology itself dictates such changes. The human brain is not fully developed in most males until at least 22 years of age. And although the human personality is likely to be shaped by some objective factors, they are by no means completely determinative of adult behaviour. What, then, made Alexander become what he was as an adult? The answer has much to do with his exposure to war from late adolescence until his death at the age of 33.

*Chapter 3*

# Alexander's Wounds

Alexander is the greatest heroic figure represented in Greek and Roman literature, and we hear of no other person's wounds as much as we hear of Alexander's. But the Alexander we read about is much more a literary creation of Greek and Roman authors than he is an historical personality. Alexander became the protagonist of legend almost immediately after his death, and much of what the ancient sources have left us is based upon 'official versions' of events.[1] Most accounts of Alexander's life portray him as a warrior hero motivated by the search for fame and glory in war. But Alexander did not die a warrior's death in battle; he died in bed of disease aggravated by his overuse of alcohol.[2] Without a glorious death to celebrate, ancient historians may have exaggerated his wounds as indicators of his 'reckless bravery' when in fact most of his wounds were neither serious nor suffered while doing extraordinary things. The ancient sources record that Alexander suffered seven wounds, some of them life threatening. If these wounds are examined from a medical perspective, however, it appears that there is significant exaggeration, if not outright fabrication, in some of their descriptions. Alexander's war record may be somewhat less than it often appears to be.[3]

Macedonia was a nation of warriors, and battle scars were the best evidence of one's bravery. When the army mutinied at Opis (Baghdad) and refused to continue campaigning, Alexander challenged his men and officers by offering to show them his battle scars. 'Who of you has toiled more for me than I have suffered for him? Come now – if you are wounded, strip and show your wounds, and I will show mine. There is no part of my body but my back which has not a scar; not a weapon a man may grasp or fling the mark of which I do not carry upon me.'[4] In fact, almost all Alexander's soldiers, certainly the senior officers and non commissioned officers who had fought with Philip for longer than Alexander had been alive, had seen more combat and likely bore more battle scars than Alexander. No one called Alexander's bluff, however, and he retired to his tent.

To assess Alexander's wounds, it is helpful to know how he was protected on the battlefield. Whether fighting on horseback or on foot, Alexander never fought alone. On foot, he was always accompanied by a seven-man bodyguard (*somatophylakes*) chosen for their loyalty and bravery in battle. Standing in front of him at all times was his shield bearer, whose task it was to use the shield to deflect arrows and javelins fired in the direction of the king. When mounted, Alexander always fought with the Royal Squadron around him, acting as a screen against attacks. Whether on foot or mounted, the primary task of the king's bodyguard was not to engage the enemy, but to protect the king, even at the cost of their own lives. At the battle of the Granicus River, the commander of the Royal Squadron, Cleitus the Black, saved Alexander's life by chopping the arm off a Persian cavalryman who was about to strike Alexander from behind. Alexander rarely led infantry attacks except during sieges, when he sometimes led his troops through the break in the walls. It is interesting that six of Alexander's wounds were from missiles (arrows and rocks) and only one from a sword, an indication of how difficult it was for an enemy to get close enough to the king to do him harm.

Alexander's helmet, body armour, and other equipment were very effective in keeping him from being wounded. When fighting on foot, Alexander was well protected by his body armour, helmet, leather boots, leg greaves, and shield, and armed with the *kopis* sword. When fighting on horseback, the Macedonian cavalryman's armour was designed to protect more from attack by infantry than by cavalry. Xenophon provides a detailed description of this cavalry armour.[5] An iron breastplate protected the cavalryman's chest and back with some sort of loose fitting collar to protect the neck 'standing up from the breastplate and shaped to the neck ... which if properly made, will cover the rider's face as high as his nose'.

If we take the Alexander Mosaic at Pompeii to be accurate and not an idealization, Alexander wore a *linothorax*, comprised of three layers of overlapping linen plates glued together creating a thickness of about half an inch.[6] Modern tests of this linen armour show it to be almost as effective as an iron cuirass in its ability to ward off penetration by the muscle-powered weapons of the day.[7] It was not uncommon for Macedonian officers to wear the linen armour over an iron breastplate for extra protection. By itself, linen armour was effective enough to resist slashing blows from a sword, while remaining sufficiently pliable to flex inward when struck to absorb much of the impact energy of missiles and thrusting weapons, and prevent penetration sufficient to reach the body. Modern kevlar armour functions the same way. Equipped with the linothorax, a Macedonian cavalry man or hoplite-equipped soldier's chest, neck, and back were almost impervious to wounding by arrows, sword slashes, slingshot, or javelins.[8]

Xenophon says that the cavalryman's head was protected by an iron helmet, and the only example of a Macedonian helmet we have recovered from the royal tombs at Vergina is an iron helmet. There is some evidence, however, that Alexander's cavalry may have worn the Boeotian helmet made of bronze. The Boeotian helmet, with its peaked forehead and ear openings, afforded good protection and better hearing on the battlefield. Regardless of which design Alexander wore, either offered excellent protection.[9] No weapon of the day, including the axe, could be wielded with sufficient power to penetrate the helmet. It requires 585 foot-pounds of energy upon a helmet to render a soldier unconscious. The most the human arm can generate in wielding a sword in a downward blow is 101 foot-pounds. Whether iron or bronze, the Macedonian cavalryman's helmet offered excellent protection.[10]

Since a wound to the left hand (the rein hand) would disable the rider, the cavalryman's left hand and arm was protected by a piece of equipment called 'the hand', or gauntlet, a leather sleeve extending from the hand to the shoulder, and secured under the breastplate. The right side of the breastplate had thick leather 'flaps' that extended down under the armpit, so when the arm was raised to strike a blow, the upper chest remained protected. The right forearm was covered with a metal greave attached to a leather sleeve that extended upward from the hand and attached under the breastplate at the armpit. The cavalryman's feet were covered by thick leather boots that extended up to his metal leg greaves. The thighs were protected by either leather or metal 'thigh pieces' that served as greaves for the upper leg. The great majority of wounds to cavalry were to the lower legs.[11]

The primary weapons of the Macedonian cavalryman, the *xyston* and the *machaira*, the lance and the sabre, were excellent self-defence weapons. The Macedonian cavalry lance was 9–10 feet long, fashioned of cornel wood with counter-balancing butt and a tip of metal, which the cavalryman wielded with one arm. The weapon was about 1½ inches around and weighed 4 pounds.[12] Grasped two-thirds the way back from its point for thrusting, it afforded the cavalryman a much longer reach than that of the infantryman's shorter *dory* spear. When aimed at a rival cavalryman *en passant*, the lance was aimed at the face and thorax of the opponent so as to strike him high and unseat him from his mount. With the shaft of the lance pressed tightly against the trunk of the horseman's body for leverage, the blade could be swept horizontally to parry other weapons, or to inflict deep cuts on both cavalry and infantry.[13]

The Macedonian cavalryman carried a murderous meat cleaver called the *machaira* as his principal close-combat weapon. The *machaira* was 25 inches long and weighed 2 pounds. Its 2½-inch wide single-edged blade was 18 inches in length and curved backward. The weight of the weapon was out at its tip, making it an excellent chopping sword, but less effective for stabbing or slashing. When the weapon was swung, the weight was carried toward the tip, where it would do the most damage as it drove the cutting edge deeply into the target. When Cleitus saved Alexander's life by striking the Persian cavalryman about to attack Alexander from behind, the force of Cleitus' downward blow was so great that it completely severed the attacker's arm at the shoulder.[14]

Even Alexander's battle dress served to reduce the chances that he would be killed or wounded. Unlike Persian and Indian field commanders who readily identified themselves on the battlefield by distinctive dress or ceremonial surroundings making them easy targets, Macedonian field commanders wore no distinctive dress or trappings of command. Thus, when Alexander entered Persepolis at the head of his army, he was wearing the same homespun clothes made for him by his sister and mother, and was indistinguishable from other Macedonian officers.[15] At Issus, Gaugamela, and the Hydaspes River, Alexander was easily able to locate the enemy commander on the battlefield by his dress, and ordered his cavalry to attack directly at him.

When a soldier of Alexander's day was wounded, he was at grave risk of death. Greek physicians had little empirical knowledge of the body's operations upon which to base sound wound treatment. They had only cautery to stop bleeding, a technique that often caused infection or death. Without the splint, bone setting was primitive, and often left the patient crippled, as with Philip when he was wounded in the leg. Even when physicians managed to prevent haemorrhagic shock, there was no way to address wound inflammation and infection. On average, about 35 per cent of a deployed battle force in antiquity could expect to suffer wounds serious enough to be abandoned on the battlefield.[16]

## Greek Medicine

An understanding of Greek medicine is important to assessing the severity of Alexander's wounds and his chances of survival. Greek medicine can be divided into two developmental phases, pre-classical (1200–550 BC) and classical (550–136 BC) medicine. The two periods closely correspond to medicine as magic and medicine as science, although even in the pre-classical period there are examples of pragmatic medicine, mostly practised by military physicians. Even after Hippocrates (460–370 BC), Greek medicine contained a strong element of mysticism and magic that coexisted alongside the empirical school, retaining both its status and clientele. There was probably never a period in Greek history before the Roman occupation when more people visited empirical medical practitioners for help than relied upon witches and sorcerers.[17]

Pre-classical Greek medicine was closely associated with magic and religion. The Greeks, like all ancient peoples, believed that disease and illness were the result of the anger of the gods visited upon humans. It was Apollo who visited plagues and epidemics upon mankind as punishment or signs of displeasure. The Greeks hit upon the idea that humans could placate the gods through ritual and sacrifice, and these practices formed the centre of early Greek religion and medicine. Glimmers of empiricism did emerge, however, especially in the practice of military medicine. The old Ionian word for physician, *iatros*, for example, meant 'extractor of arrows'.[18] It was the medical realities of the battlefield that initially engendered and sustained the empirical aspects of pre-classical medicine.

The evidence of Greek empirical medical pragmatism stimulated by war first appears in the *Iliad*. Medical treatment in the *Iliad* is carried out by both physicians and experienced warrior chieftains. Homer notes that two sons of Aesculapios, Machaon and Podalirius, were commanders of ships and 'good physicians both'. This is the first mention in Greek history of physicians present with a Greek military force.[19] There are examples throughout the *Iliad* of physicians treating the wounded. Typically, the wounded are taken from the battlefield by their comrades, often aboard a chariot, and transported to the rear to be treated in huts. A clinical picture emerges of a physician calming a wounded soldier by giving him a drink of wine, loosening his clothing in the area of the wound, washing the wound with warm water, and examining the wound. There are descriptions of spear and arrow points being withdrawn from the body by widening the entrance wound, followed by treatment with 'pain relieving herbs' or the application of the 'juice of some bitter root', and bandaging the wound with a woollen cloth. In one instance, Machaon sucked the blood from Manelaus' wound after extracting an arrow,[20] a practice that survived down to the 'woundsuckers' of the eighteenth century who attended duellists.[21]

War produced empirical techniques to deal with the wounded, and played a role in early Greek medicine. For the most part, however, magic and sorcery remained the predominant mode of pre-classical medical treatment, and it retarded the early development of a useful Greek *materia medica*. Until the classical period, Greek pharmacology was medically useless, consisting mostly of esoteric sacred potions whose value lay in appeasing the gods.[22]

As Greek society gradually recovered from the Dark Age (1200–800 BC) that followed the collapse of Mycenaean Greek civilization, the conditions that sustained a purely magico-religious medicine began to erode. By the sixth century BC, the Classical period (500–336 BC) marked by the systematic use of empiricism had begun. What was emerging was the revolutionary Greek idea, ever since the mainstay of Western medical history, that it was possible to understand the world through the rational applications of reason and empirical evidence. This new perspective placed a premium upon observation and systematic thought, and constituted the beginnings of a new epistemology of knowledge that directly challenged the way pre-classical Greeks explained the world. This development set the stage for the emergence of the more empirical practice of medicine in classical Greece.

The contribution of the most famous Greek physician, Hippocrates (460–370 BC), rested more in his method than in his medical innovations.[23] He insisted that medical theory and practice be based upon clinical observations, and firmly established medical practice in clinical applications that supported what he believed to be the natural tendency of the body to heal itself. Hippocrates was the first Greek physician to base medical diagnoses on a systematic and empirical set of observable conditions such as the patient's facial appearance, pulse, temperature, respiration, excreta, sputum, and movements of the body. This practice remains the basis of medical diagnosis to this day.[24] The Hippocratic methodology was a genuine medical advance, and with the transition of Greece into the Hellenistic period (336–168 BC), Hippocratic methodology came to embody the most important element in Greek medicine for 400 years.

Hippocrates' legacy spurred the development of the Alexandrian school of medical Empirics founded in 331 BC. The Empirics were the first Greek medical researchers, and the medical school at Alexandria was based upon the premise that extant anatomical observations were empirically inadequate and required more clinical study.[25] The Alexandrian school practised the first medical dissections in Greek history, made important investigations into the physiology of the nervous system, the brain, and spinal cord, and distinguished the sensory from the motor nerves.[26] The Greek view of pharmacy changed as well, with a new emphasis on the value of salves and ointments, a development that received considerable direction from Greek contacts with Egyptian physicians. Inevitably, this new empirical perspective on medicine influenced the pragmatics of medical treatment applied on the battlefield.

## Greek Military Medicine

It was common practice for the armies of classical Greece to have civilian physicians accompany them in war. Xenophon noted that eight army surgeons accompanied the expedition of the Ten Thousand to Persia at the end of the fifth century BC.[27] He recorded that these physicians treated his troops for frostbite, snow blindness, sickness, and gangrenous wounds suffered on the long retreat to Greece after the Battle of Cunaxa.[28] He also notes that men were designated to carry the wounded. But Xenophon mentions medical care for the troops only once, a fact that demonstrates that even at this late date Greek armies had no regular medical service corps.[29]

The presence of physicians in Greek armies was a reflection of the citizen armies of the period. These armies were small, part-time affairs that required little tactical training to implement the simple battle doctrines of the day, had no logistics trains or staff organizations, and were incapable of maintaining themselves in the field for long periods of time. Physicians were present on the battlefield, but the medical profession remained a private civilian enterprise that accompanied the army on campaign as a duty of individual citizenship. Their presence was common in much the same way as others – attendants, relatives, wives, girlfriends, prostitutes, merchants, barbers, etc. – accompanied the army. None of these, including physicians, fell under military law or discipline, and did not represent a resource that could be used in any regular manner by the military commander.

Alexander's contribution to military medicine, while still very limited, was more significant. Alexander's army was comprised of professionals who deployed on campaign for months and years on end. The presence of medical services in Alexander's army can therefore be seen as a much more integral part of a military force than it had ever been before in Greece. The names of seven military surgeons are recorded as accompanying Alexander on his initial campaign in Persia, and there are records of his doctors attending the wounded at Issus, Zariaspa, and Opis.[30] Their presence at Alexander's death is also recorded. It seems clear that Alexander recognized the importance of medical treatment for his troops, and made it a practice to recruit or dragoon whatever physicians came to hand in the captured populations. Special mention is made of his recruitment of Indian doctors in the Indus campaign to help cure his soldiers of snakebite.[31]

Alexander made provisions for wagons to serve as ambulances.[32] Wagons were normally restricted to hauling artillery pieces. While it would be going too far to suggest that Alexander developed the first military medical corps in the West, some of his physicians probably served for the same long periods of duty as the troops. Whether or not these physicians began as military doctors, there is little doubt that the experience gained on the campaign certainly made them practising military medical professionals. It would probably be correct to regard Alexander's physicians as the first medical professionals in an army of the West.

Whatever the quality of Alexander's medical support, it still did not constitute a true military medical service. The training of physicians remained a private civilian enterprise, and the army assumed no responsibility for it. The number of doctors recorded as attending various Greek armies of the period was relatively small, and clearly inadequate to any anticipated medical burden with which they would have to deal. Xenophon noted eight doctors for his force of 10,000, and only seven doctors had the responsibility for the treatment and care of over 40,000 soldiers in Alexander's first campaign. The small number of physicians present in Greek armies suggests that medical care may have been limited to high ranking officers who probably brought physicians along as personal attendants at their own expense. There is no evidence of any trained field medics or student assistants who could have provided even rudimentary care to the wounded until they could be attended by a physician.

The presence of Greek physicians with the army on campaign makes it certain that some soldiers received medical treatment for their battle wounds, and this raises the question of how effective this treatment may have been. There are scores of case studies in the Hippocratic collection dealing with war wounds. Greek physicians were quite proficient at setting broken bones and dislocations, and were among the first medical practitioners to use syringes made of animal bladders attached to thin pipes for various tasks.[33] The metal probes of the Egyptians reappeared in Greece, but there is no evidence that they were washed between examinations, and their effect in reducing infection remains doubtful. Greek physicians' ability to deal with head fractures remained generally below the skill of Egyptian practitioners, and the technique of drilling a hole in the skull, even when no fracture was present, and heating the wound to bring on infection and pus were probably lethal to wounded soldiers.[34] However, the first well-documented use of the tin pleural drain was a major Greek innovation, and improved upon similar techniques using reed drains found in earlier medical traditions.[35] Experience with penetration wounds of the chest caused by spears and arrows convinced the Greeks that it was vital to remove the pus from abscessed chest wounds. Placing a drain in the chest and applying heat to speed suppuration was probably successful in some cases.

The Greek physician's treatment of some wounds was quite good. They knew that round wounds did not heal as well as irregularly shaped wounds, and generally took much longer to heal. They introduced the practice of changing the shape of the wound to an oval which increased the chances of successful and complete closure.[36] Greek physicians were the first medical practitioners to attempt the use of the haemostatic tourniquet, and also recognized the risk of producing gangrene in the tied-off limb.[37] Most wounded soldiers in ancient armies died of blood loss and shock, and the tourniquet was one of the most potentially revolutionary medical advances of the ancient world.

Unfortunately, like other medical innovations of the Greeks, theory was not followed by systematic empirical application.

Greek physicians never learned how to stop severe bleeding, and never conceived of the arterial clamp or ligature, two procedures vital to the successful application of the tourniquet in wound surgery. Having stopped the bleeding with the tourniquet or pressure bandage, Greek physicians remained at a loss for what to do next. The result was that the main cause of fatality among wounded soldiers was haemorrhagic or neurogenic shock that killed more soldiers than infection.[38] If the tourniquet was allowed to remain, gangrene invariably set in. If the tourniquet was removed, renewed haemorrhaging killed the patient.

The tourniquet reappeared in the hands of Roman military doctors who invented the arterial clamp and had learned how to ligature veins and arteries; techniques that led to a radical increase in the rate of casualty survival.[39] After the collapse of the Roman imperium, the use of the tourniquet and the arterial clamp disappeared completely from Western medical practice. Both devices were rediscovered by the famous French battle surgeon, Ambroise Pare, in the sixteenth century. Pare is still wrongly credited in a number of medical histories with having invented the tourniquet, when it fact it was first used by the ancient Greeks.

Even granting the Greeks credit for a moderate level of skill in battle surgery, Greek methods for treating wounds failed in three important respects, all of which reduced the probability that a wounded soldier would recover from his injuries. The Hippocratic stress on 'natural processes' led Greek physicians to regard the onset of infection as an indication that the body was naturally healing itself. It was but a short step to the theoretical premise that wounds healing without infection were not being aided by the natural process of the body, and that it was necessary to stimulate the occurrence of this process. It became a common, often fatal practice to aggravate non-infected wounds to deliberately produce infection. This Greek theory of 'laudable pus' found its way into the medicine of the Middle Ages largely as a consequence of the rediscovery of Greek medical texts. The belief that infection was a normal part of the healing processes plagued battlefield medicine until at least the nineteenth century, with predictably catastrophic results in mortality.[40]

Greek physicians never developed an effective clinical technique for bandaging wounds. The issue was whether it was preferable to bandage a wound tightly or loosely. Hippocrates held that tight bandaging produced dry wounds, which he regarded as a natural state necessary for proper healing.[41]

Tightly bandaging wounds became a generally acceptable practice that drastically increased the chances of infection, tetanus, and gangrene. Tight bandaging was also accompanied by the immediate closure of wounds. These techniques were employed as standard practices until at least the First World War, when experience with horrendous rates of infection led to their abandonment.

A third shortcoming of Greek empirical practice in dealing with battle wounds resulted from the fascination of Greek physicians with chemical rather than botanical compounds for use in wound treatment. The fascination with chemicals was a result of increased contact with Egyptian physicians during the Alexandrian age. Some of the more common compounds used by Greek military physicians to treat battle wounds were lead oxide, copper sulphate, copper oxide, and cadmia. None of these compounds are useful as bactericides or bacteriostatics, and some can cause lethal tissue damage when applied to an open wound. The Greeks never truly succeeded in developing a clinical *materia medica* that was useful in treating battle injuries.

Greek wound washes, on the other hand, were generally good. The most common item used in these washes was wine, and the most common antiseptic was vinegar. The active ingredient in vinegar is acetic acid, and when used in 5 per cent strength is an excellent antiseptic for *E. Coli*, *staphylococci*, *cholera vitro*, and *E. Typhi*, all major causes of wound infection. Wine also acts as a generally effective bacteriostatic and bactericide. The important ingredient in wine is a sub-group of polyphenols called anthocyanes, the most important of which is oenoside. These chemicals are products of fermentation, and if agitated correctly produce powerful concentrations of polyphenols. Modern experiments demonstrate that when found in the proper concentrations, these polyphenols are thirty-three times more powerful as bactericides than the phenols used by Lister in 1865![42]

There is no evidence that the Greeks used special wines as wound washes, as the Romans did. The Greek preference for light wines probably reduced their medical value as wound washes. The production of polyphenols in sufficient strength to be medically valuable as bactericides requires a long process of fermentation, something not generally found in light or sweet wines. The Romans preferred strong red wines fermented to the point of almost vinegar. This strong wine, *acetum*, is very high in polyphenols. That Roman military doctors almost exclusively used this type of wine as a wound wash is demonstrated by the fact that casks of *acetum* were transported to military garrisons duty-free because the wine was classified as medical supplies.[43]

Any assessment of Greek military medicine is forced to the conclusion that while Greece produced an important methodological direction for medical research and practice by attempting to premise its medical conclusions upon empirical observation, the contributions of Greek physicians were, on balance, marginal. Whatever medical innovations were introduced by Greek physicians were never systematically applied. While medicine in Athens may be said to have been largely empirical, medical practice in Macedonia remained in the hands of sorcerers and witches right to the end. As regards military medicine, the Greek proclivity for citizen armies as a natural consequence of the fragmentation of the country into rival city-states similarly prevented any systematic application of medical technique on the battlefield. An effective system of military medical care required not only sufficient technical medical knowledge, but the organizational ability to deliver it on a regular basis. Such a task was utterly beyond the military institutions of classical Greece.[44]

## Alexander's Wounds

Successful treatment of the wounded in ancient armies given the types of wounds produced by weapons propelled by muscle power required five elements: (1) an ability to stop massive bleeding to prevent death from shock; (2) the ability to locate and extract missiles lodged in the body; (3) the ability to cleanse wounds with some sort of effective bactericide and bacteriostatic; (4) the ability to properly suture flesh, including veins and arteries, and bandage wounds; and (5) the ability to prevent infection, since no method of combating infection was available until the mid-twentieth century. All these developments were absent in armies of the Classical and Alexandrian periods. Any significant wounds Alexander suffered would have placed him at great risk of death. An examination of Alexander's wounds as recorded in our sources suggests a fair degree of exaggeration as to both the seriousness of the wounds and the heroic behaviour that Alexander is said to have demonstrated in acquiring them.

### The Granicus River (May–June, 334 BC)

Facing a mixed Greek–Persian force under the command of Greek generals, Alexander opened the battle with his light troops firing and moving toward the enemy line with a battalion of the infantry phalanx and a squadron of Companion cavalry in support. The objective was to force the enemy to expend its javelins against the light force, allowing the follow-on infantry and cavalry to force a gap in the enemy line. With Parmenio engaging on the left wing, Alexander led the Companion cavalry into the gap, and attacked obliquely towards the Persian centre, aiming for the enemy commander.[45]

Alexander was attacked by a Persian cavalryman in the initial engagement who 'brought his sword down on Alexander's head with such a fearsome blow that it split his helmet and inflicted a slight scalp wound'.[46] Arrian adds that the blow knocked off a piece of the helmet, probably some ornament, but does not record a wound at all.[47] Curtius says the split helmet fell from Alexander's head.[48] The Royal Squadron quickly surrounded Alexander, and Cleitus severed the arm of another attacker before he could reach Alexander. Diodorus says that during the battle, Alexander 'withstood two blows to his breast plate and one to his helmet'. Three other blows were absorbed by the shield that he had taken from Athena's temple.[49] It could not have been much of a fight, or the shield bearer, bodyguards, and Royal Squadron did an excellent job of protecting Alexander from danger.

The story rings of exaggeration. First, it is unlikely that a sword blow to the helmet would have split it open. It takes 151 foot-pounds of energy to split a bronze helmet and 251 foot-pounds to split an iron helmet. At the maximum, a sword swung by muscle power can produce no more than 101 foot-pounds of energy.[50] It is possible, however, that the blow shifted the helmet and caused a 'rub-wound' on the scalp, but it was not the sword blade that caused the wound. Thus, Arrian's account is probably the most accurate. The claim that Alexander took three blows to his shield is curious. Had he been fighting on foot, Alexander would have been carrying a *hoplon* shield. On horseback, however, Macedonian cavalry did not carry shields. The shield was carried by Alexander's shield bearer, and not Alexander. Alexander passed his first major test as a field commander at the Granicus River, but did not receive a genuine battle wound. There is no mention of medical treatment.

## The Battle of Issus (November, 333 BC)

Leading the Royal Squadron in a cavalry attack from the right wing against Darius' command post, Alexander suffered 'a sword-graze to his right thigh'.[51] All sources (Didorous, Justin, Arrian, Plutarch, and Curtius) mention the wound, but describe it differently. Arrian says Alexander was 'hurt by a sword thrust in the thigh', and Didorus says Alexander 'was wounded in the thigh'. That the wound was not serious or in any way incapacitating is evident from Arrian's comment that the wound did not prevent Alexander from visiting the wounded or holding a funeral for the dead.[52]

Thigh wounds were the most common wound suffered by Macedonian cavalrymen, and were rarely serious.[53] Cavalrymen wore leather boots, metal greaves, and thick leather coverings up to their thighs, and any wound was likely to be minor, as Alexander's apparently was. Cavalrymen were far more likely to be wounded by the infantry below them than by other cavalry, and this seems to be the case with Alexander at Issus who was wounded while attacking Darius' foot guard. Although the wound was minor, it is curious that all our sources mention it. This may be because it is the only wound Alexander suffered by a sword, implying that it was received in close combat. All Alexander's other wounds were caused by missiles, arrows or thrown stones which did not involve close combat. As we shall see, Alexander suffered some of his wounds while not engaged in combat at all. Again, our sources do not mention any medical treatment for Alexander's wound.

## The Siege of Gaza (September–November, 332 BC)

After mounting an infantry attack, the Macedonians were driven back by fire from the walls. As they retreated, the Persians sallied forth from the gate and engaged the Macedonians in an infantry skirmish in which Alexander 'fought courageously in the front rank'.[54] Alexander was then hit by an arrow 'which passed through his cuirass and stuck in his shoulder, from which it was extracted by Philip, his doctor'.[55] Alexander began to bleed. He ordered the bleeding to be staunched, the wound bandaged, and returned to the front. He remained on his feet 'for a long time' near the unit standards until the wound began to bleed again, at which time 'he began to faint, his knees buckled, and the men next to him caught him and took him back to camp'.[56] Arrian's version has Alexander struck by 'a missile from a catapult that pierced his shield and corselet and penetrated his shoulder . . . the wound was serious and did not easily yield to treatment'.[57] There is no mention of the missile being extracted. Curiously, Diodorus does not claim that Alexander was wounded at all at Gaza.

There are some difficulties with the accounts. If the wound was as serious as described, the claim that Alexander returned to the fighting immediately after being wounded and remained there for a long time, is difficult to believe. Curtius claims Alexander was hit by an arrow that penetrated his *cuirass*, while Arrian claims it was a catapult bolt that penetrated Alexander's *corselet* and his shield. If Alexander was wearing a bronze cuirass, then the arrow would not have penetrated at all. As noted earlier, the linen corselet was also relatively impervious to arrow fire, unless a lucky shot struck a seam. It is also difficult to believe that Alexander was struck by a catapult bolt. A catapult bolt had a thick wooden shaft approximately 28–30 inches long with a heavy metal tip mounted on the end.[58] If a catapult bolt did strike Alexander, it would likely have killed him outright, or surely caused much greater damage. It was most likely an arrow that hit Alexander's corselet and penetrated only a short distance into his body, surely less than the 2 inches required to produce a serious or lethal wound. In any event, it was a random shot fired by an archer on the wall into the infantry melee below. Alexander was doing nothing heroic that contributed to his being wounded.

Alexander's physician was able to extract the missile without removing Alexander's body armour, an indication that the depth of the wound was shallow. It is curious that Alexander's physician did not first probe the wound to determine its depth. Perhaps he could readily determine that it was not very deep from simple observation. A Persian arrow was barbed to make extraction from the flesh difficult. The ease of extraction from Alexander's corselet and his body suggests that the depth of penetration must have ended short of where the barbs on the arrowhead were located, i.e. at the top end of the 1 ¼-inch-long arrowhead. Thus, Alexander's wound could not have been as serious as the text suggests. That the bleeding could be stopped quickly also suggests a wound of shallow penetration. There is no mention of the use of the cautery or tourniquet to stop the bleeding.

The claim that Alexander passed out from blood loss is unlikely to be true. Greek physicians were well aware of fainting, and considered it a near-death condition that frequently killed a patient undergoing a surgical procedure. Bleeding sufficient to cause physiological collapse would not have been so easily stopped with a pressure bandage, and would not have stopped on its own. It is interesting that after the arrow had been extracted and the bleeding resumed, Alexander 'did not even lose colour', i.e. become pale, suggesting that the blood loss was not serious.[59] We hear nothing of further medical procedures after Alexander was removed to his camp. It is not unreasonable to suspect that the account of Alexander's serious bleeding may have been exaggerated to convey a sense that Alexander was more seriously wounded than he really was.

Within a few days of being wounded, Alexander was back on the battlefield directing the construction of a berm upon which to mount his artillery, and ordering tunnels dug to collapse the walls of the city. This short recovery would have been unlikely had Alexander been seriously wounded. The construction of the berm and tunnels must have taken at least a week. When the attack was resumed, 'Alexander himself led the advance troops, and, as he approached somewhat recklessly, he was struck on the leg with a rock. He supported himself with his spear, and though the scab had still not formed on his first wound, kept fighting in the front line.'[60] Note that the only evidence of his previous wound is a *scab* and not the much prized battle *scar*, suggesting that the wound was merely a flesh wound and not serious.

Once again Alexander was struck by a random missile, this time a rock, thrown from the battlements. How he could have remained in the fight while 'supporting himself on his spear', is unclear. But there is no evidence of broken bones or a cut to his legs. Alexander's being armed with a spear is also curious, since Macedonian infantry was armed with the *sarissa*, not the dory-like spear, and the hoplite units mostly used the sword when fighting out of phalanx formation. The most that can be said for the action at Gaza is that Alexander was unluckily struck by a random arrow that caused a minor flesh wound. No heroics were involved.

**Skirmish on the Jaxartes River (June, 329 BC)**

On the march to Marakanda (Samarkand), Alexander's foragers came under attack. After inflicting heavy casualties, the attackers withdrew to a redoubt atop a steep hill. Alexander led his troops in an attack on the redoubt. He was repulsed three times, and 'many were wounded, including Alexander himself, who was shot through the leg with an arrow and had the fibula broken'.[61] Plutarch says Alexander 'was shot in the shin, right through and a piece of his fibula was broken off by the arrow'.[62] Curtius' version has Alexander 'hit by an arrow, the head of which was left firmly lodged in his leg'.[63] Alexander was carried back to his camp.

The information in these accounts seems questionable. Macedonian hoplite infantry wore heavy leather boots covered by metal shin greaves, making a wound by an arrow to the shin very unlikely. The claim that Alexander's fibula was broken or had a piece of the bone shot off is also questionable, if only on the grounds that it would have been unlikely to determine the nature of the chipped bone without modern imaging. Any bone fragment would have likely been driven through the skin, suggesting an external wound or, perhaps, even a compound fracture, neither of which is mentioned.

The lower leg is made up of two bones, the fibula and the tibia. The fibula is the smaller of the two, and is located at the outer part of the lower leg. The fibula may be completely broken into two or more pieces, or may only sustain a crack, a condition known as a stress fracture. A break in the fibula in which both pieces of the bone are disarticulated, that is left beside each other, can leave a person permanently crippled, especially in the absence of an immobilizing splint, as in the case when Philip suffered a 'tib-fib' fracture when wounded by the Triballi.[64] If the fibula is not disarticulated or has suffered only a stress fracture, it might be possible to walk with the injury, although painfully. In modern times, an immobilizing splint is applied; in severe cases, surgery is indicated.

That Alexander was somewhat hindered by his injury seems evident from the fact that he was carried from the battlefield. Curtius notes that Alexander was transported on a military litter as the army continued its march to

Marakanda. Three days later, however, Alexander was back in action, burning villages as his army approached the city, a very rapid recovery that suggests either a cracked fibula or, at worse, a broken bone that was not disarticulated.[65]

Curtius' claim that the arrow head 'was left firmly lodged in his leg' seems unlikely in that it would certainly have caused the wound to suppurate, a dangerous condition that surely would have required medical attention.[66] The absence of any mention of infection or further treatment of the wound suggests that Alexander's injury was less serious than recorded in the texts. A more likely scenario is that Alexander was wounded in the leg by an arrow whose force was greatly reduced by first having to penetrate his thick leather boot. The arrow penetrated the skin and, perhaps, some surface viscera, but not very deeply, and its extraction was easily accomplished. The wound was probably painful, but not terribly so. The claim that Alexander was able to move around quite readily after a few days might suggest that there was no fracture of the fibula at all. The wound was neither serious nor life threatening, nor was it suffered in any heroic action. Alexander was hit by yet another lucky shot.

## The Siege of Cyropolis (Summer, 328 BC)

Alexander received his most serious wound while besieging the city of Cyropolis in Afghanistan. Curtius tells us that 'Alexander was struck so severely on the neck by a stone that everything went dark and he collapsed unconscious. The army wept for him as if he were dead.'[67]Arrian says the injury was to the back of the head and neck, while Plutarch says it was to the back of the neck and the side of the neck, that is the occipital and parietal area of the skull.[68] The Latin text can be interpreted to mean that Alexander lost his sight, and Plutarch says 'for many days he was in fear of becoming blind'.[69] We do not know for how many days Alexander was without his sight, only that he eventually recovered it, and continued to direct the attack several days later until the city was captured.

The army then marched to the banks of the Iaxartes (Syr Darya River) and constructed a camp enclosed by a wall sixty stades long, an effort that Arrian says took twenty-days.[70] A month later, Curtius tells us that Alexander had still not recovered from his wound 'and in particular had difficulty speaking'. He was so weak that 'Alexander himself could not stand in the ranks, ride a horse, or give his men instructions or encouragement'. His voice was so weak that in staff meetings he had his friends sit close to him so that they could hear 'without him having to strain his voice'.[71] At a later meeting, Alexander proposed to take the field against Spitamenes, but 'Alexander's words were spoken in a quivering voice that became increasingly feeble, so that it was difficult even for those next to him to hear'.[72] It was another several weeks before Alexander's symptoms disappeared and he was able to put on his cuirass and 'walk to the men, the first time he had done so since receiving the most recent wound'.[73] Altogether, Alexander was out of action for at least two months.[74]

The blow to Alexander's head caused a very severe concussion that resulted in transient cortical blindness.[75] Alexander's difficulties with balance, walking, and speaking, however suggest more extensive damage to the brain. The symptoms of concussion were known to Greek physicians, and appear in several case studies in the *Corpus Hippocraticum*. Most symptoms, as in Alexander's case, are eventually self-resolving. What is less evident, are the long-term emotional effects of the injury on Alexander's behaviour.[76]

The damage caused by the blow to the back and side of Alexander's head was not confined to that area. A blow to the back of the head drives the fluid surrounding the brain forward, propelling the frontal lobe of the brain into the bony structure of the skull, causing damage to the frontal lobe. In this type of 'contra-coup' injury, the functions of the frontal lobe can be greatly affected, as they appear to have been in Alexander's case. Arrian's description of the siege where Alexander was injured suggests that the injury occurred after a prolonged effort in the hot sun to gain entrance to the town. There was also a lack of water for the troops and defenders that eventually caused the defenders to surrender.[77] These circumstances can easily cause the body to become dehydrated.

Physical dehydration has two important effects on concussion. First, the reduction in bodily fluid causes the brain to contract, increasing the distance the brain must travel to strike the frontal bone structure, increasing its speed and magnifying the force of the frontal lobe impact, causing greater damage. Second, the Macedonian practice of drinking wine instead of water during an illness increases the dehydration of the body, slowing recovery and taking longer for the damage to heal.[78] Alexander continued to show physical symptoms of his concussion for at least two months after the injury.

Long-term emotional effects of concussion include depression, explosive anger, irritability, shortened temper, paranoia, memory loss, and inappropriate displays of emotion, all dysfunctions of the frontal lobe. Individuals differ in terms of their natural capacity to inhibit or control their behaviour. Certain conditions – traumatic brain injury, psychiatric disorders, and substance abuse – can create a state of reduced control over one's behaviour, impulses, attention, and emotions. Physicians refer to this condition as disinhibition, the opposite of inhibition, a state of control over one's responses. Individuals under the influence of alcohol, for example, exhibit disinhibition as a consequence of the depressant effect of alcohol on the brain's higher functioning. Disinhibition can affect motor, instinctual, emotional, cognitive, and perceptual aspects with symptoms similar to the diagnostic criteria for mania. Hyper-sexuality, hyperphagia (obsessive compulsive behaviour regarding food or drink,) and aggressive outbursts are common effects of disinhibited instinctual drives.[79] Severe concussion can, over time, also result in chronic traumatic encephalopathy, producing severe emotional outbursts and paranoid states. It is telling in this regard that Alexander's symptoms of brain damage continued to get worse over the last six years of his life, from 328 when he was injured until his death in 323 BC.

Alexander was 27 when he was injured at Cyropolis, and had been at war for seven years. As the previous analysis demonstrates, he had already begun to show symptoms of post-traumatic stress disorder: explosive anger, cruelty, paranoia, depression, heavy drinking, and suicidal impulses. The expressions of these behaviours became even more dramatic after this injury. From Cyropolis to the end of his life, Alexander's symptoms of post-traumatic stress became more severe, as he increasingly lost his ability to control his impulses, emotions, and behaviour. The year 328 began a drastic change in Alexander's personality and behaviour.

A brief review of Alexander's behaviour *after* the injury reveals this to have been the case. At Marakanda, Alexander killed Cleitus with a spear in a fit of drunken anger; his paranoia became more acute, and he had Callisthenes and the Pages executed when he believed they were involved in a conspiracy to kill him; four senior generals were executed out of fear that they could no longer be trusted; upon his return from India, Alexander ordered scores of Macedonian and Persian officials killed in a mass purge; any common soldier guilty of an offence was routinely executed without trial; his depression became worse and more frequent, and on at least two occasions he was suicidal; Alexander's homosexuality became more blatant and public, and he ordered the execution of Persian officials on the whim of his lover, Bagoas. He even had a mentally ill man who had accidentally sat upon his throne executed; and Alexander became more convinced that he was divine, paying excessive attention to even the smallest events as signs of his divinity. It was only a few months after his injury at Cyropolis that he attempted to require the Macedonians to prostrate themselves in his presence.

At Cyropolis, he ordered the death of 7,000 enemy prisoners who had surrendered. In the attack on Marakanda (328 BC), he ordered a sweep of the area, destroying every village and town, and killing every man of military age. When he captured the city, Alexander ordered the population butchered to a man. In 327 BC, Alexander returned to Sogdiana and destroyed every village, town, and tribe encountered en route of the line of march. Estimates of the losses begin at 120,000 people – 40,000 were killed in a single engagement. After taking the town of Massaga in the Kabul Valley, he granted the Indian mercenary force safe passage, then surrounded them and their families, and killed every man, woman, and child, some 7,000 people in all.

After defeating Porus at the Hydaspes River, Alexander's Indian campaign continued with the slaughter of the entire town of Sangala in 326 BC – 17,000 people were killed and 70,000 taken prisoner. The refugees fled, leaving 500 sick and wounded behind. When Alexander came upon them, he ordered them killed. Alexander moved on to a neighbouring town, bringing it under siege. He set fire to the city, burning most of the inhabitants alive. In 325, Alexander attacked the Malians, destroying their towns and villages and slaughtering the inhabitants. Some 50,000 souls were slain in this single campaign. A few months later, he encountered the Brahmins at Sambus. In a fit of anger at their resistance, Alexander once more ordered a terrible massacre. If Curtius and Diodorus are to be believed, 80,000 people were systematically slaughtered. Later, he marched through the territory of the Oreitae, killing and setting fire to homes, towns, and villages as he went, all without any provocation – 6,000 were killed in a single engagement. In 324 BC, Alexander and his army spent forty days in a campaign against the Cossaeans, again without provocation. The entire nation was put to the sword. This was done to soothe Alexander's grief at the death of his lover.

Even allowing for exaggeration by our sources, it is clear that Alexander had changed markedly, and his brutality was much worse after his injury at Cyropolis than it had previously been. Much of the slaughter seems to have had no military purpose, and was committed out of Alexander's personal anger or, perhaps, out of the psychological need to bring on the berserk state as a way of calming his turbulent mind. Whatever had inhibited Alexander's rage and psychological drives before Cyropolis seems to have lessened or disappeared altogether after he was injured. J.M. O'Brien summed up the changes that occurred in Alexander at this time. 'This change, which deepened during the last seven years of his life, was marked by a progressive deterioration of character. He became increasingly suspicious of friends as well as enemies, unpredictable, and megalomaniacal. Towards the end, he was almost totally isolated, dreaded by all, a violent man capable of anything.'[80] It would turn out that the injury at Cyropolis was the most serious wound Alexander suffered, even as it was invisible to those around him.

## Fight with the Aspasians (Winter, 327 BC)

Moving through the Swat Valley (Pakistan) toward the Indus River, Alexander entered the territory of the Aspasians and immediately attacked the first town he encountered. Arrian tells us that 'during the operation, Alexander was wounded in the shoulder by a missile which pierced his corselet. The wound was not serious, and the corselet prevented the missile from going right through his shoulder.'[81] Once again Alexander was hit by a lucky shot while doing nothing particularly heroic. There is no indication that the wound was treated in any way, or even that it pierced Alexander's flesh. If it did pierce his flesh, it must have been a minor wound, since Curtius tells us Alexander proceeded to take the town and butcher its inhabitants to a man.

## Massaga (Early Spring, 327 BC)

Alexander marched on through the territory of the Assacenians, who prepared to meet him with force. After an initial skirmish, they withdrew to Massaga, the largest town in the area. Alexander immediately took it under siege. While leading his infantry too close to the walls, he was again struck by an arrow fired from the walls that 'wounded him slightly in the ankle'.[82] Curtius tells us that 'someone on the walls hit him with an arrow which happened to lodge in his leg. Alexander pulled out the barb, had his horse brought up and without even bandaging the wound, rode around fulfilling his objectives no less energetically'.[83] Alexander's ankles were protected by thick leather boots, and it is likely that the arrow stuck in the leather without piercing his flesh. In any case, another lucky shot left Alexander unharmed.

## Sudrace (January, 325 BC)

Continuing its march along the Hydraotes River, Alexander's progress was blocked by the Malli, one of the most powerful warrior tribes in the region. He attacked their capital at Sudrace, and attempted to take it by storm. Angry that the assault was not going well, Alexander climbed a scaling ladder, gained the top of the parapet, and jumped inside the wall to engage the enemy. He immediately came under fire from archers in the towers, and was struck in the chest by an arrow.

Arrian says 'the arrow penetrated his corselet, and entered his body above the breast'. Curtius adds that Alexander was wounded 'above his right side' by an arrow that was 'two cubits long', and 'when he received his wound, a thick jet of blood shot forth'. Alexander 'dropped his weapons and appeared to be dying' when his guard finally reached him. Arrian, citing Ptolemy who was present at the engagement, says 'that the blood from the wound was mixed with air breathed out from the pierced lung. Despite the pain, Alexander continued to defend himself so long as the blood remained warm; but there was soon a violent haemorrhage, as was to be expected with a pierced lung, and overcome by giddiness and faintness, he fell forward over his shield ... Alexander was almost unconscious from loss of blood.'[84]

Rescued by his bodyguard, Alexander was taken to his tent for medical treatment by Cristobulus, a noted surgeon. The arrow had pierced Alexander's corselet, nailing the armour to his chest. The doctors 'cut off the shaft of the arrow embedded in his body without moving the arrow head'. The arrow head was barbed, and could not be removed unless the track of the wound was enlarged. Alexander refused to be held down while the wound was enlarged, and 'submitted to the knife without flinching'. The wound was enlarged, but when the arrow head was extracted, 'a stream of blood now began to gush forth. Alexander started to lose consciousness ... In vain they tried to check the bleeding with medications ... finally the bleeding stopped; Alexander gradually regained consciousness.'[85]

That the wound was serious is suggested by the time it took Alexander to recover. Arrian says Alexander remained in his tent 'for some time', and Curtius says it was seven days before Alexander, still litter-bound, continued his voyage downstream on two boats lashed together. He adds that 'Alexander's wound had still not closed', and that his condition was still 'very fragile'.[86] When Alexander reached the junction of the Hydrates and Acesines rivers where Hephaestion's army and Nearchus' fleet were waiting, Alexander was able to lift himself off his stretcher, mount his horse, and greet the troops.[87] Alexander did not make a full recovery until sometime in late August, perhaps as much as five months after he was wounded at Sudrace.

It is difficult to believe that Alexander was hit by an arrow that penetrated his corselet and his body so deeply as to puncture his lung 'above the breast' as Arrian says. The musculature in that area is considerably thicker than at or below the breast line, and would have required much greater force to penetrate the corselet and then the body deeply enough to puncture the lung.[88] Curtius may be closer to the truth when he says Alexander was struck 'above his right side'. The musculature on the side of the chest, while still substantial, is somewhat less thick than in the front. An arrow fired at point blank range may have had a better chance of penetrating the corselet and body on the right side.

The area of the wound puts the lung puncture, if it occurred at all, at the apex (top) of the lung, a location of less lung tissue area, blood circulation, and aeration function than lower areas of the lung. If punctured at the apex, the lung will collapse, but have less effect on breathing capacity, which shifts to the other lung. Over time, the lung will heal naturally, unless infection sets in. A puncture wound to a major area of the lung, however, would likely have been fatal. The description of the wound's location in the sources is generally consistent with medical reality.

It is by no means clear that Alexander's lung was punctured, however. Arrian's statement that air mixed with blood rushed *out* of the wound cannot be correct. The lungs function in a vacuum created by the plural space of the chest cavity. When the plural space is pierced, air rushes *into* the vacuum. This is why this type of wound is referred to by military physicians as 'a sucking chest wound'. It is quite possible to pierce the plural space without piercing the lung, especially at the apex of the lung where Alexander was probably hit. Any bleeding may have come from simple tissue injury, not necessarily a pierced lung. Unless an artery was cut by the arrow head, the wound's heavy bleeding would not likely have been caused by the entrance wound or a punctured lung. It is instructive that the heavy bleeding occurred only after the wound had been enlarged. We are not told how the bleeding was stopped, but that it was without the use of cautery suggests that perhaps the surgeon may have cut a vein when enlarging Alexander's entrance wound.

Curtius' statement that Alexander's wound had not closed after seven days is misleading in that he means the *outer* entrance wound. The wound would have naturally begun to heal from the *inside* very quickly. However, it would have taken at least several days or, perhaps, even weeks for the wound to heal inside sufficiently to reseal the plural space. Once this occurred, the body would begin to re-establish the vacuum in the plural space and gradually re-inflate the collapsed lung. Thus, the lung would gradually heal and recover its function, although it would take a great deal of time to do so, perhaps months. In the interim, the person would have to operate on reduced lung capacity. This is consistent with the claim that thirteen days after being wounded, Alexander was able to lift himself off the litter and meet his troops, even though his condition was 'still very fragile'. Alexander required five more months to recover fully, a length of time consistent with what modern physicians would require for him to have done so. The descriptions of Alexander's wounds by our sources merit the suspicion that some accounts may have been enhanced to convey the impression of greater severity than can be explained medically. Except for the wound suffered at Sudrace, none of Alexander's wounds were received in direct combat or under heroic circumstances. Alexander may well have been unlucky, given that most of his wounds were inflicted by random arrows or rocks fired or thrown from atop battlements. Most of Alexander's wounds were minor, while some others are clearly unbelievable from a medical perspective.

It is also curious that there are only minimal descriptions of medical treatments that may have been performed, and more curious that there are no descriptions of wounds becoming infected or even inflamed. This is especially notable of the wounds suffered in India and Afghanistan, both of which still possess very high background bacteriological environments.[89] Greek physicians believed that a non-infected wound indicated that the body was not healing properly, and required infection to be provoked by contamination. There is no mention of this in any of the wound accounts. It may simply be that our sources lacked the medical information to consider these events important. It is also noteworthy that none of Alexander's wounds, unlike Philip's, left him crippled or disfigured, allowing the sources to preserve the Greek ideal of beauty in their stories. The wound that probably did the most damage to Alexander, the blow to the head at Cyropolis, went mostly unnoticed in its importance by our sources, probably because it left no obvious physical signs.

It is possible, then, that Alexander's reputation for heroic bravery leading to serious battle wounds may very well have been exaggerated by ancient historians seeking to create a role model for moral lessons to be taught to their audiences. But Alexander's troops and officers would have known the truth. Almost all of them had been wounded in their long careers in military service, many under the heroic and badly wounded Philip. What they thought of Alexander, however, is unknown.

*Chapter 4*

# The Crucible of War

It is often believed that those who lived in ancient times were more resistant to human suffering, if only because there seems to have been so much more of it for individuals to endure. How are those of us in today's world where, in the more advanced countries anyway, the death of children is relatively rare, to comprehend the sorrow of people who watched 50 per cent of their newborns die before age 5? How to understand the suffering of the wounded where no medical care was available? How to emotionally understand the sacking of ancient cities, where all the old men and male children were slain, the women and young girls sold into slavery, and the enemy soldiers crucified? Because these events are generally beyond the experience of most of our own lives, perhaps we take some refuge in the belief that those who experienced them did so with less horror than we imagine we would.

Human nature being what it is, it is unlikely that those living in ancient times were any less immune to their own suffering than we are. War had been part of Greek life for centuries before Alexander, and the militia armies of the city-states and the almost universal practice of conscription virtually guaranteed that most men would experience battle at some time in their lives. Prior to the Peloponnesian Wars (431–404 BC), Greek warfare took the form of a rough sport in which exposure to danger was generally short-lived, casualties light, prisoners taken, civilians spared, and the demonstration of individual heroism possible. None of this, of course, prevented the occasional destruction of cities and the slaughter of its inhabitants. It's just that it happened less frequently. The length and destruction attendant to the Peloponnesian Wars changed the scope, scale, and frequency of such destruction. Armies grew larger, wars and battles lasted longer, the carnage increased, and entire cities were destroyed and their populations enslaved. The old militia armies were leavened with a new type of combatant, the professional mercenary, who travelled the land selling his skills to the highest bidder, skills that made battles more lethal. By Alexander's day, some armies had become professional standing military forces capable of inflicting damage at levels seen only rarely previously.

The increased brutality, especially to civilian populations, attendant to these wars was recognized as a great moral wrong at the time. No less an observer of war than Thucydides could remark that 'wild aggression was now seen as brotherly commitment. Concern for the future was cowardice while moderation, one of the great Greek virtues handed down from Apollo, was now seen as unmanliness or womanly. The circumspect or careful individual was really the inactive one, and the violent man was trustworthy, and anyone who spoke against him was suspect.'[1]

The idea that the Greeks accepted brutality as a normal part of their culture is grossly incorrect. Some of the West's most significant ethical treatises were written by Greek philosophers during this time. Aristotle, Plato, and Epictitus, to name but three, all wrote works on ethics in which the subject of the moral behaviour of the soldier was addressed. It was around this time, too, that Greek education began to include ethics and ethical reasoning as standard elements of its curriculum. The practice of pointless slaughter was condemned in Greek plays and in the histories of Thucydides and Herodotus. Aeschylus, Euripides, and Sophocles wrote plays that offered moral lessons regarding the immorality of the killing of the wounded, civilians, and the otherwise helpless. It comes as no surprise, then, that the most popular branch of philosophy throughout the Alexandrian and Hellenistic periods was ethics. In a world grown so brutal, moral guidelines became essential, and a number of ethical treatises were offered as advice to rulers.[2] War was viewed as a bleak, if inevitable, reality that, as Pericles remarked, gave young men a chance to win fame and glory, but was recognized as an unfortunate dimension of life grudgingly accepted as part of human existence.

The old moderation was gone, replaced by terrible and cruel, often total war with no prisoners taken, the destruction of cities, and cruelty on the battlefield. Greek awareness of the increased human cost of war was made more poignant by the increase in the wounded returning to their homes and villages, living testaments to human suffering. In his *Sayings of the Spartans*, Plutarch tells us of one Androcleidas, who reported for military duty, dragging his battle-injured lame leg behind him. Another wounded veteran made his way to the gathering place crawling on all fours, his body shattered and paralyzed by a previous wound.[3] There was a no more enthusiastic practitioner of the new form of brutal warfare than Alexander, a fact that explains at least partially why traditional Greeks were repulsed by his cruelty. That the Greeks of Alexander's day were well aware of the horrors of war is beyond question.

This awareness prompted the Greeks to develop the one area of medical practice that the modern world owes exclusively to them, the practice of military psychiatry.[4] Greek physicians were aware of mental illness caused by the trauma of war, and were the first to practice a sophisticated form of psychiatry.[5] They were the first to link psychiatric symptoms to the stress of battle.[6] Greek literature is filled with accounts of soldiers driven mad by their experience in war. Aristodemus and Pantites, two Spartan soldiers, had to be removed from the line at Thermopylae when overtaken by fear. Herodotus tells us that Leonidas, the Spartan commander, 'dismissed them when he realized that they had no heart for the fight and were unwilling to take their share of the danger'.[7] Reviled as cowards, Pantites hanged himself and Aristodemus, called 'the trembler', lived a life of isolation.[8]

Sophocles' famous play, *Ajax*, is probably the best known illustration in Greek literature of this phenomenon. After fighting at Troy for months, Ajax is 'seized with madness in the night'. Entering in to a fugue state, Ajax sets out to kill Odysseus and the other Greek soldiers who denied him his rightful share of glory. In a dream-like state, he attacks and brutalizes the cattle and other animals, believing them to be the soldiers themselves. 'Some he beheaded; of some he cut the back-bent throat or cleft the chine; others he tormented in their bonds as though they were men, with onslaughts on the cattle.' When Ajax comes out of the dream-like state and 'by slow painful steps regained his reason', he becomes concerned about how he will be thought of. Unable to bear the shame and guilt, he commits suicide.[9]

Herodotus recorded the symptoms of the first clinical case of psychiatric collapse in battle. In his account of the battle of Marathon (490 BC), Herodotus tells us that soldiers along the battle line steadied themselves for the attack. All up and down the line, men shook with fear; vomited, and lost control of their bladders and bowels. Suddenly, a projectile struck one of the soldiers squarely in the face, sending a shower of blood and brain over the man next to him. 'And then Epizelus, the son of Cuphagoras, an Athenian soldier, suddenly lost the sight of both eyes, though nothing had touched him anywhere – neither sword, spear, nor missile. From that moment he continued blind as long as he lived.'[10] Xenophon also described a case of psychosomatically induced illness due to fear of death on the battlefield. [11] That war drove some soldiers mad was evident whenever the psychiatrically damaged soldiers returned to their towns and villages.

The physically and mentally wounded often sought help at the temples of Asclepios, the most important healer god of antiquity. There patients drank of the 'water of forgetfulness' and underwent deep drug-induced sleep as a form of incubation therapy that represented a very modern and sophisticated treatment for psychiatric reactions to combat.[12] The *asclepieion* at Epidaurus was the most celebrated healing centre of the Greek-Hellenic world. Seventy case histories of patients have been preserved on *stelae* found at the centre. Among them are a number of cases involving combat veterans suffering from physical conditions, including battle wounds to the jaw, lungs, and legs. Other soldiers were afflicted with battle-induced psychiatric conditions, including hysterical paralysis, blindness, headaches, and nightmares.[13]

Some of the *stelae* inscriptions are illuminating. There was Timon 'wounded by a spear below his eye. This man, sleeping here, saw a dream. It seemed to him the god ground up an herb and poured it into his eye, and he became well.' Another veteran, Antikrates of Knidos, 'had been struck with a spear through both his eyes in some battle, and he became blind and carried around the spearhead with him, inside his face. Sleeping here, he saw a vision. It seemed to him the god pulled out the dart and fitted the so-called girls (pupils of the eyes) back into his eyelids. When day came he left well.' Another veteran, Gorgias of Herakleia, 'was wounded in the lung by an arrow in some battle, and for a year and six months it was festering so badly, that it filled sixty-seven bowls of pus. When he was sleeping here, he saw a vision. It seemed to him the god drew out the barb from his lung. When day came he left well, carrying the barb in his hands.'[14]

Greek physicians also recommended that veterans suffering from mental problems caused by war attend the productions of Greek tragedies as a form of abreaction. These plays were probably useful as a primitive form of psychodrama in which the troubled soldier identified with the tragic hero as a way of reliving and relieving his own emotions. Aeschylus' play, *Persians*, which portrays the horror of the naval battle of Salamis where Persian sailors helpless in the water were 'spit (stabbed) like tuna', is but one example. While the Greeks can be credited with inventing psychiatric diagnosis and treatment for soldiers, Greek physicians did not apply these techniques in any systematic way. The Roman army was the first army to regularly care for psychiatric casualties, where soldiers suffering battle-induced psychiatric problems were treated in the psychiatric wards of legion hospitals.[15] It was not until the Russo-Japanese War of 1905 that any Western army again attempted to deal with the problem of psychiatric casualties in a systematic manner. The Russian Army is credited with reinventing the practice of military psychiatry in the modern age.[16]

Greek society contributed the ideal of military heroism to Western thought, and it comes as no surprise that the Greeks were acutely aware of the failure of nerve that often afflicted troops in combat. The culture of heroism in which manliness was demonstrated by bravery in war permitted the Greeks to believe that psychiatric reactions did not happen as a matter of course, but as a result of poor character and lack of bravery. The fault lay with the individual soldier, and condemning the psychiatric casualty as a coward reinforced the traditional heroic culture in the face of much evidence to the contrary. The ideal of individual heroism was transmitted into the mainstream of Western culture, passed down generation after generation until modern times. From the Civil War to the Vietnam War, the problem of psychiatric collapse in war was still viewed as idiosyncratic human behaviour, the consequence of psychological or sociological 'weaknesses' in the soldier's character.[17] It is only since the Iraq and Afghan wars, with their high rates of post-traumatic stress disorder, that Western culture is becoming aware that this is not the case.[18]

There is no good reason to believe that soldiers in ancient times were any less fearful of dying or being maimed than today's soldiers. Modern studies of psychiatric collapse in war suggest that the already mentally aberrant appear most able to adjust to the horror of combat, while it is mostly the sane that collapse under its strain.[19] Whether in ancient or modern times, exposure to the stress of war is likely to seriously affect one's sanity and ability to function normally in society. It is, then, not unlikely that Alexander's thirteen-year exposure to violence and slaughter might have seriously affected his mental condition.

## The Dynamics of Psychiatric Collapse

The stresses of war impose terrible burdens on the physiology and psychology of most human beings. Physiologically, humans are as much biological animals as other animals. Humans are equipped with the normal physiological mechanisms of any animal that prepare the body to deal with and survive under stress. As in other animals, the usual accompaniment of emotion in humans is muscular action, as the autonomic system and endocrine glands bring the body to a heightened state of physical excitement to cope with perceived danger. Human instincts are the same: to recognize danger and deal with it by fight or flight.

Under stress, the body automatically reacts. The soldier's blood pressure rises, the heart beats rapidly, the body begins to sweat, muscles tense, increasing short-term strength, the mind races, and the endocrine system activates all the biological mechanisms that contribute to increased sensory awareness. Once the soldier perceives danger, few have any control over the onset of these physical reactions. Only when the danger has passed does the body's biological system gradually return to normal.

What happens when the perception of danger is of longer duration? It is not only direct perceptions of death and mutilation on the battlefield that induce stress. The military environment itself is a sensory universe of stressors: the sight of the dead, mutilated bodies, loss of comrades, the screams of the wounded, the sounds of the dying, the odour of decayed flesh, the guilt that comes with killing or having survived when others died, are but a few things that cause a soldier stress. Other physical factors such as inadequate nutrition, hunger, thirst, dehydration, heat, cold, wet weather, minor injuries caused by poor equipment (blisters from poor-fitting boots and packs, etc.), lack of sleep, tiredness from marching, carrying weapons, tents, etc., and the anticipation of battle, all work to increase the stress on the soldier's physiology. Even after the battle, the body will maintain itself in a high state of physiological tension for a considerable period. If the stress is prolonged, say a few days, the biological systems that sustain the physiology of stress will remain aroused and unable to return to normal. A soldier in this state will eventually collapse from nervous exhaustion. The body's physiology will burn out, and only prolonged rest away from the stress will reduce its enhanced state of arousal.

The mind and its imagination add another dimension to the dynamics of stress and collapse. Central to mental function is the ability of the soldier to make reasoned judgements about the circumstances he confronts, and make choices as to what actions to take. That is why it makes no sense to attribute heroism or cowardice to animals; they react in the only way they can react, guided entirely by biological responses and instinct. Humans, however, can choose what actions to pursue under danger and, to some degree, the mind can order actions that contradict and even overrule the impulses of physiology. A soldier's body exhausted by physiological reactions to stress will strongly affect the way his mind functions.

The mind can also affect the physiological operations of the body. Psychosomatic illnesses, conditions of genuine physical debilitation brought on by affective mental states in which the mind is able to produce physical ailments, are common when soldiers are subjected to prolonged stress. Conversion reactions characterized by hysterical blindness, paralysis, and surdomutism (the inability to speak) are extreme forms of such illnesses found among soldiers exposed to intense combat. Memory loss, depression, lack of energy, inability to comprehend orders, palpitations, muscle tremors, uncontrolled urination and defecation are also common, but less extreme examples of stress reactions. The first mental faculty to degenerate under stress is the ability to process information, make decisions, and render reliable judgements about what is happening, what is not happening, and what one can do about what is happening. The fog of war clouds the mind of the exhausted soldier.

But the mind is not autonomic in its reactions to stress, and is not entirely defenceless. What soldiers believe and think can have great bearing upon how they behave when confronted with danger. Jules Wasserman suggests that human psychic defence rests on three beliefs, what he calls the 'Ur defences of man', that shore up the psyche against danger.[20] The first of these is the belief that there is always a connection between a soldier's actions and what happens to him. Humans cannot remain sane in a random world, as battle often appears to be. The second is the belief that 'someone will help me', that if the soldier does all he can to survive and the danger remains or increases that someone – perhaps even God – will come to his aid. This leads some soldiers under stress to develop physically debilitating illnesses such as paralysis of the right arm, the limb used to work the rifle bolt, or to suffer the physical symptoms of a non-existent gas attack, both of which were common occurrences in the First World War.[21] By becoming incapacitated, the soldier retreats from reality and shifts responsibility for his survival to someone else to keep him safe. This often accounts for extreme religiosity among soldiers in danger who comfort themselves with the faith that God will come to their rescue.

The third belief at the centre of human psychic survival is the conviction that 'I will survive'. Even under the most trying of circumstances, soldiers must continue to believe that they will somehow survive or they will collapse. The desire to survive is so deeply embedded in our genetics and evolutionary experience as to be self-evident. When confronted with the face of death from which there seems no escape, few soldiers can retain their sanity.

Soldiers in combat are constantly confronted with stark evidence that none of these basic beliefs upon which their mental stability depends are true. The reality of battle – the noise, randomness of death, screams of the wounded, the broken bodies – can easily shake the soldier's faith in the basic assumptions of his very existence. He seeks temporary safety in the values the military has taught him, i.e., that good soldiers are brave, stand firm in battle, keep faith with their friends, and remember their training, etc. But as the evidence mounts that these nostrums offer no safety from the horror that surrounds him, the soldier's grip on reality loosens. Thus, 'the soldier is suffering from a conflict between his fear of death and injury and his own ideals of duty ... With anxiety, however, since the fear element is directed to what *might* happen and not necessarily to what *is* happening, there is nothing that can be done and the autonomic system runs riot ... the commonest process by which relief is obtained is by the conversion of the anxiety state into a hysterical symptom ... Paralysis, blindness, deafness or indeed any illness give the soldier an honourable retreat from the situation, and his conflict is solved and his anxiety relieved'.[22]

The onset of a soldier's mental debilitation can be rapid or gradual. When the onset is rapid, the condition is referred to as battle shock; when it is gradual, it is called combat fatigue. In general, about 50 per cent of all psychiatric casualties develop debilitating symptoms in less than five days' exposure to military action.[23] Some, as noted earlier in the example of Epizelus at Marathon, do so within minutes. Others develop symptoms as they approach the battle line or while waiting for the battle to begin. The remaining 50 per cent develop symptoms gradually, over a period of five to thirty days. By the end of thirty days of exposure to the combat environment, all but 2 per cent of soldiers are likely to be psychiatrically debilitated to some degree.[24] In specific instances, of course, the distribution can vary. In the invasion of Lebanon in 1982, for example, 100 per cent of Israeli psychiatric cases developed in six days or less.[25]

Almost from the moment of exposure to combat, the soldier's effectiveness diminishes, his mental state is characterized by anxiety, and his ability to function efficiently is immediately diminished to some degree. Soldiers can enter a state of fluctuating fear brought on solely by the anticipation of battle, accompanied by increased frequency and urgency of urination, intense thirst, inability to swallow, vomiting, involuntary defecation, and other reactions. During various periods of tension, almost all soldiers manifest an increase in sweating, vasomotor instability, muscular tremors, and other overt physiological signs of fear. This first stage of combat fatigue usually lasts about five to seven days, and during this period a significant number of soldiers will succumb to acute combat shock.[26]

Those who do not break down now enter a period where their confidence in themselves, their comrades, and their own fighting ability increases in a period of successful adjustment to the battle environment. In this stage, their previously heightened biological reactions to stress calm down to where they no longer interfere with the soldier's ability to perform adequately.[27] The soldier reaches his maximum fighting capability at this point, a period that lasts for some fourteen days. After this, the soldier again begins to manifest symptoms of combat fatigue to an even greater degree.

More serious symptoms of combat exhaustion begin to appear at around three weeks' exposure to the battle environment. The soldier becomes easily fatigued, only now it is not the soldier's physiology that is causing fatigue. His fatigue is being psychologically generated. The entire spectrum of fear reactions that were evident at the first stage reappear with increased intensity, as the soldier's ability to suppress them is greatly diminished.[28] The soldier is now on the verge of complete psychological collapse.

In the final phase of combat fatigue, the soldier begins to believe that he will either be killed or wounded, and that he cannot go on. The loss of friends and the casualty toll engender a feeling of helplessness and hopelessness. The soldier's mental processes begin to deteriorate, and he becomes apathetic and unable to comprehend simple orders. His memory begins to fail, and he cannot be relied upon to remember simple instructions. The soldier cannot concentrate on anything for very long except morbid thoughts of death in which the anxiety that he might be killed is replaced by the certainty that he will be.[29] If the soldier is not given substantial rest from the stress of the hostile environment, he will likely enter a vegetative coma-like state.

Very often, however, a soldier in this condition will suddenly collapse under the impact of a specific incident, such as a near-miss or witnessing the sudden death of a comrade or friend. This produces a kind of emotional explosion where the soldier might become amnesic, stuporous, unable to walk, see, or hear. Others panic and attempt to run away, while others walk toward the enemy seeking relief in death. Some soldiers fall to the ground screaming and claw at the earth. At this point the soldier has suffered a shattering emotional collapse. The simple truth is that soldiers are often crushed by the strain of war. All soldiers, whether in antiquity or modern times, are at risk of becoming psychiatric casualties, like Epizelus at the battle of Marathon.

There is no getting used to combat.[30] Exposure to war often takes a reasonably normal and sane individual and, sometimes in a matter of hours, transforms him into a completely different human being. Since the First World War, military psychiatrists have defined the major psychiatric conditions that soldiers suffer most frequently in war. These are fatigue cases, confusional states, conversion hysteria, anxiety states, and character disorders. Given human nature and its physiology as a constant, there is no reason to expect that soldiers in the armies of antiquity did not suffer the same conditions.[31]

A soldier suffering from fatigue is mentally and physically exhausted; his autonomic biological system, after repeated periods of hyperactivity maintaining his physiology at a heightened state, has collapsed. Physical exhaustion begins to erode his mental strength. Fatigue is 'prodromal' – that is, it sets the stage for further and more complete collapse that is inevitable if the soldier is not given prolonged rest. To reduce the tension, the soldier will abuse drugs and alcohol and become overly irritable. The Macedonian soldiers of Alexander's army were infamous for their heavy consumption of wine, as were Alexander and his officers. The soldier becomes prone to emotional outbursts, such as crying fits, anxiety, paranoia, and fits of rage and violence.[32] If not given sufficient respite from the perceived dangers, the fatigued soldier will develop deeper psychiatric symptoms.

A fatigued soldier can quickly shift into a confusional state marked by a general psychotic dissociation from reality. Unable to deal with the danger, the soldier mentally removes himself from it. Confusional states often involve delirium of some sort, and are likely to engender schizophrenic states of dissociation. Frequently, manic-depressive psychosis develops in which wild swings of mood and activity are evident. One often noted response is Ganzer Syndrome, where the soldier makes jokes, acts foolishly, and otherwise attempts to ward off the horror with humour and the ridiculous. The degree of affliction in confusional states ranges from the profoundly neurotic to the overtly psychotic.[33]

Conversion hysteria is one of the most pronounced and dramatic manifestations of battle shock, and is among the most common psychiatric conditions brought on by the stress of war.[34] Torn between his fears and his socially derived values of duty, courage, and honour, the soldier 'resolves' the tension by 'converting' his fears into some somatic symptom severe enough to incapacitate himself and gain relief from the terror he feels. The physical symptoms allow the soldier to gain relief with a 'legitimate' physical condition, thus preserving his self-respect and that of his peers.[35] After all, no one can rightly expect a soldier who has become blind or paralyzed to continue to fight. The advent of physical debilitation removes any notion that the soldier is himself at fault, and he is not seen as a coward or weak by his comrades.

Conversion hysteria can occur traumatically in response to a specific incident or in post-traumatic situations, especially if the soldier fears he will be forced to return to the dangerous environment his symptoms have permitted him to escape.[36] Whenever conversion hysteria occurs, it is the mind that produces the physical symptoms of debilitation. Conversion hysteria can involve massive or partial dissociative states.[37] *Massive dissociation* manifests itself in fugue states, an inability to know where one is or to function at all. It is often accompanied by a dreamlike wandering around the battlefield with complete disregard for evident dangers. Very often a soldier in a fugue state is totally or partially amnesic, blocking out parts of his past and present memory from his consciousness. Ajax wandering the battlefield in his dream, slaughtering animals while believing they were Odysseus and the Greek heroes, is an example of a fugue state. The psychosis can also take the form of twilight states, repeated passing in and out of consciousness, sometimes accompanied by severe and uncontrollable tremors. Hysteria can degenerate into convulsive attacks in which the soldier rolls into a foetal position and begins to shake violently. At the most extreme, dissociation can manifest itself in catatonia.

Among the most common afflictions associated with *partial dissociation* are hysterical paralysis, deafness, blindness, and surdomutism in which the mind forces the body to become incapacitated.[38] In the *Iliad*, Homer tells us that when Antilokhos learned of Patroklos' death, 'appalled and sick at heart, he lost for a time his power of speech'.[39] Contractive paralysis of the arm needed to operate one's rifle was epidemic in the First and Second World Wars, as was deafness in the Franco–Prussian War, and blindness from imaginary gas attacks in the First World War.[40] Plutarch reports that some of the defenders at the Roman siege of Syracuse in 211 BC suffered surdomutism.[41] Soldiers suffering from partial dissociative hysterical states can also undergo acute sensory disturbances, including somatic pain in which parts of the body feel numb or paralyzed, or chest pain simulating the symptoms of a heart attack.[42]

Soldiers suffering from combat shock often endure severe anxiety states characterized by weakness and tenseness that cannot be relieved by sleep or rest. When the soldier is able to sleep, he is often awakened by nightmares associated with battle experiences, as one of the *stelae* records happening to a soldier seeking help at Epidaurus.[43] The soldier becomes fixated on death, and interprets the events of the battlefield as being directed only at him. He becomes obsessed with death and the fear that he will fail his comrades, or that other men in his unit will discover that he is frightened. Ajax committed suicide because he *believed* his comrades knew his shame and considered him a coward. If the anxiety state persists, the soldier will develop phobic conditions, an extreme fear of some object. He may refuse to advance in formation, or mount his horse, or fire his weapon, or get out of his foxhole. Such was the case with Hori, a soldier in the army of Thutmose III in 1472 BC, who was shaking so violently from fear that he could not move.[44] In his study of over 400 Marine infantry battalions in the Second World War, S.L.A. Marshal reported that less than 20 per cent of combat soldiers ever fired their rifles, even when under attack.[45]

Anxiety can make itself felt in a range of severe somatic neuroses, such as effort syndrome, an abnormal physiological reaction to effort. It is accompanied frequently by shortness of breath, weakness, precordial pain, blurred vision, vasomotor abnormalities, and fainting. Another reaction is emotional hypertension in which the soldier's blood pressure rises dramatically, with all the accompanying symptoms of weakness, sweating, nervousness, etc. He may also develop severe palpitations, called 'soldiers heart' by Civil War physicians. A range of stress-related somatic conditions frequently develop, including vomiting, dyspepsia, backache, and emotional diarrhoea. The *Anglo-Saxon Chronicle* records that in 1003 AD, Aelfric, the English commander, was leading his men toward the Danish line when he suddenly became violently ill, began to vomit, and fell from his horse, unconscious.[46]

Obsessional and compulsive states are similar to those of conversion hysteria except that in conversion states the soldier is completely dissociated from his symptoms and is not aware that they are caused by his own fears. In obsessional states, the soldier realizes the morbid nature of his symptoms and that his fears are at their root.[47] But his tremors, palpitations, stammers, tics, etc., cannot be controlled. Two Spartan soldiers at Thermopylae in 480 BC asked to be relieved of fighting claiming they were suffering from 'acute inflammation of the eyes'. Eventually, the soldier is likely to take refuge in some type of hysterical reaction that permits him to escape psychic responsibility for his physical symptoms.

As the previous examples of Aristodemus and Panities demonstrate, sometimes the mere thought of going to war is sufficient to provoke the onset of psychiatric symptoms. Swank and Marchand's study of American Army divisions in the Second World War revealed that psychiatric symptoms began to appear whenever a unit was alerted for deployment to a combat zone. There was a great increase in the number of somatic complaints such as heart palpitations, dyspnoea, general weakness and fatigue, abdominal pain, vomiting, and backache. Many soldiers were hospitalized for these complaints and never returned to their units. There were also large increases in accidents, desertions, and self-inflicted wounds.[48]

The foregoing analysis of the symptoms of acute and gradual psychiatric collapse in war by no means exhausts the manifestations that emerge among soldiers subjected to prolonged battle stress. The human mind has shown itself infinitely capable of bringing about any number of combinations of symptoms, and then forcing them deep into the soldier's psyche, changing his personality, sometimes forever. War can exact a terrible cost on human emotions, and it is a cost that every soldier will eventually pay if exposed to the horrors of the battlefield long enough.

## War in Antiquity

But was it always so, or is psychiatric collapse only a function of modern warfare with its automatic and high explosive weapons? A number of cases of individuals in antiquity who suffered some of the psychiatric symptoms noted above have been presented throughout the previous analysis to demonstrate that psychiatric conditions fitting modern definitions can be seen to have occurred in antiquity as well. It can also be argued that the conditions of war in antiquity imposed a *greater, not lesser*, degree of stress upon the soldier, and in the absence of the means for psychiatric diagnosis and treatment, it is likely that the rate of psychiatric casualties was even higher than in modern conflicts, even if it was not clearly recognized as such.

What was a battle like in Alexander's day? As the armies approached one another, they would encamp somewhere between one and seven miles apart, depending upon the advantages offered by terrain and availability of water.

Cavalry and light infantry, sometimes performing reconnaissance, foraging, harassment, or movements to contact, would engage in skirmishing. This might go on for days until one side deployed its main force to offer battle and the other accepted. Sometimes the armies remained facing one another for days without further action until one side decided to attack.

The initial encounter of the main forces usually involved an infantry charge preceded by a discharge of missiles (arrows or javelins). The opening attack might occur all along the battle line or in just one segment of it. If the charge was ferocious enough, the other side might quickly lose its nerve, turn tail, and run. More often, however, the enemy would meet the charge and hand-to-hand combat would ensue.[49] The engagement would last probably no longer than a few minutes, the lines remaining in contact, hacking at one another until one side tried to break off the fighting and move back a short distance out of harm's way. The attackers, too, would break off the fight, eager to be out of danger. Then the attackers might move forward for a few yards taking up the positions without fighting previously occupied by the adversary, but remaining a few yards apart. The attackers usually would not press the attack once the adversary gave ground. Sheer exhaustion, fear, and high casualties militated against continuous contact.[50]

The two sides continued facing each other only a few yards apart, yelling and waving their weapons, daring the other side to attack. As the tension and noise rose, perhaps a few brave soldiers might sally forth and engage in individual combats. Then the lines, or perhaps only segments of them, would clash again, engage for a few minutes, until one side fell back and the other advanced into the once contested space before breaking off the fighting again. And so it might go on for hours. A superior force might succeed over time in pressing the other side back for several hundred yards, but do so in bursts and pulses of combat action.[51] During the lulls between pulses, the wounded would be recovered, reinforcements from the rear moved into their places, and commanders might take the opportunity to rearrange their formations by altering their depth or length.

Then the battle would begin again until one side broke from exhaustion or fear or some tactical manoeuvre. In Alexander's day, this manoeuvre was usually a cavalry attack that flanked or penetrated the enemy line, destroying the tactical cohesion of the enemy formation, causing its troops to lose their will to fight or take flight. Safety lay in retaining the integrity of the fighting formation. Once this was lost, the will and ability of the soldier to resist declined rapidly. 'This kind of dynamic stand-off punctuated by episodes of hand-to-hand fighting could continue for some time until one side finally lost its ability to resist, thereby breaking the bonds of mutual deterrence and encouraging the opposing troops to surge forward and begin killing in earnest, their gnawing tension and fear now released and converted into an orgy of blood lust.'[52]

The presence of disciplined cavalry made it almost impossible for a soldier to flee the battlefield alive. Cavalry could easily ride down and kill the hapless victims, many of which had thrown away their arms and shields in their desire to escape. A rear or flank cavalry attack was likely to force the defeated enemy into the centre of the line, where it continued to be pressed from the front by the attacking infantry. Under these circumstances, the defeated soldiers would find themselves closely packed together without any formational integrity with which to resist. The press of humanity would become so great that the soldiers would be unable to use their weapons effectively to defend themselves. As Livy said of the Romans at Cannae, surrounded and packed together, the victims were slaughtered like cattle.

My earlier study of casualty rates in fourteen ancient battles in the Bronze and Iron ages suggests that a defeated army in antiquity, on average, would suffer 37.7 per cent of its combat force killed and another 35.4 per cent wounded. Seven out of ten soldiers who took the field could expect to be killed or wounded. The victorious army suffered much fewer losses, with only 5.5 per cent killed and 6 per cent wounded.[53] Comparative figures for American armies in all wars from the Civil War to the Korean War were 17.7 per cent killed and 46.1 per cent wounded.[54] Thus, the chances of a soldier being killed or wounded in antiquity were much greater than in modern times, suggesting that the levels of stress engendered by the fear of being killed or maimed were at least the same, if not greater, in ancient as in modern battles.

There was one factor, however, that suggests that the stress suffered by ancient soldiers was considerably greater. All the killing in ancient battles was done with muscle-powered weapons inflicted upon the victim at close range, so that the slayer directly witnessed the fate of the slain that he caused with his own hands. Studies have shown that the strength and duration of the psychological impact of killing at close range is much greater than killing at a distance.[55] Soldiers that have killed 'at knife range' are more likely to suffer psychiatric symptoms of stronger intensity and for longer duration than soldiers who killed at more distant ranges where the victims were seen only as a fleeting image in the distance. The greater distance permits the modern soldier to believe he has never really killed anyone, or at least, probably did not, because he never saw the results of his actions up close. Soldiers in ancient battles could sustain no such illusion. The gory business of close killing – blood, screams, torn flesh, terror in the victim's eyes, etc. – was immediately evident to the killer, and the impact of these visions upon the killer's psyche was likely to be very strong.

When trying to assess the stress endured by the ancient soldier, it is important to recall that stress in a military environment arises from other factors besides close combat. The basic physical conditions of life in an army on the march or garrisoning a hostile country are, by themselves, sufficient to cause psychiatric breakdown. Jonathan Shay in his seminal work, *Achilles in Vietnam*, criticizes Homer when he notes that in the *Iliad* battlefield shortages of everything at one time or another are treated by Homer as if they never happened. Shay remarks, 'His complete silence on the deprivations suffered by men in combat screams out for correction. Where are thirst, hunger, and lack of sleep, maddening heat, and agonizing cold? Where are filth, squalor, and inability to wash the body, pants sticky and reeking from dysentery, the utter lack of privacy? Where are lice, rats, ants, scorpions, snakes, mosquitos?'[56]

The Alexander sources tell us that his soldiers froze to death, endured days of driving rain, were bitten by snakes, suffered from dysentery and disease, and succumbed to heatstroke. But we are not told of the effect of these difficulties on the individual soldier or the fighting ability of the army. Alexander himself seems to have suffered from heatstroke and from dysentery. Although dysentery is the disease that has caused more casualties throughout history than any other, our sources tell us nothing about its effect on Alexander's army. In all probability, the Macedonian army in Alexander's campaign suffered frequently from disease and infection, especially in the tropical areas of India and Pakistan.[57]

Injuries were another cause of stress in the life of the ancient soldier. Alexander's army of 65,000 men and 6,000 cavalry arranged in column ten abreast stretched for sixteen and a half miles, not counting baggage animals and pack trains.[58] This forced the army to move in as compact a mass as possible. Otherwise, it could not move at all. The air breathed by the men in the centre of the column was putrid. The dust choked their nostrils, eyes became irritated, and lungs became congested. In a single day, nosebleeds, eye irritation, and respiratory problems caused injury of such severity, that men would begin to drop out of the march formation to be left behind. It was even worse in cold climates. When Alexander crossed the Hindu Kush with his army of 100,000, he arrived thirteen days later with only 64,000, a loss rate of 36 per cent. An ancient army on the march was a medical disaster. In just a few days, an army of 10,000 could expect to lose 400 men to heatstroke or exhaustion, and 1,700 to routine injuries.[59] Then, as now, military life tended to be dangerous to the soldier's health.

The general conditions of military life are sufficient in themselves to cause psychiatric casualties. Comparing the rates of post-traumatic stress disorder in the American army across three wars, Vietnam, Iraq, and Afghanistan, it becomes clear that military life is very stressful indeed. Of soldiers in these three wars *who experienced direct combat*, only 12.5 per cent (on average) reported symptoms of post-traumatic stress disorder. In Vietnam, 54 per cent of the soldiers reporting post-traumatic stress disorder symptoms *had not been in combat at all*; similarly, 45 per cent of soldiers in Iraq/Afghanistan reporting symptoms had no combat exposure. It is a remarkable testament to the general stress of war that more men suffered psychiatric symptoms from being in the war zone (area of operations) than from exposure to combat![60]

A similar finding emerges when suicides for veterans of Afghanistan and Iraq are examined. Some 30 per cent committed suicide *while deployed* overseas, and 35 per cent *after returning* from deployment. But 35 per cent of suicides were committed by soldiers *who had never been deployed to a war zone, much less experienced combat*.[61] The armies of antiquity had very short 'tails', that is logistics and supply trains, and every soldier was expected to take his place in battle when the time came. In modern armies, only a small percentage, 10–15 per cent, of the total deployed force is likely to actually be exposed to combat. Even so, for a substantial number of soldiers, the general stress of military life, even without exposure to battle, is enough to cause them to develop psychiatric symptoms and become debilitated. There is no reason to believe that this was not so in antiquity.

The conclusion to be drawn from the foregoing analysis is that the same objective and subjective factors that drive modern soldiers to psychiatric collapse affected the ancient soldier in exactly the same way. Even the behavioural symptoms associated with specific psychiatric conditions are largely the same. There is no reason, then, to expect that Alexander's troops did not manifest the same psychiatric conditions and symptoms at approximately the same rates as modern soldiers.

*Chapter 5*

# Alexander's Psychology

One of the more intriguing questions about Alexander is how he managed to survive the trauma of war and slaughter for thirteen years, and how that experience affected his character and actions. Studies of military psychiatry over the last century have clearly demonstrated that prolonged exposure to these events can drastically alter a person's character and even destroy it. The place to begin answering this question is to analyse Alexander's personality using modern psychiatric concepts and diagnostic criteria employed by military psychiatrists dealing with combat trauma victims. Alexander's behaviour at war can then be examined to assess how the prolonged exposure to combat and the military environment may have affected him.

In attempting to uncover the key elements of Alexander's personality, we have the advantage of being able to examine his behaviour over most of his adult life, at least as revealed by the ancient sources. These accounts can serve as a case study, elements of which can be associated with Alexander's personality traits. This approach may raise concerns about the validity of 'psychohistory' as a method of historical analysis. But whenever any historian attempts to discern a subject's motives or describe his or her actions, that historian is really attempting to make sense of the subject's psychology, if only by implication. One cannot read Arrian, Curtius, Diodorus, and Justin's accounts of Alexander without being drawn into their understanding of Alexander's psychology.

What, then, can modern psychology tell us about Alexander's personality? Nasser Ghaemi, in this book *A First-Rate Madness*, has developed eleven modular personality types based on an examination of the lives of eleven world leaders.[1] The personality that most resembles Alexander's is that of William Tecumseh Sherman, the famous American Civil War general. Both suffered from what are called biologically abnormal temperaments, meaning both had traits that were divergent from average behaviour. Abnormal temperaments are to be distinguished from mental illness in that there is no implication that the subject suffers from the presence of a mental disease (manic-depression, bi-polar disorder, borderline personality, etc.), but only that the demonstrated personality traits are divergent from the norm. Temperament abnormalities resemble lesser expressions or milder versions of mental disease, but with the caveat that the abnormalities *are present all the time* while mood episodes like manic phases and deep depression are episodic.[2] Neither Sherman nor Alexander were manic-depressives, but both possessed abnormal temperaments with characteristics that were milder versions of manic-depressive illness.

Alexander and Sherman closely match Ghaemi's definition of a hyperthymic personality, a condition genetically related to bi-polar disorder, but less severe. Individuals possessing this type of personality tend to be highly self-confident, possess high energy levels, need little sleep, are given to rapid speech and impulsive behaviours, including a tendency toward explosive anger, can be doggedly determined in their pursuit of a task, often avoiding contrary evidence and experience, and are strongly resilient in dealing with objections and hardship.[3] Hyperthymic personalities are also creative thinkers in their ability to think and see things in broad terms, a trait psychologists call 'integrative complexity'.[4] They often make connections between seemingly disparate things, leading to divergent thinking that others find difficult to follow or comprehend. Integrative thinking, the tendency to link things together in different ways, is the basis of creativity, but can also lead the person to formulate grandiose plans that only make sense to him. Hyperthymic personalities are risk-takers, often ignoring or not seeing the obstacles to their goals. Divergent and creative thinking can lead to paranoia, with the person suddenly believing himself surrounded by enemies and spies. Hyperthymic personalities tend toward heavy alcohol use and an active libido, activities that sooth them.[5] Hyperthymic personalities are not disconnected from reality the way the mentally ill often are, but have a distorted view of what's happening when measured against 'average' or 'normal' comprehension of occurring events.[6]

There appears to be a genetic link to the development of hyperthymic personality, and Alexander's father seems to have possessed some of the characteristics associated with the type. Philip had high energy, was a workaholic, a heavy drinker, possessed an elevated libido, was given to risk-taking, was ambitious and sociable.[7] There is, however, no evidence that Philip suffered from depressive moods, grandiose thinking, paranoia, or suicidal impulses, traits evident in the behaviour of both Sherman and Alexander.

To whatever degree genetics plays a role in the development of personality, Alexander seems to have more resembled his mother than his father. Like Olympias, Alexander was headstrong, arrogant, and incapable of tolerating criticism. Both mother and son kept their associates under close scrutiny, and any sign of disloyalty was met with outrage and vindictiveness. Both were grimly serious, given to fits of ungovernable anger. Alexander's well-known sensitivity to even minor criticism, what psychologists call 'narcissistic injury', was also evident in his mother. This led both of them to see themselves as victims. Both needed constant reassurances of their position, and both were very dependent upon the frequent praise of others to feel reassured about themselves. Alexander's well-known religiosity was also shared by his mother, an extravagant practitioner of the Dionysian cult.[8] With Philip emotionally remote from his son and often away on campaign, Alexander was raised by his mother and her relatives. He grew very close to her, and remained loyal to her until the end. It is no exaggeration to say that Olympias was the dominant personality in Alexander's life.

Ancient historians offer a far simpler perspective on Alexander's personality, and have offered two explanations as to why Alexander behaved and thought the way he did: first, that he was jealous of his father and wanted to surpass him in achievement and reputation and, second, that his mother, Olympias, instilled in him the idea that he could be a greater man than his father by following the example of Olympias' ancestor, Achilles.[9] That Alexander wanted to emulate his father and surpass Philip as a great leader is beyond question. It was, however, no easy task since Philip was the saviour of his country, a valiant warrior, a hard drinking field general beloved by his troops, and the greatest national king of his time.

Alexander grew to resent his father in almost every way. Plutarch tells us of this resentment when he says 'and so every success that was gained by Macedonia inspired in Alexander the dread that another opportunity for action had been squandered on his father'.[10] By the time Philip was assassinated, Alexander had become convinced that Philip no longer intended Alexander as his heir.[11] Alexander's resentment seems to have persisted throughout his life, and he could fly into a rage whenever anyone praised Philip in his presence. Alexander killed Cleitus the Black in a fit of drunken rage after Cleitus had the temerity to praise Philip and criticize Alexander in front of the officers gathered at a symposium.[12]

It was also likely that the reason Alexander had Parmenio murdered was Parmenio's frequent disagreements with Alexander over strategy and tactics. As chief of staff of the army and Alexander's second in command, Parmenio frequently gave the inexperienced Alexander advice, military and otherwise, sometimes disagreeing with him in front of other officers in war councils.[13] Alexander was very sensitive about his lack of combat experience, and resented Parmenio's advice. Parmenio's criticisms could only have served to remind Alexander that the old general did not consider Alexander his superior, much like a grizzled combat-hardened old sergeant criticizing an inexperienced young platoon leader, but at best an equal and at worst a subordinate needing instruction in things military. One might imagine that when

Parmenio gave young Alexander advice, he reminded the boy of Philip himself. After Parmenio had served Alexander well on the battlefield in defeating the Persians, Alexander had the old bull murdered.

Alexander's desire to emulate Achilles may well have been inculcated by his mother, whose family claimed lineal descent from Achilles. This maternal inspiration supposedly led Alexander to regard the *Iliad* as his favourite book, and to take it with him on campaign. He is said to have slept with a copy of the *Iliad* and a dagger under his pillow. It was from these ancient, if somewhat suspicious accounts, that historians concluded that Achilles came to serve as the heroic model that Alexander sought to emulate in his desire to outdo his father. Many of Alexander's brutal actions on and off the battlefield do indeed mimic the behaviour of Achilles as recounted in the *Iliad*. But in seeking to imitate Achilles, Alexander does not seem to have grasped that he was emulating the behaviour of a man driven to insanity by war. It is because of this, Achilles' descent into madness, that Plato called the *Iliad* a work of tragedy written by the first of the tragedians.[14]

The *Iliad* is not about Achilles' heroism so much as about his descent into madness as a result of his experience of war. Homer's poem is about Achilles' rage, first brought about by his betrayal by his commander who takes from Achilles a slave girl the army had awarded Achilles as a prize of war. This reduced Achilles' status in the eyes of his comrades, and his first reaction was to draw his sword and kill Agamemnon, only to be stopped by the goddess Athena.[15] Achilles had been at war for almost nine years, and was suffering combat fatigue. His first reaction to insult is to kill his commanding officer! It might have been the first recorded instance of 'fragging' a superior officer had Athena not descended from heaven and stayed his hand. In response to Agamemnon's betrayal, Achilles withdrew from the fight at Troy and sulked, knowing that without their best warrior the Greeks would suffer badly in the battles ahead, as they did.

After the Greeks had suffered several defeats at the hands of the Trojans, Achilles' adopted brother and second in command, Patroklos, came to Achilles with the idea that he borrow Achilles' armour and enter the battle in disguise to boost the morale of the Greeks by convincing them that Achilles has returned to the fight. Achilles agrees, and sends his brother into battle dressed in Achilles' armour. When Patroklos is killed by Hector, the Trojan's great warrior, Achilles blames himself for having abandoned Patroklos and for sending him out alone. He laments, 'I could not help my friend in his extremity ... He needed me to shield him or to parry the death stroke ... Here I sat, my weight a useless burden to the earth.'[16] Achilles' guilt moves quickly to passing sentence upon himself as being responsible for Patroklos' death, and he is filled with the impulse to kill himself. He is prevented from doing so when 'Antilokhos ... bent to hold the hero's hands when groaning shook his heart: Antilokhos feared the man might use sharp iron to slash his throat'.[17] Prevented from killing himself, Achilles' grief now transformed itself into a murderous rage, what military psychiatrists call a 'berserk state', in which all human values are abandoned in pursuit of bloody revenge or 'payback'.

And that is the point. Achilles has now become insane, the prototype of the berserker. Homer's narrator calls Achilles' brutal actions against the Trojans 'shameless' and 'an outrage', the exact opposite of the Greek ideal of heroism. The god Apollo makes his disgust with Achilles clear:

> Murderous Achilles ...
> A man who shows no decency, implacable,
> barbarous in his ways ...
> The man has lost all mercy;
> he has no shame.
> A sane one may endure
> an even dearer loss; a blood brother;
> a son; and yet, by heaven, having grieved
> and passed through mourning, he will let it go ...
> Not this one.[18]

Before Achilles suffers the psychological injuries of betrayal, survivor guilt, and a descent into madness, Homer tells us that Achilles was a good warrior who used to take prisoners, respect the enemy dead and not defile them, and to ransom prisoners rather than kill them. In his berserk state, Achilles kills pointlessly, cuts the throats of prisoners, defiles the corpses of his victims, and loses all compassion for any human being, even his fellow Greeks.[19] He taunts the dying Hector, telling him he will kill him and eat his flesh![20] In complete defiance of the Greek ideal of an ethical warrior, no living human has any claim upon Achilles any more, not even the claim of being well-remembered. No restraint of any kind limits Achilles' actions during his berserk state – no prudence, ethics, piety, personal gain, compassion, fatigue, or physical pain, not the rational requirements of victory or even fidelity to his dead friend. Even the ghost of Patroklos reproaches Achilles for his actions saying, 'thou hast forgotten me, Achilles'.[21]

Modern military psychiatry tells us that Achilles' rage is not passion, but the negation of all emotion, a 'psychic numbing' that negates all other emotions, that constitute the normal human feelings – compassion, empathy, sympathy, fairness, love, etc. – that make communal life possible. The berserk state is also addictive in that it produces neuro-hormones, specifically endogenous opiods, which have psychoactive tranquilizing properties that produce a state of calm in the berserker. If a soldier survives the berserk state, the experience 'imparts an emotional deadness and vulnerability to explosive rage to his psychology, and often a permanent hyper arousal to his physiology', two characteristics typical of soldiers suffering post-traumatic stress disorder.[22] As early as the First World War, military psychiatrists recognized that the berserk state often resulted in permanent deformation of the soldier's personality, leading to episodic recurrence in civilian life. This, then, is the Achilles that Alexander's mother urged him to emulate.

Alexander's emulation of Achilles represents a perversion of the traditional Greek ideal of heroism, not its realization. Closely related to heroic behaviour is the idea of manliness. For Greeks, manliness in war is the highest value in defining a man's social worth in the community. But it is by no means the only requirement. A good man is one who knows how to behave in civil life as well, and even to behave humanely on the battlefield by not killing the wounded, being willing to take prisoners, taking care to treat even the enemy dead properly, and to be fair in treating his fellow soldiers. No matter how brave a soldier may be, if he lacks these requirements he is not regarded as heroic.

Sheer brutality on the battlefield is not heroism. Matthew Gonzales has identified the traits of the Homeric warrior that constituted the warrior's ethical world. They include: excellence (*arete*), being a good man (*agathos*), honour (*time*), glory (*kudos*), renown (*kleos*), reverence (*aidos*), a sense of shame (*eleos*), and a sense of avoiding moral ruin (*ate*).[23] Note that all the heroic virtues are *social* in nature in that they require proper behaviour toward *other human beings* or the gods. The Homeric warrior's virtues address the way he ought to treat others, and not just how to serve his own interests, desires, or sense of personal virtue. The tragedy of Achilles lies in his abandonment of these social virtues and the triumph of personal rage over them.

A central element in Alexander's personality was his desire to prove his manliness within the Macedonian and Greek cultural context. In so many ways – his effeminate physical appearance, lack of military training, lack of battle experience, homosexuality, and failure to perform the usual acts of bravery required of youthful warriors – Alexander lacked the overt characteristics of manliness expected of a Macedonian warrior and royal heir. To overcome these shortcomings, Alexander set out to emulate Achilles' battlefield prowess as a way of proving he was a man. There was a deep sense of insecurity at the root of Alexander's personality even before going to war, and he feared that others would discover it. Plutarch confirms this when he tells us that from an early age Alexander was intensely concerned about how he appeared to others, and that 'above all, if anybody spoke ill of him, his judgement was apt to desert him and his mood would become cruel and merciless'.[24] Arrian, too, hints at it when he says 'it was for praise alone for which he [Alexander] was absolutely insatiate'.[25] Alexander required praise to reassure himself that he was a man in the Greek heroic sense.

Not all soldiers who suffer lingering symptoms from exposure to war become berserkers like Achilles. As noted earlier, prolonged exposure to war and the hardship of life in the field can drive men to become psychiatric casualties. There are a number of specific events that can precipitate psychic wounding, including betrayal, insult, or humiliation by a superior; death of a close friend; being wounded or injured; being overrun by the enemy and surviving while one's comrades are killed; seeing dead comrades mutilated by enemy fire or deliberate butchery; and unexpectedly surviving from what seemed certain death.[26] Deep guilt can also arise when the soldier realizes he has killed another human being or, worse, engaged in the kind of barbaric behaviour – rape, torture, murder, wanton destruction, slaughter, etc. – that often occurs in war. Any of these events can produce long-term psychological effects, a phenomenon recognized as post-traumatic stress disorder.

It is noteworthy that Alexander experienced *every one* of the events that can precipitate post-traumatic stress disorder. He felt betrayed by Philip when he came to believe that his father no longer regarded him as his heir; he interpreted Parmenio's criticisms and advice as humiliation, an insult to his status as a superior; Alexander witnessed the death of many companions in battle, including some of his friends; he was wounded seven times; the nature of ancient weapons made bodily mutilation a frequent occurrence in ancient warfare, and Alexander would have witnessed it often; sometimes mutilation was done deliberately to weaken enemy morale, as when the Persian king Darius chopped the hands off the Macedonian wounded at Issus before sending them back to Alexander; at the siege of Malli, Alexander found himself alone, surrounded, wounded, and trapped behind the enemy battlements, facing certain death before being unexpectedly rescued by his officers.

The subject of Alexander's atrocities will be addressed in detail in the next chapter. Suffice it to say that Alexander's brutality put Achilles to shame who 'brought twelve radiant sons of Troy whose throats I'll cut, to bloody your great pyre ...'[27] by exterminating an entire people to soothe his terrible grief over the death of his friend, Hephaestion.[28] Even Alexander's later developed sense that he was immortal has its roots in war trauma. The belief that one cannot be killed is often a psychological reaction to having survived some harrowing circumstance.[29] Given his experiences, it would not be unreasonable to expect that Alexander may have suffered from the symptoms characteristic of post-traumatic stress disorder.

The American experience in treating psychiatric casualties in the Vietnam, Iraq, and Afghan wars has produced a detailed knowledge of the symptoms of post-traumatic stress disorder among soldiers exposed to war.[30] These symptoms can range in severity, and not all soldiers will demonstrate all symptoms at the same time. However, the presence of even a single symptom can have devastating effects on the soldier's behaviour, and can set the stage for the development of more stable personality traits associated with severe character disorders. The longer the exposure to war, the more likely the soldier will develop post-traumatic stress disorder. In the case of Alexander, his exposure to multiple traumatic events over a period of thirteen years made the development of post-traumatic stress disorder almost a certainty.

Among the more dramatic symptoms of post-traumatic stress disorder is the 'persistent mobilization of the body and the mind for lethal danger, with the potential for explosive violence'.[31] Once exposed to the dangers of war, the body can remain physiologically mobilized to meet these dangers, even when they no longer objectively exist. A constant state of physiological arousal creates other symptoms of illness, such as insomnia, agitation, headaches, rapid heartbeat, gastrointestinal disorders, etc. The soldier's capacity for a sense of well-being, self-respect, confidence, and satisfaction erodes, and he can become full of dread. Life under these physical and psychological conditions can become extremely irritating, leading the soldier to explosive outbursts, often including violence.[32] As we shall see, Alexander was given to fits of explosive violence of which the killing of his friend, Cleitus, is the most famous, but hardly the most dramatic example. In another instance, he ordered the extermination of an entire village after they surrendered, because their very existence somehow set him off.

A soldier's prolonged exposure to war can create an almost constant sense and expectation of betrayal by those around him, destroying any capacity for trust and leading to the individual's psychological isolation.[33] Research has shown that soldiers in this condition are seven times more likely to suffer major depression and eleven times more likely to suffer a dysthymic disorder, a fluctuating state of depression.[34] Alexander nursed a sense of betrayal that developed into deep paranoia. As his wars went on, he began to see enemies everywhere, even among his closest friends and comrades. In every case, Alexander dealt with his fear by having the 'conspirators' killed. At the end of his life, he trusted only one person, his long-time lover, Hephaestion.[35]

A battle-hardened soldier either quickly acquires a set of survival skills or he dies. The soldier's hyper-vigilance is accompanied by the need to react quickly and with violence. Soon, the soldier may lose an ability to respond to simple disagreements or other social situations in any other way, leading to the activation of combat survival skills in other than combat situations.[36] This explains why a simple misunderstanding can often lead to a violent physical attack, say, in a bar, when a combat veteran perceives himself insulted or being stared at. Alexander, like many veterans, seems to have forgotten how to deal with even the most minor difficulty with anything but violence. In India, he hanged a group of Indian philosophers who had the temerity to disagree with him, and had the defeated Persian commander at Gaza dragged around the city behind a chariot because the man remained silent when Alexander threatened him. Achilles' first reaction to Agamemnon's order to turn over the slave girl was to reach for his sword and kill his commander.

Alcoholism and drug use are common symptoms of post-traumatic stress disorder, and both are employed by the soldier as a way to 'numb' the psychic pain that afflicts him, and reduce the effects of his other symptoms. There is no doubt that by the end of his life, Alexander was surely a heavy drinker and, perhaps, even an alcoholic in the clinical sense. His increased drinking coincided with the clearer emergence of other symptoms of post-traumatic stress disorder and character disorder.[37]

Post-traumatic stress can lead to suicide. Two of the most common triggers of suicide in veterans are guilt and despair. Watching one's comrades die in situations where you have survived, or having ordered soldiers to do something that cost them their lives, often produces 'survivor guilt', a sense that 'it was my fault' or 'it should have been me that died'. Guilt can also arise from having committed some horrible act from which one seeks redemption. Achilles tried to kill himself out of guilt after the death of Patroklos, but was prevented from doing so by Antilokhos. Despair and isolation can also trigger suicide, leading the soldier to take risks that obviously threaten his life, hoping to achieve escape from his pain through death, or to redeem himself by being killed before the eyes of his comrades. At the Battle of Platea, Aristodemus charged 'forward with the fury of a madman in his desire to be killed before his comrade's eyes' to redeem himself for his cowardly behaviour at Thermopylae the year before.[38] Alexander tried to kill himself twice for reasons similar to those of Achilles and Aristodemus.

It is clear from Xenophon's account of the Spartan general, Clearchus, with whom he served in Cyrus's army in Persia, that the Greeks were familiar with the behaviour that results from post-traumatic stress. Beginning at the age of 19, Clearchus had spent twenty years fighting in the various campaigns of the Peloponnesian War, more than enough exposure to war to bring on post-traumatic stress. Lawrence Trittle outlines Xenophon's description of Clearchus.[39] Clearchus was a man who was fond of war, who could have lived in peace but always chose war (*Anabasis*, 2.6.6); a man who preferred hardship and a difficult life to one of leisure and pleasure (*Anabasis*, 2.6.6); a man who spent money on war the way a man lavishes gifts upon a mistress, with the result that he never had much money (*Anabasis*, 2.6.6); a man who was fond of adventure, who always desired to lead the attack, and whose forbidding demeanour and appearance became relaxed in times of great danger (*Anabasis*, 2.6.7.10); a tough and difficult man who possessed a harsh voice, was a brutal disciplinarian, and incapable of personal relationships (*Anabasis*, 2.6.11.13); and a man who could not serve under the command of another officer (*Anabasis*, 2.6.11.13). Clearchus had seen a lot of war, and that experience had taken its psychic toll by turning him into a grim soldier that was only truly alive when excited by the dangers of war. War had made Clearchus incapable of normal human emotions and feelings, a condition that made it impossible for him to sustain personal relationships. The Greeks called a man like this *philopolemas*, or a war lover.

Clearchus' post-traumatic stress disorder is also evident in his tendency to explode in rage over even small difficulties, and to resort to his combat survival skills as the best way to deal with any difficulty. Xenophon tells us that one of Clearchus' soldiers fell into a dispute with a soldier from another general's command, Meno of Thessaly. Clearchus decided that his soldier was in the right, and had Meno's soldier harshly beaten. Two days later, as Clearchus passed through Meno's camp he was greeted by a hail of stones and whatever other missiles Meno's troops could lay their hands on. Clearchus flew into a rage, ordered his troops to prepare for battle, and was about to attack his assailants. Proxenus, another general, tried to calm Clearchus, only to have Clearchus threaten him with violence. Only when Cyrus himself, commander of the army, arrived could Clearchus be controlled and his anger lessened.[40] This kind of explosive anger is usually referred to by psychiatrists as 'pervasive hyper-alertness', and is typical of soldiers suffering from post-traumatic stress disorder.[41]

Post-traumatic stress disorder is a serious psychological condition that can provoke a range of behavioural abnormalities. Over time, however, as in the case of Clearchus' twenty years and Alexander's thirteen years of war, the condition can become deeply embedded in the soldier's psyche and permanently deform his personality. One set of permanent psychiatric reactions to prolonged war stress are called character disorders. The terms are somewhat misleading in that they seem to imply that the soldier's character has been disordered by conscious action. This is not the case, however. Correctly understood, character disorder is a condition in which the prolonged stress of war creates problems so deeply seated that they become part of the soldier's personality. Character disorders include stable obsessional states in which the soldier becomes fixated on certain actions or things; paranoia accompanied by irascibility, anxiety, and depression, often accompanied by the belief that the soldier is surrounded by enemies who threaten his safety; schizoid trends leading to hypersensitivity and isolation; epileptoid character reactions in which the soldier becomes irritable, stubborn, egocentric, and aggressive, accompanied by periodic rages; the development of extreme dramatic religiosity, and, ultimately, the degeneration into a psychopathic personality. Character disorders represent a fundamental altering of the soldier's personality that is extremely difficult to reverse. All too commonly the symptoms accompany the soldier for the rest of his life.[42]

The foregoing analysis attempts to present a description of Alexander's personality by drawing upon information from modern diagnostic psychiatry as well as upon the insights offered by the accounts of ancient historians as to Alexander's psychological motivations. While the modern perspective offers more detailed and precisely defined concepts with which to work, it is important to note that there is nothing in the two approaches that stand in contradiction. Human motivation is complex, and probably does not lend itself well to single factor analysis. In some instances, the motivations attributed to Alexander by the ancient historians may prove to be more valuable in comprehending Alexander's behaviour than those offered by modern psychiatric analysis. The following chapters seek to analyse Alexander's behaviour at war with both approaches in mind.

*Chapter 6*

# Anger and Atrocity

It can be said with certainty that the one area in which Alexander surpassed his father was in cruelty and atrocity. Alexander was one of antiquity's most notorious mass murderers. He slaughtered thousands of innocent victims, mostly women and children, and, at times, his own countrymen. Almost every one of his military campaigns was marked by an atrocity. Alexander's murdering ferocity falls into five categories: the sheer carnage he inflicted upon enemies on the battlefield; the routine slaughter of defenders and civilians in sieges; the wholesale and genocidal extermination of tribes and villagers during his guerrilla wars in Iran, Afghanistan, and Pakistan; the toll taken on his own soldiers and their thousands of camp followers during his crazed and unnecessary crossing of the Gedrosian Desert; and the crass murders of his rivals, family, and an entire generation of Macedonian generals and officers that Alexander, in his paranoia, came to see as threats.[1]

Alexander's record of murder and atrocity stands in marked contrast to Philip's. In over twenty years of war, Philip participated in more than thirty-four battles and sieges,[2] during which only two examples of atrocities can be found, the complete destruction of the city of Olynthos (348 BC) and the slaughter of the Scythian males of military age during the Scythian campaign (339 BC).[3] In both cases, however, Philip had sound strategic reasons for doing so, and coldly acted upon them.

Olynthos was the leader of the Chalcidian League, and had to be destroyed if the strategic Chalcidian peninsula and all its cities and towns were to be incorporated into the Macedonian state. Moreover, Olynthos had given two of Philip's brothers refuge and support in their attempts to raise armies to replace Philip as king of Macedonia. In Scythia, the area was too important in grain production to leave a large hostile tribe to its own interests. Philip killed the military-age males, and transported the young boys and women to Macedonia to be sold into slavery. In his expansion of Macedonia, Philip captured more than a score of cities. Except for Olynthos, Philip allowed the civilian populations to remain unmolested or incorporated them into the Macedonian state. In not a single case is it reported that Philip ordered military action out of personal anger. Unlike Alexander, there are no accounts of Philip flying into a rage and ordering the death or destruction of a military or civilian population, or even an individual. When it came to anger, cruelty, and atrocity, Alexander truly surpassed Philip.

Alexander's experience with murder began within days of assuming the throne after Philip's assassination. Perhaps on the advice of Antipater and/or Eumenes, Alexander had his cousin, his half-brothers, his step-sisters, and their entire families put to death. He ordered the execution of Philip's new wife and her young child, as well as her extended family, to include Attalus, a well-known general and her guardian. These murders are often excused on the grounds that Macedonian court politics were often lethal, and that Philip had his rivals for the throne murdered as well.[4] The two cases are not comparable, however.

All three of Philip's step-brothers left Pella in search of allies to mount military expeditions against him. Argaeus obtained the support of Amphipolis, Archelaus of Olynthos, and Cotys the support of the king of Thrace. Over the next few years, each of the step-brothers were killed by their hosts in order to obtain Philip's friendship for their larger interests. Philip's nephew, the child of his slain brother, and the first heir to the throne, Amyntas IV, lived peacefully alongside Philip for his entire life. Nor is there any evidence that the wives and families of Philip's step-brothers were harmed.[5] Alexander's murders, on the other hand, were cold-blooded dynastic politics that took the lives of anyone remotely capable of raising a claim to the throne.

If Alexander had any hesitation about murder, he seems to have grown accustomed to it very quickly. Later, he had the great general, Parmenio, and his son, Philotas, a first-rate cavalry commander, murdered, and then killed the four-man, hand-picked assassination team of Cleander, Sitalces, Heracon, and Agathon who had murdered Parmenio on his orders. Alexander had Callisthenes, his official court historian and nephew of Aristotle put to death, and threatened Aristotle in a letter with a similar fate. Alexander killed Cleitus, who had saved his life at the Granicus and whose sister, Lanice, had been Alexander's nurse, in a fit of drunken rage. After his return from the Indian campaign and the catastrophic Gedrosian desert crossing, Alexander launched a purge of his administrators and satraps that consumed hundreds, many of whom were fellow Macedonians. Besides the Macedonian officers we know about from ancient sources, there were a host of lesser-known bureaucrats who were summarily killed on suspicions of disloyalty, incompetence, and intrigue.[6]

The more Alexander was exposed to war, the more explosive anger and violence characterized his behaviour. Curtius tells us that, 'at the end of his life, his degeneration from his former self was so complete that, though earlier possessed of unassailable self-control, he followed a male whore's judgement to give some men kingdoms and deprive others of their lives'.[7] Justin summed up the difference in personality between Philip and Alexander by saying 'Philip preferred to be loved while his son, Alexander, preferred to be feared.'[8]

The analysis that follows examines those events recorded by the ancient historians that comprise a list of atrocities committed by Alexander during his Persian, Afghanistan, and Indian campaigns. The purpose of the analysis is to investigate the motives for Alexander's actions in each case, and to determine if these motives can be reasonably explained as the result of Alexander's prolonged exposure to war and its effects on his personality (character disorder) or his psychology (post-traumatic stress), or if there are other explanations. The cases are presented in chronological order, each occurring at a time when Alexander's exposure to war stress was greater than in the case before.

### The Destruction of Thebes (October, 335 BC)

In 335 BC, Alexander was conducting his Illyrian campaign in the Balkans when a rumour began to circulate in Greece that he had been killed. With Philip dead, and Alexander away on campaign, the Thebans saw an opportunity to withdraw from the League of Corinth that Philip had forced upon them after their defeat at Chaeronea. Along with some other members of the League, all neighbouring states and enemies of Thebes, Alexander attacked Thebes in 335 BC to put down the revolt. He turned his troops loose on the city without pity, and slaughtered the civilian population. Diodorus tells us that 'as the slaughter mounted and every corner of the city was piled high with corpses, no one could have failed to pity the plight of the unfortunate'.[9] More than 6,000 Thebans were killed, and 30,000 more sold into slavery.[10] Alexander assembled his allies in council who voted that Thebes, one of Greece's oldest and most renowned cities, the birthplace of Hercules, Oedipus, Pindar, and Epaminondas, be razed to the ground. When Alexander was finished, nothing remained but two huge mounds of rubble. It was Alexander's first case of ethnic cleansing. There would be many more.

Alexander had not yet been exposed to real war, so it is unlikely that battle stress had much to do with his motive to destroy Thebes. Some historians have excused the slaughter on the grounds that Alexander wanted to frighten the Greek states into obedience while he campaigned in Persia.[11] Curiously, only Diodorus hints at this reason when he says that Alexander 'decided to destroy the city utterly and by this act of terror take the heart out of anyone else who might venture to rise against him'.[12] But Alexander came to this conclusion only after twice attempting to get the Thebans to come to a peaceful accommodation. Diodorus tells us that when the Thebans refused, Alexander realized 'that he was despised by the Thebans', and when they publically rejected his second offer, Alexander 'flew into a towering rage'. Only then did he decide to massacre the Thebans and destroy their city.

Here we see two of Alexander's character traits. First, his extreme need for praise and agreement, and his sensitivity to criticism and second, explosive rage. When he realized that the Theban's 'despised him', he aroused such a state of anger within himself that it turned to rage. It was while in this state of rage that he ordered the brutal attack on Thebes 'with the extremity of punishment'.[13] Once the city was taken, it might have been expected that Alexander would have calmed down and reflected on his original intention. He did not.

The decision to destroy Thebes also reveals Alexander's lack of sound strategic sense. Philip could have destroyed Thebes after Chaeronea. He did not because a moderately strong Thebes was critical to Philip's strategic array to keep both Athens and Sparta from threatening the hegemony of the League. Thebes had been the critical fulcrum between Athens and Sparta for centuries, keeping them in check in the classical balance of power that brought peace to central Greece. Philip's policy was to weaken all three states, but allow each to retain some military capability to serve as a check against the others, should any one of them seek to recover their former military prominence.

Alexander's destruction of Thebes weakened the new security regime that Philip put in place. Sparta was now free to attempt to loosen the fetters that Philip had placed upon it. Three years later, the king of Sparta, Agis III, led a serious revolt against Macedonia, and came within an ace of defeating Antipater at the battle of Megalopolis. Alexander despised Antipater for his victory, calling it 'the battle of the mice'. But had Antipater been defeated, all of Greece would have risen in revolt, forcing Alexander to return from Asia. Moreover, Alexander's cruel destruction of Thebes made the Greeks despise him, and right to the end more Greeks fought against Alexander than for him.

## The Battle of the Granicus (May–June, 334 BC)

After allowing Alexander to land in Asia unopposed, the Persians sent a small army to block his further advance. The armies met at the Granicus River. Alexander's attack succeeded in breaking the Persian infantry line, scattering the cavalry, and driving the Persians into retreat.[14] The phalanx of Greek mercenary heavy infantry fighting for the Persians was brought into the battle late, and their formation was still intact when the battle ended. The mercenaries offered to surrender and join Alexander's service, an accommodation typical of the time. Instead, 'Alexander quickly had them surrounded and butchered to a man, though one or two may have escaped notice among the heaps of the dead.'[15] Some 18,000 Greek mercenaries were mercilessly slaughtered by Alexander's cavalry and infantry.[16]

Plutarch tells us that the action against the mercenaries cost Alexander more Macedonian casualties, killed and wounded, than he had lost in the battle itself![17] The slaughter was pointless from a military perspective, since the mercenaries could have been sent home, sent to the mines in Macedonia, or incorporated as selected units into Alexander's army, a common practice in Greek warfare since the Peloponnesian Wars. Why, then, did Alexander murder more Greeks in a single day than the entire number that had fallen to the Persians at Marathon, Thermopylae, Salamis, and Plataea combined?[18]

Plutarch says that Alexander's slaughter of the Greek mercenaries was 'guided rather by passion than judgement', but does not tell us the reason for that passion.[19] This was Alexander's first major battle as commander of the Macedonian army, and he may have intended to demonstrate his heroic manhood by being as brave as Philip. Unlike the old Macedonian generals who wore clothes indistinguishable from their troops, at the Granicus Alexander dressed ostentatiously, galloped to the front, plunged into the fight, and led his troops in riding down the fleeing survivors, all intended to demonstrate his bravery and military competence before the eyes of his troops. He surely succeeded, but 'left the legacy of a battle commander who enjoyed killing, a modern Achilles who measured his worth by his own skill in personally spearing, stabbing, and unhorsing as many of the enemy as he could get his hands on'.[20] Alexander passed his first test as a combat soldier and field commander at the Granicus, but in doing so revealed a penchant for slaughter that was to mark almost all of his future campaigns.

## The Siege of Tyre (January–July, 332 BC)

After defeating the Persians again at Issus, Alexander marched down the Mediterranean coast, capturing or accepting the surrender of the towns that served as ports for the Persian fleet. This permitted him to secure his line of sea communications with Greece that were protected by the Macedonian fleet augmented with Athenian naval squadrons. Before approaching Tyre, the last remaining port city before Gaza, Alexander dismissed his combatant fleet, keeping only a few Macedonian transports to ferry his siege equipment. Alexander's reputation preceded him, and the Tyrians met Alexander as he approached the city, welcomed him, and told him 'they had determined to abide by any instructions Alexander might give', presumably including taking the Tyrian ships out of the Persian naval coalition.[21] Instead of accepting what amounted to the surrender of an important port, Alexander demanded that he be permitted to sacrifice to the gods in the ancient temple of Baal, the most sacred Tyrian and Carthaginian god, located in the island city. The Tyrians refused, saying that only their priests were allowed in the sacred precinct. Anyone else would be committing sacrilege. They offered Alexander the opportunity to sacrifice in another temple in the old city on the mainland.

Denied what he had demanded, Alexander flew into a rage, and brought Tyre under siege. The siege lasted seven months, and the Macedonian army suffered badly under the prolonged conditions. Arrian hints at Alexander's glory-seeking once more when he notes that 'Alexander himself was in the thick of it, fighting like the rest, and ever on the watch for any act of conspicuous courage in the face of danger'.[22] When the Macedonians finally broke through the fortifications and entered the city, 'the slaughter was terrible – for the Macedonians ... went to work with savage ferocity'. Some 8,000 were killed, and 30,000 men, women, and children sold into slavery.[23] As a final outrage, Alexander 'crucified all the men of military age. These were no less than 2,000.'[24] Alexander's decision to reduce Tyre and punish its people was produced by his personal rage at having his will thwarted, and not any military calculus.

There was no need or military advantage in attacking Tyre, whose government had already agreed to abide by Alexander's commands. If he doubted their word, he could always have left a garrison in the old mainland city to keep the island city in check. Cut off from supplies from the mainland, the Tyrian fleet could hardly have remained an important combat asset to the Persians. Alternatively, Alexander could have foregone his request and marched on.[25] He already had control of the Phoenician cities to the north, and only Gaza remained in Persian hands to the south. The conquest of Tyre proved of little value except to bolster Alexander's now growing reputation for needless cruelty. Whatever else, there was no reason to slaughter the citizenry and crucify the soldiers except, perhaps, to demonstrate that Alexander was not a man to be angered without great risk.

## The Siege of Gaza (September–November, 332 BC)

Alexander continued down the coast to Gaza, the strategic key to Egypt, and took the city under siege. The siege lasted two months. When the city fell, Alexander permitted his troops to murder the city's inhabitants at will. All the males were murdered, some 10,000 Persians and Asiatic civilians were killed, and thousands of women and children sold into slavery.[26] Macedonian losses were significant as well, forcing Alexander to dispatch ten triremes to Macedonia to transport a new levy of recruits.[27]

Betis, the Persian governor of Gaza, though greatly outnumbered by the Macedonians, showed great military ability and put up a stiff and costly fight.

When he was captured and brought before Alexander, Alexander threatened him with execution. Betis was a large man, and stood before Alexander covered with his own blood and that of the Macedonians he had personally slain in battle. Betis also wore several exposed wounds suffered in the defence of his city. He must have been an imposing figure.

When Alexander told Betis that he could expect 'to suffer whatever torment can be devised against a prisoner', the Persian gave Alexander 'a look that was not just fearless, but downright defiant, and uttered not a word in reply to Alexander's threats'.[28] Curtius tells us, 'Alexander's anger turned to fury, his recent successes already suggesting to his mind foreign modes of behaviour.' Curtius continues, 'Thongs were passed through Betis' ankles while he still breathed, and he was tied to a chariot. Then Alexander's horses dragged him around the city while the king gloated at having followed the example of his ancestor, Achilles, in punishing his enemy.'[29] In a spasm of cruelty, Alexander himself drove the chariot that dragged Betis around the city, just as Achilles had done with Hector.[30]

The fact that Alexander took personal pleasure in the torture and death of Betis suggests the presence of a sadistic streak in Alexander's personality that would make itself evident again and again in the future. Later, Alexander personally witnessed the torture of Philotas, ordered the stoning of suspected conspirators, crucified thousands of captives, and occasionally murdered or tortured victims himself.[31] Alexander had now been at war for almost four years, and the experience was taking its toll.

## The Capture and Burning of Persepolis (February–May, 330 BC)

In October, 331 BC, Alexander crushed the Persian army at the battle of Gaugamela, driving Darius and the remnants of his army to the east. During the next three months, Alexander advanced through Babylonia and Sittacene, to Susa, into the land of the Uxii, and through the Persian Gates to the Persian capital at Persepolis.[32] In February, 330 BC, Alexander approached the walls of Persepolis, the seat of the Persian kings.

Darius and the remnants of his army were on the run, and there were no Persian military forces to defend the city. Tiridates, the regional governor, offered to surrender the city to Alexander. Instead, Alexander attacked the city by storm. Alexander told his troops that he wanted to avenge the burning of Athens by the Persians in the first Persian War, more than 150 years earlier. Diodorus tells us that 'the Macedonians raced into it slaughtering all the men whom they met and plundering the residences'.[33] Curtius says that 'cruelty as well as avarice ran amok in the captured city; soldiers laden with gold and silver butchered their captives ... and cut down people they came across at random anywhere'. The slaughter was so great that some citizens committed suicide by 'hurling themselves down from the walls with their wives and children ... some to burn themselves alive along with their families'.[34] Once again, Alexander visited a pointless slaughter upon helpless civilians.

Alexander and his army remained in Persepolis for four months. In May, 330 BC, 'a madness took possession of the minds of the intoxicated guests', and at the suggestion of the 'drunken whore', Thais, an old concubine of Philip's and now the paramour of Ptolemy, a drunken Alexander was the first to cast a blazing torch into the palace, setting it afire and burning it to the ground.[35] Some historians have excused this destruction on the grounds that Alexander wanted to demonstrate to the Persians that there was no alternative to his rule as new king. If so, it backfired badly. Persepolis was the holiest city in Persia, the seat of the national religion, equivalent to Rome or Jerusalem. Alexander's destruction provoked a genuine national insurgency against him that went on for years.

Here is the first clear example of Alexander's use of alcohol affecting his military decision-making. The old bull, Parmenio, had warned Alexander that destroying the royal palace made Alexander look like a conqueror passing through their country, and not a future king of the Asiatics, a warning that turned out to be prophetic as the Persian countryside rose against the Macedonian invader.[36] Curtius tells us that even though Alexander was still in a dangerous position in Persia, he was attending day-time drinking parties.[37] As events unfolded over the next few years, Alexander's use of alcohol and his resulting violent behaviour increased markedly, confirming Curtius' judgement that all Alexander's positive qualities 'were marred by his inexcusable fondness for drink'.[38]

## The Mardi and Alexander's Horse (August–September, 330 BC)

After destroying Persepolis, Alexander marched north to Hycarnia along the coast of the Caspian Sea. Some of the tribes in the region sent emissaries to honour Alexander and assure him of their support. One tribe, the Mardi, refused to send an ambassador and recognize Alexander as king. This angered Alexander who grew 'indignant that one people could prevent him from being invincible'.[39] Alexander set out to bring the Mardi to heel. Finding them in battle formation in a hill pass, he attacked and killed 8,000 of them, driving the rest into the hills.[40] He then set about wasting the countryside with fire and murder.

In the mayhem, some natives stole Bucephalas, Alexander's favourite horse. Alexander was furious, and 'his anger and grief surpassed the bounds of propriety'.[41] He ordered that every tree in the land be cut down. He summoned the local leaders and threatened to lay waste the entire country 'to its furthest limits and its inhabitants slaughtered to a man'.[42] Wisely, the natives returned the horse, no doubt convinced that Alexander would indeed kill their entire people. This failed to appease Alexander, however, who began making preparations to assault the Mardian positions anyway. Finally convinced, the Mardians surrendered, fortunate indeed to have escaped the genocidal wrath of Alexander the Great.

### The Slaughter of the Branchidae (Spring, 329 BC)

In the spring of 329 BC, Alexander crossed the Hindu Kush, entered Bactria, and continued his hunt for Bessus, Darius' satrap of Bactria, who had raised an insurgency against Alexander. During the hunt for Bessus, Alexander came upon a people known as the Branchidae living in a small city. They were Greek civilians, supposedly *émigrés* from Miletus in Ionia whose ancestors were transported by Xerxes when he returned from his Greek campaign in 479 BC, more than a century earlier. The Branchidae welcomed Alexander as a fellow Greek, surrendered, and opened their city to him. In response, Alexander surrounded the city, brought it under attack, and ordered the population killed to a man. 'The unarmed and defenceless Branchidae were butchered throughout the city, and neither community of language nor the olive-branches and entreaties of the supplicants could curb the savagery.'[43] Alexander ordered the city destroyed down to its foundations, and even uprooted the sacred groves dedicated to Greek gods 'so that nothing would remain after the removal of the roots but empty wasteland and barren soil'.[44]

The slaughter of the Branchidae is perhaps the most curious of Alexander's many cruelties.[45] There seems to have been absolutely no reason for it. The story that Alexander considered these Greeks traitors for having followed Xerxes into Asia is not at all credible. Why would Xerxes have ordered them to be transported? The story is probably another gloss put on the slaughter by Callisthenes, the official court historian, to explain the horror in somewhat more reasonable terms. A more plausible explanation, however, is that Alexander was suffering from acute combat fatigue. He had been in the field pursuing Bessus for almost two years, attacking and slaughtering villagers, being attacked, suffering losses, and living a generally miserable life on campaign. Prolonged combat and time in the field under harsh conditions brings about physiological changes that serve to deaden pain and hunger, and even to suppress sexual desire, often resulting in an emotional coldness and indifference. Under these conditions, the adrenaline 'rush' associated with killing is pleasurable, producing opiate-like substances in the brain that can bring about a certain calm and relaxation that comforts the soldier both physically and psychologically.[46]

Alexander may have ordered the slaughter of the Branchidae after a period of prolonged fighting and military activity for the pleasure, stimulation, and relaxation it would bring him in an effort to arouse his 'deadened' physiology. Killing for this reason, indeed killing anything, even animals, is not uncommon among soldiers who have succumbed to battle stress, and this is what may have happened to Alexander. The slaughter of the Branchidae was a merciless killing that had no strategic or tactical military purpose. It was done to fulfil Alexander's psychological needs.

## The Torture of Bessus (June, 329 BC)

After the battle of Gaugamela, Bessus fled with Darius in the direction of Bactria to continue the resistance against Alexander. He and his fellow-conspirator, Nabarzanes, betrayed Darius and killed him. Bessus then assumed royal dress and took the title Artaxerxes as king of Persia. He was betrayed in turn and turned over to Ptolemy in the summer of 329 BC. Ptolemy sent a messenger to Alexander asking how he wished Bessus to be brought into his presence. 'Alexander replied that he must be stripped of his clothes and led in a dog-collar and made to stand on the right [side] of the road on which he [Alexander] and his army would pass.'[47] When Alexander approached, he ordered Bessus to be scourged; 'and at every lash a crier was to repeat the words of reproach he had himself used as he asked the reason for his treachery.'[48] Alexander later had Bessus brought before an assembly of Macedonian officers, and ordered Bessus' nose and ears cut off, a punishment that the Macedonians regarded as barbaric.[49] Bessus was then sent to Ecbatana and turned over to Darius' brother, Oxyathres, with the order that Bessus should be crucified before his countrymen.[50] Alexander also ordered that the vultures be kept away from Bessus' body. This was a gruesome order. The Zoroastrian religion required the dead to be devoured by birds. To deny this to Bessus was the equivalent of the Geek denial of burial.[51] Again we find Alexander witnessing torture committed at his order, and again with no point except to exercise his cruelty.

## Butchery in Sogdiana (Spring–Summer, 328 BC)

In the spring of 328 BC, Alexander began his campaign to pacify Sogdiana, the area northeast of Bactria. Sogdiana was the easternmost province of the Persian Empire centred around modern Samarkand and Bukhara in Tajikistan and Uzbekistan. The area was occupied by a loose coalition of warrior states that served as a protective buffer between Persia and Scythia. Urged on by

Spitamenes and the other leaders of the Persian insurgency, the tribes and towns of Sogdiana rose in revolt against Alexander.

The leader of the revolt was Spitamenes, the man who betrayed Bessus, and whose name suggests a connection to Zoroastrianism. The founder of this Iranian religion was Zarathustra, also called Spitama. Alexander's destruction of Persepolis, the religious centre of the Iranian priesthood, had added a religious dimension to the national insurgency. When the Macedonians attempted to prohibit the Zoroastrian practice of exposing the dead to dogs and vultures, this alienated the general population even more. When Alexander's army began to confiscate cattle, they committed the only sin that was explicitly condemned in the Zoroastrian creed. The Sogdian revolt had strong religious as well as national overtones.[52]

Seven garrison towns located along the Persian–Scythian border were involved in the revolt. Alexander moved quickly to suppress the uprising. He attacked Gaza (not to be confused with Gaza in Palestine), first, where 'all males in the town were killed, by Alexander's orders; the women and children were treated as prizes of war, and carried off with anything else of value. Then, without delay, Alexander proceeded to the next settlement, took it the same day and in the same manner, and dealt with the inhabitants with the same severity. Thence he went on to the third, and on the day following took this, too, at the first assault.'[53] At the fifth town, Alexander sent his cavalry ahead with orders to surround it. When Alexander approached leading his infantry, the town's population fled, 'running straight into the cordon of mounted troops and were nearly all killed'. These 'towns' were really villages, and the victims were all civilians.

Alexander now marched on Cyropolis, the largest of the towns, founded by Cyrus the Great. He ordered Craterus to surround and blockade the town. Meanwhile, Alexander himself attacked the sixth town, took it by storm, 'and gave the signal for the execution of all the adult males ... The city was demolished so that its destruction could serve as an example to keep the others in line.'[54] This accomplished, Alexander linked up with Craterus and attacked Cyropolis. The tribe inhabiting the town were the Memaceni, a people noted for their military prowess. They prepared to resist Alexander. The town was fortified, and Alexander was forced to reinforce his army with troops from Meleager and Perdiccas' commands to bring the town under siege. 'But the stubborn resistance of the people so inflamed his rage that after its capture he ordered it to be sacked.'[55] Of the 15,000 men defending the town, 8,000 were killed and 'the rest took refuge in the central fortress'.[56] Alexander surrounded the fort, and a day later, its 7,000 defenders surrendered for lack of water. Citing Aristobulus who was there, Arrian says the 7,000 defenders were then slaughtered to a man.[57]

Once again, Alexander committed mass murder out of personal rage. It is likely that after so much exposure to war, Alexander was no longer in complete control of his emotions. To quote the First World War poet Siegfried Sasson, himself driven to psychiatric collapse by war, Alexander had become 'a stone cold killer', just like Achilles.

**Marakanda (Winter, 328 BC)**

Alexander had been in Afghanistan and Sogdiana for two years, with little to show for it. Bessus' successor, Spitamenes, was fighting a national-religious war, and had given Alexander more trouble and cost him more troops than had all the battles with Darius.[58] Spitamenes and the Sogdian barons had turned Bessus over to Alexander, and Spitamenes now made the pretence of going over to Alexander as well. Alexander summoned Spitamenes to a meeting. No fool, Spitamenes refused, and laid siege to Marakanda, modern Samarkand.

Alexander responded by attacking the outlying forts (see above), and sent a small force toward Marakanda itself. Spitamenes ambushed the force of 2,360 men, killing three Macedonian generals, and executing all the prisoners. It was the worst defeat Alexander had ever suffered. Spitamenes withdrew from Marakanda and disappeared into the desert to fight another day.

As Alexander approached Marakanda, he divided his force, one element taking up positions outside the city and the other, led by Alexander, set out in pursuit of Spitamenes. After a few days with no results, Alexander returned to Marakanda. Now he ordered his men to sweep the general area, seize and demolish every fort, village, and town, burn all the crops, and kill every man of military age among the natives.[59] Whenever he entered a town, he rounded up the population and 'had them all butchered'. When he was finished, much of Sogdiana was in ruins, much of the population was dead, and the refugee population very large indeed.[60] Alexander's cruelty only served to drive the general population into the arms of the rebels. Once more, Alexander had accomplished nothing by his merciless reign of terror against civilians.

**Sogdiana Again (Spring–Summer, 327 BC)**

In late spring of 327 BC, Alexander and his army crossed the Hindu Kush from Bactria into Sogdiana. The objective of the campaign was to march through modern Afghanistan pacifying the countryside and towns, again in revolt, as Alexander made his way eventually to the Indus River and India. He had learned from his previous campaigns that his army could move faster separated into columns, each commanded by an experienced officer. Two columns swept south past modern Jalalabad and Kabul, while Alexander's columns swept north, and then descended through the Swat Valley, finally linking up with the other columns at the Indus River in early spring of 326 BC.

Alexander's route was chosen so the columns could pass through or near important tribes, towns, and cities that he wanted to 'pacify' to secure his rear communications. By pacify, Alexander meant slaughter. The columns attacked and slaughtered the populations of every town, village, and people they encountered en route, taking no prisoners, razing and burning villages and towns to the ground, and pillaging the land. Alexander's Macedonians met resistance with overwhelming force and terrible retribution. He showed no mercy or conciliation until he had shed great quantities of blood.[61] Estimates of the number of women, men, and children killed begin at 120,000 and climb considerably higher.[62] Arrian and Curtius report events where a population of 40,000 were destroyed in a single engagement. Alexander's own losses, some 7,000 men, represented a significant part of Macedonian strength, perhaps as much as 20 per cent.

When the operation was over, much of the local population was dead, and many of the towns and cities were in ruins or destroyed altogether. The destruction was so complete in one area that Alexander put Hephaestion in charge of rounding up the survivors to plant new settlements. With a trail of blood and death behind him, Alexander and his army marched on to the Indus, no doubt confident that they had 'pacified' the area behind them. There would be no more peasant revolts because there were no more peasants! If Alexander thought this, he was wrong. Within a year the region flared into revolt again.

Alexander's campaign in its intent and brutality closely parallels the Soviet Union's military operations in Afghanistan during ten years of war there. On Christmas Day 1979, the Soviet Union sent military forces into Afghanistan to rescue the regime. Within a month, the Soviets had deployed 750 tanks, 2,100 combat vehicles, and 80,000 troops to Afghanistan. Over the next few months, they sent an additional 300 combat helicopters, 130 fighter aircraft, several squadrons of heavy bombers, and began carpet-bombing Afghan villages. The Soviets deployed their troops in a base network from which to launch 'destroy and search' missions.

Like Alexander, the Soviets made no attempt to win the 'hearts and minds' of the Afghan population. Instead, the Soviets repeated the methods they had used in the Ukraine in 1937, and attempted to rip the country up by the roots as a prelude to reconstructing a new society. They depopulated the country-side with air power. Mi-24 Hind helicopter-gunships operating in waves attacked villages and towns, after which assault troops landed to probe the ruins for weapons and insurgents. Survivors were routinely shot. Fixed-wing aircraft laid mines in the narrow valleys, and crops and orchards were doused with napalm. Herds of goats and sheep were gunned down from the air, and farmland was sown with mines to prevent further cultivation. Hundreds of thousands of 'butterfly mines' were dropped over the country, and brightly coloured cluster munitions disguised as toys designed to injure children were also used.

By mid-1984, 3.5 million Afghans had become refugees in Pakistan, and another 1.5 million were driven into Iran. Some 2 million more became displaced persons in their own country. The Soviets pursued a policy of 'migratory genocide'. Moscow expected little resistance, and planned to stay for less than three years. They were there for nine years, one month, and eighteen days.[63] Within months of the Soviet withdrawal in 1989, Afghanistan once more rose in revolt, driving the regime left behind by the Soviets from power and precipitating a civil war. Similar events followed Alexander's departure for India.

## Murder of the Mercenaries at Massaga (Winter, 327 BC)

Alexander marched down the Kabul Valley on the way to India. En route, he was opposed by a people called the Assacenians in the northwest Punjab. Alexander first engaged the Assacenians in a skirmish outside the main town of Massaga, and quickly drove them from the field. He pursued them to Massaga, and brought the city under siege. Four days later, with the Macedonians about to break through the walls and their own commander killed, the townspeople offered to surrender. Alexander accepted.

A group of Indian mercenaries who had been fighting for the Assacenians negotiated their free passage out of the town with the promise to serve in Alexander's army. The mercenaries encamped on a hill away from the city with their women and children. But 'Alexander, nevertheless, nursed an implacable hostility toward them.' He followed them with his army and stationed his whole force in a ring around the hill. Diodorus tells us that Alexander was guilty of great treachery, and 'fell upon them suddenly and wrought a great slaughter'.[64] The mercenaries fought to the last man. Alexander then killed all the women and children. In all, 7,000 were slain to satisfy Alexander's anger.[65]

The slaughter at Massaga reveals Alexander's developing paranoia. The mercenaries had agreed to join Alexander. But Alexander came to believe that they really intended to desert under cover of night and disperse to their homes.[66] Alexander could have simply let them leave, and that would have been the end of it. But the suspicion that they had lied to him and were planning some sort of attack created an 'implacable hostility' in Alexander's mind. As always when faced with real or imagined 'threats', Alexander responded with unrelenting fury. He simply killed everyone … again.

**India (Spring, 326 BC)**

Alexander crossed the Indus River into India in spring, 326 BC, and immediately skirmished with a group of Indians that confronted him. He drove them before his cavalry, followed them to their town, and took it under siege. Curtis tells us that Alexander wanted 'to strike terror right at the start into a people which had, as yet, no experience with Macedonian arms'.[67] He ordered his troops to show no mercy to the town's inhabitants. When Alexander's troops entered the city, 'the inhabitants were butchered to a man, and [Alexander] even unleashed his fury on its buildings'.[68]

**Sangala (June, 326 BC)**

Alexander sailed down the Acesines River to the junction of the Hydaspes, where he encountered a tribe called the Sibians (Curtius/Diodorus) or the Cathaei (Arrian). Alexander attacked Sangala, their main town, and took it by storm. The capture of Sangala cost the Indians 17,000 dead and 70,000 taken prisoner. The cost to Alexander was 100 dead and a 'disproportionately large' number of wounded.[69] When the news of the fall of Sangala reached two neighbouring towns, their inhabitants fled into the countryside to escape Alexander's wrath. He immediately set out to hunt them down. The fleeing inhabitants had abandoned 500 sick and wounded in their haste to escape. Angry that the others had eluded him, Alexander ordered the sick and wounded slaughtered on the spot.[70] This done, Alexander gave up the pursuit of the refugees, returned to Sangala, and razed the city to the ground. The few adult males that had survived the initial attack on the city were executed, and the rest of the population sold into slavery.[71]

Both Curtius and Diodorus report that Alexander now moved against a second city. The city put up fierce resistance, and Alexander's attempt to take it by storm was driven back with heavy Macedonian casualties. Alexander then brought the city under siege. This demoralized the inhabitants and 'the townspeople lost all hope of saving themselves, and set fire to the buildings, burning themselves in the blaze along with their wives and children'.[72] Diodorus' version has Alexander, angry at the resistance, ordering the city set afire 'and burned most of the inhabitants with it'.[73]

All this killing was inflicted upon the Indian populace simply because they would not acknowledge Alexander as their king as he passed through their region. One might reasonably ask why the local tribal rulers didn't simply agree to do so, pay a tribute mostly in needed supplies, and wait for Alexander to disappear down river. Or why Alexander didn't simply sail on when he met resistance. Why the pointless killing? Most probably, because Alexander now enjoyed it too much. It was what he did as a field commander, what now gave his life meaning. By this time, after all, there were no more new worlds to conquer. Alexander, like Achilles, found his true personality in fighting and killing. Both had come to equate the excitement of battle and the killing of their enemies with military glory. It mattered not a whit that most of the 'enemies' were women and children.

### The Mallians (January, 325 BC)

It was now January, 325 BC, eight years since Alexander had begun his campaign against the Persians. Sailing down the Hydaspes River, Alexander encountered a tribe called the Mallians who, along with the Oxydraci, controlled the passage at the confluence of the Hydroatis and Hydespes Rivers. The two tribes who barred his way were 'the most numerous and warlike of the Indians in that part of the country'.[74] Alexander fought a number of running battles with them in which he slaughtered large numbers of civilians and soldiers caught by surprise, or who had fled to their towns for safety.[75] J.F.C. Fuller points out that these towns ought not be thought of as fortified in any significant way, and probably resembled many present-day Indian villages – 'conglomerations of mud-huts, the circumference of which formed a protective wall of no great height or thickness'.[76] As he approached the Mallian main town, Alexander confronted an Indian force of 50,000 men.[77] After an initial skirmish, the Indians retreated behind the town walls.

The Macedonians quickly breached the wooden walls, and Alexander was wounded in the process. The Macedonian army stormed the town. 'Now the slaughter began; neither women nor children were spared.'[78] According to Curtius, 'old men, women, and children – none were spared … mass slaughter of the enemy finally appeased their rage'.[79] If Curtius is correct about the size of the Indian force, then some 50,000 soldiers were slain, not counting the untold number of women and children who were also killed. No effort was made to spare a single person. Having suffered few casualties, Alexander sailed on, recuperating from his wounds aboard his transport.

### Sambus and the Brahmins (August–November, 325 BC)

Alexander sailed down the Indus River, attacking and slaughtering tribes as he went, to no apparent military purpose except, perhaps, to vent his frustrations for having to bring his Indian adventure to an end.[80] When he came upon the kingdom of Sambus, 'he ravaged the kingdom of Sambus, enslaved the population of most of the cities and, later destroyed the cities.'[81] Then Alexander crucified the king. The Brahmin priests had urged the population of the area to resist, which they did until Alexander took Harmatelia, the Brahmin capital. The Brahmins urged resistance in other towns, and Alexander took it personally, executing all the priests and their families he could get his hands on. Citing Cleitarchus as their source, Curtius and Diodorus say that in this campaign against the Indian tribes Alexander killed 80,000 Indians in this region and captured many others.[82]

The reason for Alexander's terrible anger at the Brahmin priests is unclear. They were non-warriors whose task was to teach philosophy and perform the old religious rituals brought to India by the Indo-European invaders more than 1,000 years before. The Brahmins were pacifists, but had urged the populace to resist Alexander. They also reviled the Indian princes who went over to him. Perhaps it was their willingness to defy Alexander even at the cost of their lives that angered him so. When Alexander was in Taxila, he had met Dandamis, the leader of the Brahmins, who ridiculed Alexander's claim that he was the son of a god. Dandamis pointed out that every human being was descended from the gods.[83] For whatever reasons, Alexander exterminated thousands of Brahmin priests. When he could not kill them in large numbers, he seems to have preferred hanging them individually.

**The Oreitae (September, 325 BC)**

Upon reaching the ocean at the Indus delta, Alexander sent Nearchus ahead by sea along the coast and through the Strait of Hormuz, intending to link up with him later. Alexander burned his boats, and proceeded overland on his return route to Persia. His route of march took him through the territory of several tribes. Alexander divided his forces into three columns, ordering Ptolemy to plunder the district along the coast and Leonatus to lay waste the interior. 'He himself devastated the upper country and the hills. At one and the same time much country was wasted, so that every spot was filled with fire and devastation and great slaughter … and the number of persons killed reached many myriads.'[84]

This horrendous slaughter of thousands of human beings – Leonatus killed 6,000 in a single engagement – occurred before Alexander had met the enemy or encountered any resistance.[85] It was the prelude to the main attack on the Oreitae, whose only sin was they 'had long been independent and hitherto made no gesture of friendship toward Alexander and his army'.[86] When he finally reached the main villages of the Oreitae, the battle was short and deadly and 'all the natives who attempted resistance were killed'.[87] Although none of the other tribes had risen against him, Alexander's frightful slaughter of the

Oretiae terrified them into further submission. Having slaughtered thousands once more, Alexander marched on.

## Hephaestion's Death and Murderous Rage (October, 324 BC)

In October 324 BC, Hephaestion, Alexander's closest friend and lover since their teen-age years and commander of the Companion cavalry, drank himself to death. Arrian says that Alexander 'flung himself on the body of his friend and lay there nearly all day long in tears, and refused to be parted from him until he was dragged away by force by his Companions; and again, that he lay stretched upon the corpse all day and the whole night too'.[88] For more than a month, Alexander plunged into a deep depression, where he ate little, 'paid no attention to his bodily needs,' and 'lay on his bed now crying lamentably, now in the silence of grief'.[89]

Gradually, Alexander recovered, if not entirely, by mid-winter. After he had arranged for Hephaestion's funeral, Alexander assembled the army and led his men a short distance north against a nomadic tribe called the Cossaeans that lived in the Zagros Mountains between Ecbatana and Susa. Without any provocation, Alexander spent forty days attacking village after village, burning and killing everything in his path. There are no reports of prisoners or collecting the women and children to be sold into slavery. As Alexander had done many times previously, the Cosseans were exterminated in a vile act of ethnic cleansing.[90]

Alexander's extermination of the Cosseans was an act of murderous rage rooted in guilt. Arrian says that Alexander blamed himself for Hephaestion's death, in the same way that Achilles blamed himself for the death of Patroklos. Alexander had seen Hephaestion drinking too much and blamed himself for making no attempt to stop him.[91] Alexander cut his hair short, just as Achilles did in mourning for Patroklos. In an act that Greeks would have considered sacrilegious, Alexander destroyed the local temple of Asclepios, the god of healing. With his guilt having turned to rage, like Achilles, Alexander went berserk and set out to purge his emotions in a spasm of killing, just like Achilles, seeking the opiate-like calm that often follows such violent episodes. Plutarch says as much when he notes that 'then seeking to alleviate his grief in war, Alexander set out on a campaign, as if the tracking down and hunting of men might console him ... This was called a sacrifice to Hephaestion's ghost.'[92] As Achilles had done for Patroklos, Alexander offered human sacrifices to honour the spirit of Hephaestion.

Alexander's atrocities cannot be explained as military or strategic necessities. Some historians have gone to great lengths to overlook or explain Alexander's brutality on the practical grounds of military necessity. Historians like Tarn, Fuller, and Wilcken, while recognizing that Alexander's actions were often 'dreadful', nonetheless suggest that they were either militarily necessary or, at least, useful in achieving his objectives. In their view, Alexander employed brutality in a deliberate manner as part of his larger strategy to root out the opposition 'root and branch' in the various theatres of conflict. However, the evidence does not support the argument, and has served mainly to keep historians from inquiring into other causes for Alexander's actions.

If Alexander thought brutality would reduce resistance, much as the Soviets believed it would during their war in Afghanistan, Alexander's own experience should have convinced him otherwise:

- Despite the massacre and destruction of Thebes, far more Greeks fought against Alexander than ever fought with him. He never regained support in Greece after the Theban massacre, and Sparta rose in open revolt three years later. When Alexander died, all Greece rejoiced.
- Because of the hatred of the Greeks, Alexander was never able to make good use of the Athenian navy because he couldn't trust them. When he disbanded his fleet at Tyre, he kept a few squadrons of Athenian ships and crews with him to use as hostages in case of Athenian treachery.
- The sieges of Halicarnarsus and Miletus, as brutal as they were, did not frighten Tyre into surrendering. Alexander still had to take the port city by force.
- The massacres at Tyre did not stop the Persians at Gaza from putting up a six month fight that almost killed Alexander.
- The burning of Persepolis did not stop the Persian nobility from leading a three year insurgency against Alexander. The destruction of Persepolis, the religious capital of the country, only created popular support for the insurgency.
- Afghanistan was a disaster that cost Alexander thousands of troops and gained him nothing. Despite slaughter after slaughter, the next town or tribe always resisted, often to the end. The Soviet policy of 'migratory genocide' in Afghanistan over ten years had the same effect.
- The victory over Porus had no strategic effect except to unify the Indian tribes on the other side of the river to rally and prepare to fight Alexander together. Confronted with this opposition and the mutiny of his troops, Alexander was forced to abandon his Indian campaign.
- The transit down the Indus River saw Alexander perpetrate one slaughter after another. None of them convinced the next tribe to forego resistance. If Alexander thought his brutality would reduce resistance, he was grossly mistaken.

It must be borne in mind that Alexander did not just order these atrocities to be committed, but he was an enthusiastic participant in them. He enjoyed wading into the slaughter, almost as if he could not stop himself. Arrian suggests as much in trying to explain Alexander's dangerous leap behind the walls of the Malli, an impulsive act that almost got him killed. 'The truth is that ... such was his passion for glory that he had not the strength of mind, when there was action afoot, to consider his own safety; the sheer pleasure of battle, as other pleasures are to other men, was irresistible.'[93] Whether he fought on foot or on horseback, Alexander's killing was bloody business indeed, where he could see the fear in his victim's eyes, hear their cries of pain, and feel the splash of blood and the warmth of their hacked flesh upon his own skin. And yet, like Achilles, he was drawn to it again and again.

Except for the death of Hephaestion, the texts reveal few expressions of Alexander's remorse or pity for suffering of any kind, not even for his own troops or his friends. His soldiers died in windrows from wounds, battle, disease, and exposure to days of rain, heat, ice, snow, snakebites, and the slow painful death from poisoned Indian arrows. Only once did he visit the wounded. Only once, when Alexander feared that Ptolemy might die from his wounds, do we find any expression of concern or sorrow for the loss of a comrade in arms. By the end of his life, Alexander was emotionally dead, incapable of any human emotion beyond the exhilaration produced by the excitement of killing.

Alexander had become Achilles.

*Chapter 7*

# Paranoia, Suicide, and Depression

One of the most lethal aspects of post-traumatic stress and one of the most common is the destruction of the capacity for social trust that creates a persistent expectation of betrayal and exploitation in a soldier suffering from prolonged exposure to war.[1] This condition is a consequence of the soldier's loss of authority over some of his mental functions, especially memory and the ability to make perceptions that the soldier can trust to be accurate. With confidence in his own perceptions lost, the soldier's world seems uncertain in every aspect. The uncertainty creates anxiety, leading to a persistent expectation of betrayal by friends and everyone else.

A battlefield is a very uncertain place, where one's very existence can no longer be assumed. Already suspicious by nature, Alexander's prolonged exposure to war and slaughter, much of it occasioned by his own orders and often accomplished with his own hands, created the circumstances in which he could no longer trust anyone or even his own assessments of reality.

That something was psychologically wrong with Alexander must have been clear to his officers and troops. It was certainly clear to our sources. Cleitarchus, a main source for Curtius' history, authored an influential history of Alexander (now lost) in 310–301 BC that painted a dark psychological picture of Alexander as corrupt, an alcoholic, a tyrant, and a murderer. Cleitarchus' work seems to have been drawn from the eyewitness accounts of common soldiers, suggesting that Alexander's behaviour did not go unnoticed by his troops and was widely known.[2] Much of Arrian's history of Alexander is based upon the lost history of Aristobulus, one of Alexander's staff officers who accompanied him on campaign.[3] We have no accounts of Aristobulus participating in battles, and his post as a staff officer afforded him a degree of detachment from the events he witnessed. Aristobulus began writing his history of Alexander during the Indian campaign, after Alexander's cruelty had already been displayed in Afghanistan and was becoming genocidal in India. He was a friend of Alexander's father and among Alexander's admirers. Aristobulus was able to reconcile his admiration for Alexander with the terrible events he witnessed by introducing the *pothos* literary motif into his accounts.

*Pothos* means 'longing', and Aristobulus employed it as a literary device to explain Alexander's 'inner drives'. The *pothos* motif was incorporated by almost all later ancient historians, including our main sources, usually in the form that Alexander was driven by a desire to see foreign countries or seek new knowledge. W.W. Tarn incorporated the device into his nineteenth-century work on Alexander, transforming it into Alexander's desire to spread a unity of mankind to different cultures through the importation of Hellenism. One of the attractions of the *pothos* device is that it removes any need to explain Alexander's otherwise strange behaviour, since it could be attributed to or explained away by his *pothos*.

But *pothos* is more than a literary device. It is also a description of a psychological condition. Understood in the Greek context, Pothos was the god of sexual desire and sexual longing. The Greeks understood that sexual desire was one of the most powerful human motivations, and often assumed uncontrollable proportions that produced disastrous consequences. In this sense, *pothos* is strongly akin to mania, a state of intense excitement bordering on compulsion, in which the individual cannot control his behaviour. It is interesting that some sources use the term interchangeably with 'seizures', in that Alexander sometimes entered a reverie in which a 'longing' for something would overtake him.[4] This condition seems to be what Aristobulus was describing and attributing to Alexander as an explanation for the events he witnessed in Afghanistan and in India, when he first began to write his history. If so, it is evidence that Alexander may have already lost some authority over his mental functions of memory and trustworthy perception as a consequence of post-traumatic stress. But whatever it was that afflicted Alexander, it did not escape the attention of Aristobulus and, we may reasonably assume, Alexander's officers and men.[5]

## Paranoia

There is almost no disagreement among modern historians that by the end of his life Alexander had become a paranoid whose delusions of conspiracy and betrayal had proved lethal to a number of his officers, men, and Persian officials.[6] But the signs of paranoia were evident long before Alexander's life neared its end in 323 BC, and those around him lived in terror that they might be next to be executed for some imagined conspiracy. Ephippus, one of Alexander's officers who helped administer Egypt and was later present in Alexander's court in Babylon, wrote that 'none dared approach him without reason because he [Alexander] aroused great fear; his pride and good fortune had raised him to the position of tyrant'.[7] Ephippus writes further that 'a religious stillness and silence born of fear held fast all who were in his presence. For he was hot-tempered and murderous, reputed, in fact, to be melancholy-mad.'[8] Bosworth described Alexander's court as 'a court in terror and a king lost in savage brooding'.[9]

Given Alexander's prolonged exposure to war, it is hardly surprising that he would have succumbed to paranoid thinking. After a traumatic experience, and in Alexander's case repeated and prolonged traumatic experiences, the human system of self-preservation goes onto permanent alert, as if the danger might return at any moment, with the result that physiological arousal continues unabated.[10] When this physiological condition is compounded by the soldier's loss of social trust, the consequence is a persistent expectation of betrayal by friends and others around him.[11] The result is paranoia. Paranoid states induced by war stress can be intermittent and of short duration (hours or days), but can also develop into a permanent condition over time. The sources are clear that as time went on, Alexander's paranoid episodes became more frequent until, as he approached the end of his life, it was a characteristic element of his personality and behaviour.[12]

Paranoia is a mental condition in which one's thought processes are heavily influenced by anxiety and fear. It is typically characterized by persecutory beliefs or beliefs of conspiracy concerning perceived threats toward oneself. Paranoia is marked by a profound distrust of others, and a constant scanning of the environment for signs that validate the paranoid's fears. The need to be constantly vigilant results in a constricted emotional life in which the victim has a reduced capacity for emotional involvement and empathy for the circumstances of others.[13] Other characteristics of paranoia included a tendency to bear grudges and a refusal to forgive slights, a tendency to distort experience by misconstruing neutral or friendly actions of others as hostile, preoccupation with conspiratorial explanations of events, and a sense of excessive self-importance.[14] Paranoia is often accompanied by major depressive disorder, obsessive-compulsive disorder, and alcohol or drug abuse.

A review of Alexander's behaviour reveals a series of imagined conspiracies, allegations of conspiracies, and attempts to anticipate conspiracies that may well be unequalled in the life of any other great leader of antiquity.[15] Immediately after his confirmation as king, Alexander had the two sons of Aeropus of Lyncestis executed on the grounds that they had conspired to kill Philip. A third son, Alexander, Antipater's son-in-law, was spared and entrusted with command of the Thessalian cavalry. He was later arrested on charges of conspiring to kill Alexander in service to Darius, imprisoned, and executed in September 330 BC. Next, Alexander had Attalus killed with the help of Parmenio, again on a charge of conspiracy. Alexander's cousin, Amyntus, the child of Philip's brother and original heir to the throne, was killed to remove any threat to the throne based on lineage. We hear nothing of trials before the assembled army to which Macedonians were entitled by law and tradition. Alexander's response to these 'conspiracies' was outright murder with no pretence of legality.

By 330 BC, Alexander had destroyed the Persian army, occupied the country's capital at Persepolis, and was attempting to put down the insurgency led by Bessus. He now turned his attention to murdering Parmenio and his oldest son, Philotas, commander of the Companion cavalry and one of Alexander's boyhood friends.[16] Philotas was arrested on charges of conspiracy shortly after returning from his brother's funeral in Ecbatana (modern Hamadan). The plot against Philotas seems rooted in the personal ambitions of his accusers, all of whom were rewarded with promotions and major commands.[17] Philotas had made no secret of his opposition to Alexander's claims to be the son of a god ever since the events in Egypt, and had been disliked and suspected for years before his arrest.[18] Like his father, Parmenio, Philotas opposed Alexander's orientalising pretensions, and it must be more than coincidence that Philotas was arrested shortly after Alexander first dressed and behaved undisguisedly as the Persian Great King while in Parthia.[19] Philotas was tortured until he confessed to the trumped up charges. He was dragged before the army and his confession read. Alexander himself called for the death penalty. The army agreed, and Philotas was executed.

With Philotas dead, Alexander moved against Parmenio, who had been removed from his combat command and was in charge of troops protecting the rear supply lines in Media. There is evidence to suggest that Alexander struck at Philotas as a deliberate prelude to bringing down his real target, the old general Parmenio. With his son murdered, Parmenio could be expected to react against Alexander with force, perhaps calling on his fellow Macedonians to remove the king. To pre-empt this, Alexander sent an assassination team to do his work. Betrayed by one of his own officers, Parmenio was stabbed to death, beheaded, and his head sent to Alexander.[20] Again the charge was conspiracy; again there was no trial.

Parmenio was a constant reminder of Alexander's hated father, and Alexander had resented Parmenio's habit of disagreeing with him in matters of tactics and strategy since the very beginning of the campaign. Parmenio was a proven warrior beloved by his troops and officers, something Alexander longed to be. There were also disagreements over Alexander's policy of continued conquest, with Parmenio and the veteran officer corps wanting to put an end to war and enjoy the fruits of their victories. Alexander resented most the old general's opposition to his claims of divinity and to his behaviour as an oriental king. Justin offers evidence of the reasons behind Alexander's actions.

He tells us that 'what most incensed him [Alexander] was that reflections were cast upon him in the common talk of the soldiers for having cast off the customs of his father, Philip, and his country. For this offence, Parmenio, an old man [he was in his mid-seventies], next to the king in rank, and his son Philotas, were put to death.'[21] Justin also captures Alexander's developing anger toward those around him when he says, 'Alexander, meanwhile, began to show a passionate temper toward those about him, not with a princely severity, but with the vindictiveness of an enemy.'[22]

Parmenio's murder sent tremors of fear through the army and the officer corps. Macedonian law provided for the death penalty for the relatives of persons who had plotted against the king. Curtius tells us that some officers 'committed suicide and others fled into remote mountains and desert wastes as sheer terror spread through the camp'.[23]

Alexander played upon the fear he had created. He urged his soldiers to write to their relatives in Macedonia, then intercepted the letters and read them. 'Having learned from them what everyone thought of him, he put all those who had given unfavourable opinions of his conduct into one regiment [a disciplinary battalion] with an intention either to destroy them [by wasting them in battle] or to distribute them in colonies in the most distant parts of the earth.'[24] The entire Parmenio affair and the reaction of the troops and officers served only to reinforce Alexander's anxiety that he was more feared than loved, and that his troops and officers required constant watching along with everyone else.

While our sources tell us that Alexander intercepted the letters of his troops, they are silent on the letters of the officers. It is reasonable to assume, however, that these letters were also read by Alexander, who now had a good idea of the restlessness in the officer ranks that his policies had engendered. Curtius tells us a number of Macedonian officers were executed in the aftermath of Parmenio's murder.[25] They included Demetrios, a bodyguard and important Macedonian noble, who was removed and later replaced by Ptolemy. Alexander of Lynkestis, the surviving brother of the two brothers executed for Philip's murder and who Alexander had arrested years ago on a charge of conspiracy, was finally murdered. The list of victims includes the names of six other Macedonian officers whose identities cannot be determined. The four sons of Andromenes, a client of Parmenio, were tried and found innocent by the army.[26] This was not the end of it, however. Parmenio's brother, Asander, was still alive while these events were taking place. He had been sent to Media to gather reinforcements. He arrived in Bactra a year later, and was never heard of again. He may reasonably be counted among the victims of Alexander's lingering resentment of Parmenio.

Alexander now began to suspect even those closest to him, including members of his bodyguard. Badian argues that Alexander's suspicions of betrayal by his *hetairoi* and his personal guard are evident in the events surrounding the murder of Cleitus at Marakanda in fall of 328 BC.[27] The matter of Cleitus' murder will be treated in detail in the next section of this chapter. Here it is sufficient to describe only the outline of events that frame Alexander's killing of his old friend in a fit of drunken rage.

Alexander and his officers had gathered at one of their late night drinking parties. After hearing Cleitus come to the defence of Philip and his officers, Alexander became enraged, grabbed a lance from the hands of a guard, and tried to attack Cleitus. Ptolemy and Perdiccas grabbed Alexander around the waist to stop him, and Lysimachus and Leonnatus wrestled the weapon away from Alexander.[28] Alexander called out for his Guard, and when no one came to rescue him, he cried out, 'What? Have I nothing left of royalty but the name? Am I to be like Darius, dragged in chains like Bessus and his cronies?'[29] Apparently, Alexander thought that he was the victim of a plot by his personal guards, and that he would be killed in the same manner that Bessus had been killed by his closest comrades. Alexander struggled free, however, grabbed another lance as his attendants made no further effort to stop him. He waited in ambush in the hallway of the banquet hall, and killed Cleitus.

We hear nothing more of conspiracy for a year until late summer of 327 BC when what appears to have been the first genuine conspiracy against Alexander occurred at Bactra. Alexander had gone on a boar's hunt accompanied by some Pages when he was attacked by a wild boar. Hermolaus, one of the Pages, saw the charge coming and moved to protect Alexander. He speared the boar, and probably saved Alexander's life. Alexander was furious at the incident for reasons that are unclear, and had Hermolaus whipped in front of the other boys. Hermolaus vowed revenge, and recruited five Pages in a plot to kill Alexander in his sleep, when the Pages served as his night guard.[30] Loose talk among the conspirators caused the plot to be discovered, however, and the Pages were arrested, tortured, and forced to confess.

When Hermolaus was brought before the army for trial, he offered a defence of his actions with a list of grievances that made it impossible, he said, for an honourable Macedonian to continue to serve their king. He accused Alexander of the murder of Attalus, Philotas, Parmenio, other officers, and Cleitus. He criticized Alexander's assumption of Persian dress, the introduction of the Persian habit of genuflection, his heavy drinking, and his rejection of Macedonian values and Philip's achievements. Hermolaus declared that he wanted Alexander dead to free all Macedonians from these evils.[31] Hermolaus and his co-conspirators were executed. The incident must have focused Alexander's attention, for Hermolaus publicized what Alexander knew many of his troops and officers were already thinking. None of the conspirators were sons of important Macedonian nobles. Still, the Pages' conspiracy was yet another indication that Alexander's behaviour was weakening his hold on the army and its officer corps, and that their disenchantment with him was growing. None of this allayed Alexander's fears.

Proof of Alexander's fear followed quickly upon the execution of the Pages. Within days, Callisthenes, the official court historian, colleague of Aristotle, and boyhood friend of Alexander, was arrested as an accomplice in the Pages' conspiracy and summarily executed. Callisthenes was an Olynthian, and not entitled to the Macedonian right of trial.[32] Alexander's dislike of Callisthenes may have rested in the man's reputation for speaking his mind honestly and in public. Callisthenes' irritating habit aroused suspicion when at a banquet he publically criticized Alexander's claim to have a divine father (Ammon) and his demand that Macedonians follow the Persian custom and prostrate themselves (*proskynesis*) before him. Only two months before, Alexander had announced his policy requiring prostration of all Europeans. He then went ahead and married Roxane, a Bactrian princess. Both actions were repulsive to most Macedonians.

Once more opposition to Alexander's policies had surfaced in public, this time before a combined audience of Macedonian and Persian nobles. Alexander knew well enough that the Macedonians found Callisthenes' views 'very much to their mind'.[33] Even if he could not keep his officers from thinking what they would, Callisthenes' execution was probably intended to silence any further public criticism of Alexander's behaviour.

By now, Alexander must surely have realized how incendiary his policies and claims had become, and he announced that he would not enforce the Persian practice of prostration. The judicial murder of Callisthenes was met with resentment among the Greeks, and probably among some Macedonians as well, for everyone knew that Callisthenes was a man of the finest character and innocent of any plot to kill the king. His only fault was that he could not keep his opinions to himself. In the atmosphere of fear that pervaded Alexander's court, Callisthenes' fault proved fatal.

Alexander had massacred the old Macedonian officer nobility that Parmenio and his sons represented, putting an end to any real threat from that quarter. He replaced the murdered officers with officers who had taken part in the arrest of Philotas, making them marshals of the empire. Hephaestion now became his second in command. Other positions were filled by toadies that Alexander felt he could trust. Most were men of no distinction. For the moment at least, Alexander felt safe, and continued his campaign to bring India under his rule. Over the next eleven months, Alexander enjoyed great success, campaigning in the Swat Valley, capturing the Aornus rock, crossing the Indus, and defeating Porus at the battle of the Hydaspes River. In June, he pressed on across the Acesines River, reaching the banks of the Hyphasis in late July. And then disaster struck.

Weary of war and frightened by reports that they were outnumbered by the troops of the Mauryan Indian Empire that lay in wait for them on the other side, the Macedonian troops refused to carry out Alexander's order to cross the Hyphasis River. The mutiny seems to have been a spontaneous event in which the older troops had simply had enough of hardship and war, and desired to return home.[34] Alexander's response was to appeal to the officers to bring the troops back into line, only to discover to his horror that the officers supported the troops. Most significant for Alexander's sense of security was that the spokesman for the soldiers' demands was none other than Coenus, one of the recently promoted marshals. Coenus, Parmenio's son-in-law, had been one of Philotas' accusers, and had participated in the plot to murder Parmenio. Now here he was publically supporting a mutiny that not only threatened Alexander's authority, but everything else Alexander had hoped to accomplish when he invaded India. Coenus was obviously not a man to be trusted. Unable to rely upon the support of his officers, Alexander suffered his first defeat (as Arrian has it), and agreed to the army's demands to turn back. He was furious with his betrayers.

Alexander was not one to forgive easily, if at all, and ordered the army to retreat down the Indus to the sea. He could have easily retraced his steps back through Porus' kingdom to Afghanistan and on to Persia where supplies were plentiful en route and the opposition to his passage minimal. Instead, Alexander deliberately chose the more difficult route through hostile territory, forcing his army to endure harsh conditions on the march and much desperate fighting that was largely unnecessary from a military point of view. From November 326 to August 325 BC, more than nine months, the army was forced to fight its way through one tribe after another. Alexander made the mutineers suffer like they had never suffered before, and in the process got a good number of them killed or wounded in pointless battles. Others he simply abandoned. Alexander founded the city of Alexandria on the east bank of the Hyphasis River, leaving behind many of the older and injured veterans with little hope of ever returning to Greece or Macedonia. Nature itself took revenge on Coenus, who died shortly after the mutiny from disease.[35] As Badian observes, 'Alexander never recovered from the shock he had received. He had no sooner achieved his objective of gaining untrammelled power than he found that he was more than ever dependent on others, and that absolute power meant eternal vigilance.'[36]

After joining the Indus River at Patalla (modern Hyderabad), Alexander set sail down the river to the sea. He divided his forces, sending half by sea to Susa under the command of Nearchus. The other half was to accompany him on a march through the Gedrosian desert.[37] Gedrosia is the Greek name for an area that corresponds to the Makran Desert in modern Baluchistan. It runs from the Indus River to the southern edge of the Strait of Hormuz. Alexander's reason for the difficult trek was rooted in his desire to punish the troops and officers who had mutinied at the Hyphasis for, like the battles against the Indian tribes, it had no military purpose.

Arrian, drawing on Nearchus, says 'Alexander did not choose the route because he was unaware of the difficulties it would involve; he chose it because, apart from Semiramis on her retreat from India, no one . . . had ever succeeded in bringing an army safely through.'[38] Arrian continues, '. . . for it is a fact that Cyrus came here with the intention of invading India, but found the going so bad and the country so wild and barren that he lost nearly all his men before he could do so. Alexander heard these stories; they inspired him to go one better than Cyrus and Semiramis.'[39] As always with Alexander, the desire for fame and glory was unquenchable. Waldemar Heckel argues that Alexander was still punishing his troops for their refusal to cross the Hyphasis River, and denying him his chance to conquer India.[40] Given Alexander's personality, it is just as likely to have been a desire to punish those who betrayed him as it was his desire to seek further glory. Or it may have been that Alexander did not want to allow another opportunity to fight and kill to pass. War was now a normal way of life for Alexander. Like Achilles and the berserkers of other wars, Alexander enjoyed it too much to let it slip away. He needed it psychologically.

Alexander drove his army through an unrelenting wasteland on a death march that lasted for sixty days.[41] Starting with an army of 60,000–70,000 men, Alexander lost at least 12,000 soldiers in addition to thousands of camp followers, livestock, and most of his baggage train.[42] Plutarch places the figure much higher, saying the losses amounted to three-quarters of the army.[43] The decision to challenge the Baluchistan desert out of revenge or in search of glory must be regarded as the greatest blunder in Alexander's Asiatic campaign. Wasting thousands of battle experienced troops and thousands of camp followers, many of whom were the wives and children of his soldiers, destroyed whatever faith the army and officer corps still placed in Alexander. Many never forgave Alexander and, later, mutinied again. Already paranoid,

Alexander sensed he was once more at risk of betrayal. As soon as he reached the city of Gedrosia, he struck first.

Upon his arrival, Alexander ordered the governor of Gedrosia executed for his failure to provide supplies to his army during the desert crossing, only to discover that the governor was already dead, killed in action in some minor skirmish. When Alexander arrived in Carmania, he and the troops went on a seven-day drinking binge. He was met in the capital by the four senior officers – Cleander (Coenus' brother), Sitalces, Heracon, and Agathon – who had engineered the murder of Parmenio. They had been serving in Parmenio's old command in Media after the old bull's murder. Alexander had all four executed without trial. To pre-empt any resentment that their troops might harbour, 600 of their subordinates, many probably junior officers, were also executed.[44]

The purge was expanded to include the governors of the empire's provinces, almost all Macedonian senior officers, and continued for months. Eight of the twenty-two provincial governors were executed. A number of others died of natural causes, some died violently, and still others were removed and ordered to court, some of which were never heard from again. Counted together, only four of the governors escaped death or removal.[45] The fear surrounding Alexander's actions was so pervasive that his old and trusted friend, Harpalus, the Imperial Treasurer, took as much money as he could carry and fled Babylon with a number of loyal troops, intending to make his way back to Greece.[46]

The pervasiveness of Alexander's fears is illustrated by three anecdotes recounted by Arrian and Plutarch. When Alexander arrived at Parsagardae, he was visited by Atropates, the governor of Media, who had brought with him a man he had arrested for wearing his cap upright in royal fashion and proclaiming himself king of the Persians. The man was obviously mentally ill. Nonetheless, Alexander had him executed along with several of the man's associates. In another instance, a simpleton somehow made his way into the royal tent and sat upon the throne. Alexander was furious, charged the man with 'treasonable design', and had him killed. In a third incident, Alexander's hat blew into the water while he was sailing down the Euphrates. The royal diadem-ribbon wrapped around the hat fell off and stuck to a reed. Anxious to be of service to the king, a sailor swam to retrieve the royal ribbon. Seeking to keep it dry, he wrapped it around his own head. The court seers told Alexander that this was a bad omen, and Alexander had the sailor beheaded.[47] Arrian tells us that 'Alexander ... had become readier to accept as wholly reliable the charges which were made to him against officials, and to inflict severe punishment even for minor offences'.[48] No threat was trivial enough to ignore.

Having dealt with the officer corps and the royal governors, Alexander next tried to expunge his fear of his own troops. Over the years, considerable numbers of Greek mercenaries who had originally served in the armies of the Persian satraps were absorbed into Alexander's army. Other Greek contingents were serving in the armies of the royal satraps under Macedonian commanders. Alexander had never trusted these Greeks, and had forcibly settled large numbers of them in the towns and colonies in Asia he established during his campaigns. This reduced their ability to become a threat, but also made it impossible for them to return to Greece. The forced settlement led some of the colonies to revolt.

Alexander's treatment of the Greek mercenaries engendered hatred among them, and Alexander feared that they would mount a revolt against him. In the spring of 324 BC, Alexander ordered all mercenary contingents serving in the satrapal armies dismissed from service, immediately depriving them of home and livelihood. Within months, Asia was plagued by groups of armed men wandering around the countryside seeking a means of keeping body and soul together, often by violence. Alexander's actions created an even greater danger to himself, for now the number of Greek mercenaries who wanted to kill him and who possessed the weapons, skill, and courage to try was legion.[49]

A few months later (August, 324 BC), Alexander was faced with another mutiny. The army was encamped at Opis (Baghdad), on the Tigris River when Alexander announced that all Macedonian soldiers who were unfit for service because of age or injury were to be discharged and sent home. He promised to reward them handsomely, 'enough to make their friends and relatives envy them' when they arrived home.[50] The depth of resentment toward their commander for his past ill-treatment boiled over in a spontaneous outburst of anger and insult. They insulted Alexander, demanded that anyone who wanted should be allowed to return home and, as Arrian says 'in bitter jest', told him that on his next campaign he could take his father with him meaning, of course, the god Ammon whom Alexander claimed as his real father.

Of significance is that a handful of officers supported the troops, as Coenus and others had done at the Hyphasis mutiny. One of the officers taken into custody confronted Alexander. 'How long are you going to indulge in this self-gratification with such executions, and executions of a foreign kind at that?' [This is a reference to Alexander's increasing use of torture and mutilation, both Persian practices and foreign to the Macedonian practice of being speared or stoned.] 'Your own men, your own citizens, are being dragged off to punishment without trial – led away, alas, by their own captives' [i.e., Persians in Alexander's service]. 'If you decide that they have deserved death, at least change the executioners!'[51]

Curtius gives us some insight into Alexander's temperament at this time when he says 'Alexander had begun to be quick to order summary execution and also to believe the worst in people … and at the end of his life his degeneration from his former self was complete'.[52] Alexander leapt from the platform from which he had been speaking in a rage, pointed out the men who had been hurling the insults, and 'they were all marched off to execution' without trial.[53] The officers and troops were horrified at this display of oriental absolutism.

In the end, however, Alexander had to give in. Some 10,000 Macedonian soldiers were discharged, including many who were neither old nor unfit, but were discharged upon their own request.[54] Curtius adds that Alexander's force in Asia now totalled only 13,000 infantry and 2,000 cavalry, an army of 'only modest size'.[55] Over the years, Alexander had received several large contingents of Macedonian reinforcements sent by Antipater.[56] Now, all that was left of the great Macedonian army was a handful of troops. The rest had been killed, wounded, left behind in remote colonies, or simply grown too old in service to be of any use. Others more fit had become disgusted with their king and asked to be sent home.

By late summer 324 BC, Alexander was completely isolated from any base of support upon which he could rely to enforce his will or protect his person. The remnants of the army that had stayed behind in Asia were no more likely to serve Alexander loyally than the old veterans who had left, if only because most of them had been in service for several years and witness to Alexander's poor treatment of his troops. He was, as Plutarch says, 'feared by his men for his relentless severity in punishing any dereliction of duty'.[57] The Macedonian senior officer corps had been decimated by Alexander's paranoid delusions of conspiracy, and even those promoted to higher rank had shown themselves unreliable. The surviving officer corps, mostly junior officers, lived in fear, and even Alexander's bodyguard had come under suspicion, with at least one having to be removed and likely executed.[58] The only man Alexander completely trusted was Hephaestion, his long-time friend and lover, who served as his second in command.

Hephaestion's death from alcohol abuse in late October, 324 BC was a serious blow to Alexander's psychological stability. He knew Hephaestion was a heavy drinker, and blamed himself for not trying to stop him. In another of his paranoid episodes, Alexander became convinced that Hephaestion's death had been caused by his personal physician, Glaucias, and ordered the physician executed by impalement, the traditional Persian punishment for traitors. Alexander began to drink even more heavily. If we can believe Plutarch, he was often drunk for days at a time. He began to make grandiose plans for future conquests, became obsessed with getting the Greeks to recognize his divinity, and became even more obsessed with portents and conspiracies. Plutarch describes Alexander's condition in stark terms. Alexander became 'so much obsessed by his fears of the supernatural and so overwrought and apprehensive in his own mind that he interpreted every strange or unusual occurrence, no matter how trivial, as prodigy or a portent, with the result that the palace at Babylon was filled with soothsayers, sacrificers, purifiers, and prognosticators'.[59] His mind 'was filled with unreasoning dread ... and he had become a slave of his fears'.[60]

In the winter of 323 BC, Alexander launched an attack against the Cosseans that lasted for forty days, and completely annihilated the entire people. Alexander's slaughter of the Cosseans is a typical example of extreme post-traumatic stress: the berserker seeking relief in violence. Plutarch tells us as much when he says Alexander attacked the Cosseans 'seeking to alleviate his grief [at Hephaestion's death] in war'.[61] Alexander had again become like Achilles, seeking to calm his troubled mind with the solace that accompanies slaughter for those so afflicted with post-traumatic stress that they are already insane.[62]

## Suicide

Suicide was a phenomenon well-known to the Greeks, and is recorded in the works of the Greek historians (Thucydides, Xenophon, and Herodotus) and tragedians (Sophocles and Aeschylus). It was also an important topic of discussion among Greek philosophers.[63] The Greek view of suicide is modern in terms of its causes, although the Greeks saw the causes as different for men than for women. Men were thought to commit suicide out of shame, guilt, despair and cowardice, while women did so because they had been raped, left alone by the death of a husband, or out of deep sorrow for the death of a child, particularly a son. Central to male suicides were the Greek concepts of heroism and honour. A man who failed to perform adequately in war suffered public shame and disgrace, resulting in the loss of his status as a heroic male. Pantites, the Spartan who showed cowardice at Thermopylae, returned to Sparta to find himself in such disgrace that he hanged himself. Aristodemus, another Spartan who asked to be relieved from the line at Thermopylae, suffered public infamy until he regained his honour by trying to get himself killed in front of his comrades by engaging in a pointless frontal attack at

Platea. Spartans who did not perform well in battle were often shunned and unable to find wives.

The Greek idea of suicide differs from modern interpretations in that it did not regard suicide as an irrational act resulting from madness or any mental aberration. The Greeks viewed suicide as a completely rational human action that was instrumental in nature, that is, the victim was attempting to achieve something by it. Thus, suicidal obedience to orders in battle was seen as praiseworthy, and suicide at the command of the state (institutional suicide) carried no stigma. Like the Japanese samurai, suicide resulting from shame, guilt, or fear of dishonour was commendable, and suicide to restore one's honour was greatly praised. The intent of the suicide was, therefore, of central importance. Accordingly, suicide driven by cowardice, laziness, or even physical suffering was condemned.[64]

Psychologists today treat suicide as a mental aberration in which the victim's thinking is corrupted by emotional trauma or disarray. This is especially, though by no means completely, the case when dealing with soldiers exposed to war who have succumbed to post-traumatic stress. Suicide rates among soldiers are often high. In 2012, the suicide rate in the US Army was 24/100,000, and the rate during the Iraq war was 17.3/100,000. When suicide for veterans of Afghanistan and Iraq is examined, 35 per cent of the suicides were committed by soldiers who had never been deployed to a war zone, much less experienced combat. For a substantial number of soldiers, the stress of military life, even without exposure to battle, is enough to cause them to develop psychiatric symptoms and kill themselves.[65]

Suicide among stress victims may arise in two ways: an impulsive act in reaction to an immediate triggering trauma, emotional event, or sudden availability of the means (weapons, drugs, etc.) to carry out the act, or as result of some extended consideration in which the victim chooses or arranges the time, place, and circumstances of his actions that are intended to lead to his death. The second type of suicide is consciously seen by the victim as having some instrumental objective in which the victim's death is regarded as a means to that objective. One of Alexander's two suicidal episodes falls into the first category, and one in the second.

Alexander's first suicidal episode occurred in autumn 328 BC at Marakanda. For almost two years Alexander and his army had been in the field attempting to put down a national insurgency led by Darius' senior officers. The campaign had not gone well, and the insurgency was growing despite Alexander's brutal treatment of the native population. The death of Darius and Bessus had accomplished nothing, and the insurgency went on under the command of Spitamenes, an even better field general. After a particularly difficult campaign season in Sogdiana and Bactria, Alexander captured Marakanda, where he remained for ten days to rest his army. Alexander's officers, troops, and animals were exhausted.[66]

It was at Marakanda that Alexander's murder of Cleitus occurred. Cleitus was at least twenty years older than Alexander, the brother of Alexander's childhood nurse, Lanice, whose two other brothers had been killed in Alexander's service. Cleitus was the commander of the Royal Cavalry Squadron, and probably had held this post under Philip. It was Cleitus who had saved Alexander's life at the Granicus.

Alexander and his officers had finished eating and settled in to one of their typical drinking bouts when the conversation turned to praise of Alexander's accomplishments. Some servile officers began to denigrate the accomplishments of Philip. Cleitus, drunk by now, came to Philip's defence and the achievements of his officers, particularly Parmenion. It was the reference to Parmenion that angered Alexander.[67] Some of the officers tried to calm Cleitus, but to no avail. Cleitus went on to remind Alexander that he had saved the king's life. Alexander always resented being reminded of this fact, and 'even the memory of it annoyed the king'.[68] Cleitus does not seem to have realized the risk he was running. The persistent mobilization for violence, as we have seen, is one of the veteran soldier's persistent modes of behaviour, making him ready to spring into action at any provocation, to kill if necessary.[69] What drove Alexander over the edge, however, was Cleitus' taunting Alexander with the murder of Attalus and his ridicule of Alexander's claim that Ammon was his father.[70] At this, Alexander flew into a rage, grabbed a lance from a guard, and waited in the vestibule for Cleitus. When Cleitus appeared, Alexander stabbed him. Bespattered with the dying man's blood, Alexander cried out, 'Now go and join Philip, Parmenion, and Attalus.'[71]

Curtius and Justin agree on what happened next. Curtius tells us that Alexander 'pulled the spear from the dead man's body and turned it upon himself'.[72] Justin adds that Alexander 'would have committed suicide had not his friends interposed' and taken the weapon from his hands.[73] Alexander was carried to his tent, where he shut himself away for three days. Both Justin and Curtius record that Alexander was in such a depression that 'he was determined to die'. The king's dangerous depression did not escape the attention of his bodyguards who burst into his tent and put him under guard – a suicide watch – for more than a week. During that time Alexander suffered through a deep depression in which the ghosts of the others he had killed, 'Parmenio, Philotas, his cousin Amyntas, his stepmother and brothers, Attalus, Erylochus, Pausanias, and other slaughtered nobles of Macedonia, presented themselves to his imagination.'[74]

Curtius tells us that the next ten days were spent 'mainly devoted to restoring Alexander's self-respect'.[75] Had Alexander succeeded in killing himself, he would at least have redeemed his honour. Having failed, however, the problem of restoring Alexander's honour remained. Justin says it was Callisthenes, his old friend and fellow student under Aristotle, who came to him and finally convinced Alexander that he had to go on. In the Greek warrior context, however, Alexander's physical recovery itself was insufficient. His honour had to be restored by some public act. Curtius explains that 'to ease his feelings of shame over the killing, the Macedonians [the army in assembly] formally declared that Cleitus' death was justified, and they would have refused him burial had not the king ordered it'.[76]

The sources suggest that the reason the army exonerated Alexander was their fear that if he died, they would be left leaderless and unable to find their way home. The argument is not convincing, although the army's concern is proof enough that the officers believed that Alexander was quite capable of killing himself at the time. The Macedonian army was a professional army, not a conscript force, whose veteran troops and officers had served together for years. Justin notes that all the officers had fought under Philip at some time, and that more than soldiers, these troops and officers were 'masters in war'.[77] The army was highly cohesive, and troops looked to their combat commanders for orders and leadership, not to their king, who was mostly remote from day-to-day operations. Moreover, the army was highly organized around a general staff system that kept the army running. The death of Alexander would have made little difference to the Macedonian army's ability to fight, supply itself, or navigate across Persia to return home.

There is no reason to doubt that Alexander tried to kill himself as Achilles did when he learned of Patroklos' death. Achilles and Alexander blamed themselves for the death of their friends, and their guilt prompted both to attempt impulsively to commit suicide. Alexander's reactions to killing Cleitus also reveal Alexander's emotional instability after exposure to seven years of war. In the space of a few minutes, Alexander's emotions ranged from anger at Cleitus' praise of Parmenion, to rage at Cleitus' insult of Alexander's divine father, to fear that he was going to be killed by his own bodyguards when they attempted to stop Alexander from attacking Cleitus, to rage-filled violence when Alexander stabbed Cleitus, to guilt at realizing what Alexander had done, to an impulsive suicide attempt, and finally to a deep depression that lasted for days.

The range and intensity of Alexander's emotions in so short a time present themselves as a classic case of severe post-traumatic stress exploding into a berserk state. Moreover, Alexander's stress symptoms were surely aggravated by the severe concussion he had suffered during the siege of Cyropolis barely two months before the incident at Marakanda. The evidence points to severe disinhibition across the whole range of Alexander's emotions as a result of that concussion. Curtius was only partially correct when he noted that Alexander could barely control his temper even when sober. In fact, Alexander was no longer in control of any of his emotions.

Alexander's second suicidal episode occurred in January, 325 BC during the assault on the Malian stronghold in India. The army's mutiny in July, 326 BC had greatly affected Alexander's emotional balance, and he never seems to have wholly recovered from the shock of his officers and troops refusing to obey him.[78] But it was more than the army's disobedience that shook Alexander to his emotional core. As Plutarch notes, Alexander 'valued his glory and reputation beyond his life or kingdom'.[79] After the mutiny, Alexander's megalomaniacal dream of conquering India like Hercules and, in the process, discovering how to become a god was no longer possible. He had achieved all he could. There were no more worlds to conquer.

By now he was drinking heavily, depressed, and angry at having had his will frustrated. The central element in Alexander's psychological self-identity had been taken away. In his anger, he decided to take his army home along the most difficult route possible, forcing them to fight, suffer, and die along the way. But there was little glory in massacring tribes, and nothing in the way of conquest to be had. He could punish his troops for their disloyalty, but he could not restore the dream and achieve the great ends he had set for himself. Alexander's purpose in life had been lost.

In November, the army set sail down the Hydaspes with columns moving on foot along the river banks to protect the flanks. Over the next three months, the army fought a number of skirmishes and engagements with Indian tribes encountered along the way. In January, 325 BC, the Macedonians engaged the Malians in a series of pitched battles, eventually driving them back to their stronghold, which the Macedonians quickly placed under siege. It was during the siege that Alexander tried to take his life in true Homeric fashion.

Arrian says that Alexander was not satisfied with the pace of the siege, and seized a scaling ladder from a soldier, set it against the walls, climbed the ladder, and stood alone atop the battlement. He stood there in his shining armour for some time, deliberately exposing himself to the archers stationed in the wall's towers. Climbing the ladder behind him were his shield bearer, Peucestas, and Leonatus, one of Alexander's bodyguards.[80] Before they could reach him, 'With a wild leap, Alexander flung himself into a city full of his enemies.' The Malians recognized Alexander, and unleashed a torrent of arrows, one of which struck Alexander in the right chest, bringing him to his knees. Fortunately, his bodyguards arrived in time to drive off the attackers, and carry Alexander to safety.

Alexander's actions at Mali were clearly self-destructive, a fact that did not escape the notice of our sources, all of which record that Alexander was seeking a heroic death now made more attractive by the demise of the central purpose of his life. With his dreams shattered, all that was left was an honourable death in combat. Curtius says that 'his desperation provided a keen incentive to gain an honourable death ... even though he could barely hope to die in combat without uselessly sacrificing his life'.[81] Diodorus tells us that 'Alexander was eager to make this, if it were the last feat of his life, a supremely glorious one.'[82] Arrian adds, 'if it was his fate to die, death would come ... as the crown of an exploit which would live upon the lips of men.'[83] Denied the ultimate goals that had defined his identity as a warrior, Alexander tried to kill himself in one final blaze of glory by deliberately putting himself in harm's way before the eyes of the very men who had betrayed him. Alexander was imitating Aristodemus, the Spartan who tried to regain his honour by making a suicidal attack on the enemy line at Platea.

It is likely that Alexander's attempt to die heroically at Mali was the type of suicidal episode that required some extended consideration. Alexander's anger at the mutiny continued over some period until it developed into depression, as often happens when anger is not resolved. If he did nothing, he would be remembered for having been forced to abandon his goal of Herculean conquest and his opportunity to be recognized as a god among men. As Arrian noted, Alexander would be remembered only for his failures. As his depression deepened, Alexander sought a solution to the problem of restoring his identity. In the Greek ethos of heroism, the answer was to die a heroic death in battle. The Malian fortress was no Troy, but if he died well it would serve the purpose of restoring Alexander's honour.

Beyond his rationalization, it is possible that Alexander no longer cared very much about anything, even his own life. He had been at war for years, his friends and the soldiers he had sent into battle had died in windrows. He had murdered other friends and comrades. Thousands of civilians, women and children, had died before his eyes and at his command. If his experience had proved anything, it was that life was cheap, perhaps even his own, and that it might be taken or forfeited without any great loss. Like most people suffering from depression, there were times when death itself might appear preferable. Mali may have been one of those times.

And so, Alexander found a way to separate himself from his battlefield bodyguard, climb the ladder before anyone knew he was missing, make himself a target by standing atop the wall, and just as his bodyguards were about to reach him, elude them by jumping into the enemy's midst. It was by all indications a well-thought-out suicide attempt. Although Alexander failed to kill himself, his wounds were serious enough to regain some of his stature with the army, who interpreted his actions as but another example of his 'reckless bravery' which our sources extol far too much.

## Depression

Depression was an integral part of Alexander's psychology, and a number of his depressive episodes have already been noted in the previous pages. Ephippus, in eyewitness testimony, tells us that Alexander was often so depressed that he was, in his words, 'melancholy-mad'.[84] Alexander's reaction to the death of his closest friend, comrade, and lover, Hephaestion, offers an interesting insight into the dynamics and depths of depression of which Alexander was capable near the end of his life. Alexander's depression over Hephaestion's death was exacerbated by guilt rooted in Alexander's belief that he was responsible for his friend's death. Arrian tells us that Alexander knew that Hephaestion had been drinking too much, and felt guilty that he had made no attempt to stop him.[85] Grief, guilt, and depression combined in Alexander to produce an extreme emotional reaction: 'he flung himself on the body of his friend and lay there nearly all day long in tears, and refused to be parted from him until he was dragged away by force by his Companions; and again, he lay stretched upon the corpse all day and the whole night too.'[86] Alexander retired to his tent where he 'lay on his bed now crying lamentably, now in the silence of grief'.[87] It took Alexander three months to regain his emotional stability, and even then he continued to suffer. It was, as Plutarch tells us, 'to seek relief in war' that Alexander massacred the Cossean people. It is a disturbed person indeed for whom the din and slaughter of the battlefield is needed to drive away one's grief.

It had been so for Achilles, and it was now so for Alexander.

*Chapter 8*

# Alcoholism, Religiosity, and Megalomania

To understand the role that alcohol played in Alexander's life, it is important to understand the contexts within which extreme alcohol use becomes established in an individual. In Alexander's case, three contextual influences – cultural, familial, and social military – need to be understood. We may immediately dismiss Alexander's apologists, both ancient and modern, who claim that Alexander was not an alcoholic, for the evidence is overwhelming that he was. Even Plutarch, an admirer of Alexander, had to retract his earlier claim that Alexander did not drink heavily, and finally admit that Alexander drank 'immoderately'.[1] Arrian, himself a military man and a defender of Alexander, had to concede that 'Alexander had taken to new and barbaric ways in drinking' before the events at Marakanda.[2] Tellingly, Arrian seems to have reached this conclusion only after the murder of Cleitus, and after Alexander had suffered the head injury at Cyropolis two months before. Curtius tells us that Alexander's judgements 'were sullied by an excessive love of wine',[3] and Justin says Alexander was like Philip in being 'too fond of wine'.[4] Some modern scholars have reached the same conclusion. T. Africa speaks frankly of Alexander's 'dependence on alcohol', and Peter Green is clear in noting Alexander's 'advanced alcoholism'.[5] Given the Greek world in which Alexander was raised (cultural context), the drinking habits of his parents (familial context), and his life as a soldier (social military context), it would have been surprising indeed had Alexander not become an alcoholic.

The Greece of Alexander's day, and Macedonia in particular, was saturated with alcohol. Greece was a highly productive wine growing area, Macedonia especially so, and wine was cheaply available to all classes. Drinking acquired a civic status in which groups of men gathered for the purpose of drinking and discussing of civic events. The *symposium* of Alexander's day, though much maligned by critics of the Macedonian practice, was common in all Greek city states except Sparta. The Spartan military code required temperance, and according to the laws of Lycurgus, Spartans were allowed to drink wine only to quench their thirst.[6] They were the only Greeks not to have institutionalized drinking parties. To drive home the point to their warriors, Spartan leaders held public events in which Helots were forced to get drunk to provide a negative example of the dangers of drink for young warriors.[7] Wine was consumed on a daily basis by most Greeks, and even more during shortages of potable drinking water that often plagued Greece in the summer months when wine was used to quench one's thirst. Armies in the field drank wine often, especially on the march where wine was carried in barrels on the sides of wagons or on pack animals where it could be easily accessed by a thirsty soldier. Wine contains 8–12 per cent alcohol, however, and is more likely to exacerbate thirst rather than quench it. It also contributes to dehydration.

Wine was so central to Greek life that its manner of use became a primary means of determining social and cultural status. The 'civilized' Athenians diluted their wine in a common mixing bowl, a *krater*, in a proportion of three or four to one of water to wine as a means of preventing drunkenness. For Athenians, moderation was the rule, gulping wine considered vulgar, and getting drunk the mark of a barbarian. Macedonians, Byzantines, and Thracians were regarded as barbarians because they drank their wine unmixed, and did so until drunk. Macedonians, as noted earlier, were prodigious drinkers who regarded drunkenness as a sign of manliness and strength, and saw the symposium as the perfect forum to drink oneself into unconsciousness. Ephippus summed up the Greek view of Macedonians as a people 'who never understood how to drink in moderation'.[8]

Wine and drunkenness were strongly established in Greek religion, particularly in the cult of Dionysus. Originally the god of a Thracian cult of vegetation and fertility, in Greece Dionysus became the god of wine who travelled far and wide to spread the gift of wine to humanity. Drinking to intoxication allowed the god himself to enter a person, so that man and god were, for a time, one and the same.[9] The purpose of the god's gift was to liberate mortals from their suffering and pain, by granting them relief from their difficulties on this earth. In his play *The Bacchae*, Euripides describes the attraction of Dionysus:

> For filled with that good gift, suffering mankind forgets its grief; from it comes sleep; with it oblivion of the troubles of the day. There is no other medicine for misery. And when we pour libations to the gods, we pour the god of wine himself that through his intercession man may win the favour of heaven.[10]

Beyond the promise of temporary relief from life's suffering lay the greater promise of an afterlife, an attractive creed indeed for those living amid the often terrible hardships of life in antiquity. This was especially so for soldiers, whose experiences with the horrors of war required more frequent and prolonged relief from their own memories. It is no accident that from time immemorial soldiers have been thought to be heavy drinkers and drunkards. Perhaps they needed Dionysus' gift of relief more than most.

The Dionysus cult enjoyed wide popularity, and seems to have been most popular in those areas of Greece that Athenians thought to be the most primitive, like Macedonia and the quasi-tribal areas like Epirus, the birthplace of Alexander's mother, Olympias. The cult's popularity was such that most Greeks in antiquity would have looked upon those who abstained from drinking with suspicion. Failure to imbibe at a Dionysiac festival could lead to charges of impiety. There was, then, a strong cultural force in ancient Greece that encouraged drinking that was even stronger in Macedonia, where drinking was regarded as an important element in being a warrior. Intoxication, often to the extreme, was justified by religious sanction.

Alcohol use also had a strong influence on Alexander's family life as a young man. Much of Alexander's religiosity is said to have come from his mother, and she, too, was influenced by alcohol.[11] Olympias was an enthusiastic devotee of the cult of Dionysus, and spent lavishly and often on the god's festivals. She may already have been an initiate of the cult before she met Philip at one of these festivals when she was 18. Plutarch tells us of her religious devotion when he says, 'it was Olympias' habit to enter into the Dionysiac states of possession and surrender herself to the inspiration of the god with even greater abandon than others.'[12] In short, she got very drunk very often.

We have little information on Alexander's drinking as a young man other than the incident at Philip's wedding when he hurled his cup, presumably full of wine, at Attalus. Plutarch tells us that Alexander did not make a habit of attending the drinking parties given by his father, and that he drank only modestly as a young man.[13] Given his mother's religious fervour and drinking habits, however, it is likely that Alexander was raised in an atmosphere where drinking to intoxication was seen as a normal and legitimate activity. Under these circumstances, it is not surprising that Alexander may have later turned to alcohol when seeking relief from his troubles.

Philip was also a heavy drinker, although we are given only a few instances by our sources when Philip was drunk, far fewer than we have for Alexander. Unlike Alexander, we have no examples when Philip's decision-making was affected by his drinking. Theopompus, who makes much of Philip's tendency to drink to excess, allows that Philip was always clear-headed when it came to making decisions. No Macedonian warrior needed encouragement to drink. But Philip suffered from five serious wounds, leaving him with unset bones and in constant pain. Alcohol likely helped reduce his suffering.

Philip's reaction to alcohol was decidedly different than Alexander's, however. Philip could accept criticism even when he was drunk, and could laugh at himself. Diodorus tells us that after his great victory at Chaeronea, Philip got raving drunk, danced on the corpses of the dead, and ridiculed the Athenian prisoners. When one of the prisoners, Demades, publically criticized Philip's behaviour, Philip 'abandoned his revelry' and freed Demades as a reward for his courage in speaking out.[14] Alexander, by contrast, was incapable of accepting criticism drunk or sober. When drunk, his reaction was explosive outbursts of anger and violence. The only safe course when dealing with an intoxicated Alexander was agreement and flattery.

Psychologists classify the children of alcoholics into two types: Type 1 begin drinking before age 25, while Type 2 do not drink as adolescents and begin drinking after age 25, often in response to their life experiences as adults.[15] If we accept Plutarch that Alexander did not drink excessively as a young man, then Alexander may have been a Type 2 child of a family that had strong alcoholic tendencies. Interestingly, Type 1 drinkers show little influence of heredity on the formation of their drinking habits, while Type 2 drinkers show a substantial transmission of alcoholism and anti-social behaviour from father to son.[16] Most Type 2 drinkers are male and possess 'high-profile personalities'. They frequently experience a loss of control when drunk, and are given to impulsive, aggressive, and violent actions, all characteristics of Alexander's behaviour when inebriated.[17]

Another primary characteristic of Type 2 drinkers is that they are 'novelty seeking personalities', risk-takers and seekers of adventure and the unusual. They are also extremely curious.[18] When Alexander learned about naphtha while in Persia – the fire that could not be extinguished by water – he decided to see if that was the case by soaking his bath attendant in the liquid and lighting him on fire! Sure enough, water would not put out the flames, and the attendant was badly burned. It is worth considering, if only in passing, that what our sources took for Alexander's *pothos* – his adventurism, curiosity, and willingness to seek the unknown – may have been ultimately rooted in an alcoholic personality.

If Greek culture and family background disposed Alexander to excessive drinking, an even stronger and proximate influence was the social life expected of a Macedonian soldier, particularly a combat commander. Even if Plutarch is right that Alexander did not drink in his youth, he could hardly not have become a heavy drinker once he became king and commander of the Macedonian army. Macedonian nobles and officers drank heartily, and they expected their king to do so as well. Alexander would have been expected to keep up with his officers. One can only imagine what it must have been like in the early days for the young king with no battle experience, no wounds, and little experience in drinking to attend these meetings with a group of drunken battle hardened warriors. It may well have been that he took to drinking with his officers as a way to compensate for his obvious lack of military standing and for obvious physical attributes like his fair skin, long blond hair, beardless face, small stature, high voice, etc. Drinking may have been the way Alexander could feel himself at one with a group of combat officers.

Drinking bouts had a long history in Macedonia. The king and his officers were expected to gather together often and drink until they were intoxicated. When on campaign, these meetings were usually held when the army was safely protected behind city walls. The Macedonian tradition was that the king was first among equals and expected to hear straight talk and criticism from his brother officers. This democratic element of the military symposium was reflected in the arrangement of the couches and tables in a circle or a square, with no head table for the king or the senior officers. Drinking was done in rounds, and it was almost impossible for anyone to remain sober.

The symposia were mighty drinking contests and Alexander often sponsored these contests, with expensive gifts going to the winner. One might have thought that Alexander's small stature might have made him particularly susceptible to inebriation, but from all accounts he could drink with the best of his officers. In one incident reported by our sources, Alexander is said to have drunk to the health of all twenty participants and then accepted another round of twenty toasts in addition.[19] None of this implies that Alexander remained sober, only that he remained conscious. As Borza so candidly reminds us, the purpose of these drinking parties was to get drunk, and the party 'continued until fatigue, boredom, drunkenness, violence, unconsciousness, or sleep intervened'.[20] In some cases, drinking competitions led to the death of some of the participants!

Psychologically, however, the symposium served a more important purpose, especially for soldiers long exposed to war and trying to come to grips with their own emotional turmoil. In a real sense, the symposia were therapy sessions in which soldiers imbibed alcohol as a means of loosening their inhibitions, releasing their emotions, and making them willing to share their innermost feelings with their fellow warriors. Lawrence Trittle, himself a combat line officer in Vietnam, describes why soldiers get drunk in the company of comrades. Trittle writes, 'among soldiers, however, drinking takes on a much different role. Drink becomes a means of forgetting what you have done and seen, a means of coping with pain – not only psychic pain but also the type associated with wounds.' After having suffered several battlefield injuries, you take to drink in order to simply cope with the realities around you.[21]

One of the difficulties that complicates the social relationships of suffers of post-traumatic stress disorder is the sense that one is the only person who has ever suffered in this way. Drinking and emotionally opening up to fellow soldiers is an attempt to reach out to others who have gone through similar experiences. Often, just to hear other soldiers relate their experiences and pain – sometimes accompanied by crying, shaking, and soldiers holding each other in comfort – provokes emotional relief from the guilt and fear soldiers suffer. Being drunk in the company of fellow sufferers provides reassurance that all the released feelings will be washed away, forgiven, and forgotten when everyone sobers up. American GI's travelling home in troopships after the Second World War frequently reported hearing soldiers crying, sobbing, and being comforted by their comrades. There is no reason to believe that Alexander and his officers were any less affected by what they had seen and done in war than any soldiers before or since. The symposium was the primary forum for dealing with the burdens of post-traumatic stress disorder, and it is likely that Alexander used it in just this way to gain some relief from his own emotional trauma.

Alexander seems to have accustomed himself to the symposia with little difficulty, and the first evidence of a drunken Alexander comes from Diodorus who notes that Alexander sponsored a nine-day festival in Dium in 334.[22] In 333, a drunken Alexander crowned a statue at Phaselis.[23] In November of the same year Alexander held a banquet to celebrate his victory at Issus at which he is drunk again.[24] By 333, Alexander had been at war for three years, and had been wounded once. All of the reported incidents of drinking occur at symposia. We hear no more about Alexander's drinking until May 330, when at the end of a four month period of resting his army in Persepolis, he set the royal palace on fire in a fit of drunken mania.[25] It was during his stay in Persepolis that Alexander first began to show signs of explosive anger and to regard his colleagues with suspicion. At Persepolis, Alexander 'yielded to dissipation' and began attending drinking parties during the day, followed by 'drinking and mad revelry throughout the night'.[26] From this time to the end of his life, Alexander remained a heavy drinker.

Most reports of Alexander's drinking are contained in our sources' description of various symposia that Alexander attended. From 334 to 323, Alexander held and attended twenty-six symposia that we know of, twenty-one of which were held after Alexander suffered a severe concussion at the siege of Cyropolis in 328.[27] As we shall see in the next chapter, Alexander's concussion probably resulted in significant brain damage that produced severe disinhibition, and possibly hyperphagia, so that from this point forward his ability to control his drinking was severely diminished.

In almost every one of the reported symposia, Alexander is described as either drunk or drinking heavily. It must be kept in mind, however, that the reports of his drinking are only part of the story. Our sources tend to report only one symposium at each location, usually to highlight some significant event. That does not rule out the possibility that other symposia were held as well, but at which nothing unusual occurred. In addition, the daily use of wine at meals, to quench one's thirst during the day, and for simple relaxation in the evening must also be considered. Alexander was also a frequent guest at banquets given by his officers, where he also found opportunity to drink and sponsor drinking contests.

One can point to at least five incidents in which Alexander's alcohol use affected his behaviour in a significant way. The burning of Persepolis in 330 took place when Alexander was in a state of drunken mania. In 328, Cleitus was struck down by a drunken Alexander consumed with violent rage. In Pakistan in 327 at Nysa, the city marking the farthest of Dionysus' mythical journeys, Alexander held a ten-day revel for the army in which Alexander himself became 'possessed by Dionysus, raised the Dionysiac cry, and rushed hither and thither in the Bacchic way'.[28] After the crossing of the Gedrosian Desert and reaching Carmania in 325, Alexander led the army on a week-long drunken march, putting the army at serious risk of exposure to attack. Following the death of Hephaestion in 324, Alexander entered a drunken depression that lasted for at least a month, after which he ordered the extermination of the Cossean people down to the last child. Hamilton notes that from this point Alexander's drinking became worse and 'Alexander now approached more and more closely to insanity'.[29]

In autumn of 324, Alexander moved his army across the Zagros Mountains to Ectabana, the summer retreat of the Persian kings. He remained here until the spring of the next year, when he moved to Babylon where he died on 10 June, 323. The time at Ectabana was spent in festivals and drinking bouts, and evidence is clear that Alexander had lost control of his drinking and was drinking or drunk almost every day. A passage in the *Ephemerides* or Royal Diaries (now lost) is cited by Aelian that reveals the extent of Alexander's drinking a year before he died. It is quoted in full below:

> They say that on the 5th of the month Dius he drank at Eumaeus', then on the 6th he slept from drinking; and as much of that day as he was fresh, rising up, he did business with the officers about the morrow's journey, saying that it would be early. And on the 7th he was a guest at

> Perdiccas' and drank again; and on the 8th he slept. On the 15th of the same month he also drank, and on the following day he did the things customary after drinking. On the 24th he dined at Lagoas'; the house of Bagoas was 10 stades from the palace; then on the 28th he was at rest. Accordingly, one of two conclusions must be true, either that Alexander hurt himself badly by drinking so many days in a month or that those who wrote these things lie.[30]

It seems likely that Alexander continued his hard drinking until he died a year later, if only because there was no good reason to stop even if, which seems unlikely, he could control his need for alcohol.

The unresolved question is whether Alexander's alcoholism was the result of post-traumatic stress disorder as a consequence of his prolonged exposure to war, or the result of the severe concussion he suffered at Cyropolis in 328, or both. Alexander was already drinking heavily before Cyropolis and manifesting other symptoms of post-traumatic stress. The head injury may have reduced Alexander's emotional inhibition across his entire emotional spectrum, as evidenced by his increased manifestations of violence, anger, and cruelty after the injury. The head injury may also have produced hyperphagia, further stimulating Alexander's appetite for alcohol, until he was unable to control his drinking at all. The conclusion that Alexander was an alcoholic for much of the time he was campaigning in Bactria, Sogdiana, Pakistan, and India seems reasonable. It must be noted, however, that alcoholics can often achieve remarkable things. This is what Graham means when he says that 'Alexander the great was an alcoholic. But the same alcoholism-created ego that led him to murder trusting subordinates, also drove Alexander to try and conquer the world.'[31]

**Extreme Religiosity**

One element of Alexander's personality that is often given less attention than it deserves is his strong sense and practice of religion. Arrian tells us that he was a deeply religious man who was unfailing in his performance of the ceremonies required by Macedonian religious custom.[32] He continued to perform the required daily sacrifices even when wounded and being carried on a litter.[33] As king, Alexander was the chief priest of Macedonia, and required to perform daily religious rituals, just as Philip had done, although Philip could hardly have been called religious in any genuine sense. Alexander's mother was also a sincere practitioner of religion, and may have had much to do with inculcating the importance of religious devotion in her son. Alexander paid serious intention to oracles and portents all his life, and his life ended surrounded by seers and soothsayers in a spasm of religious fanaticism.[34]

Macedonians worshipped the Olympian gods in the same way as Greeks in other states, but did so in a cultural context that was characteristic of Archaic or even Homeric Greece. Within this context, the gods were closer to humans in time and deeds, and were regarded more as historic personalities than they were in more rational, philosophical Athens or Thebes. The great heroes of the Homeric past were real to Macedonians, humans whose *arete* (excellence) conferred upon them a quasi-divine status, and who were honoured with statues and cult-like ceremonies of respect. The idea that one could become like the great heroes of the past was much more credible to a Macedonian than it was to an Athenian. It was certainly credible to Alexander, who seems to have believed it from his youth until the end of his life.

To comprehend Alexander's religious madness, it is necessary to understand the relationship between gods and humans in Greek religious thought. There had always been a clear distinction between gods and men based on the impassable gulf between mortality and immortality. The gods consorted with humans in various ways, and sometimes fathered sons with mortal women. These 'sons of god' after a lifetime of virtue and achievement, could become heroes who could be honoured with the establishment of some sort of sacred precinct within which sacrificial offerings might be proffered. But these hero cults were essentially cults of the dead, and their rituals were fundamentally different from those observed toward the gods.[35]

Being born the son of a god did not convey any fact or implication of divinity. Simply put, sons of gods were not gods. Mortals who became heroes through achievement and virtue might be permitted, after death, to consort with the gods in some limited way (demi-gods), but were not considered fully divine. Achilles, Perseus, and Hercules all had mortal mothers and were great heroes, but were not considered divine. Only one person born of a mortal mother, Dionysus, became a genuine god, and then only after death. The idea that a human being could become divine while still alive was regarded as false, outrageous, and blasphemous by Greeks and Macedonians alike. As the later king of Macedonia, Antigonous Gonatas, said of Alexander's claim to be divine, 'even my piss-pot bearer knows better.'[36]

Alexander's madness rests in his claim to be divine and to be worshipped while he was still alive.[37] Callisthenes had the temerity to remind Alexander at a symposium in 327 that no Macedonian or Greek had ever claimed to be mortal and divine.[38] In response, Alexander had Callisthenes murdered, a clear indication as to how seriously Alexander regarded his claim to be a god. What, then, was at the root of Alexander's obsession with his own divinity?

The seed of Alexander's obsession may have been planted by his mother. Olympias had first encouraged Alexander to emulate Achilles. Plutarch suggests that sometime after Philip's death and before Alexander left for Asia, Olympias confided to her son that Philip was not his real father, and that she had actually been impregnated by Zeus.[39] It would, of course, have been foolish – and dangerous – to circulate such a story while Philip was alive. But the story gained currency early in Alexander's career and became widely known.

That Alexander took the story seriously is evident by his visit to the oracle of Ammon-Zeus at Siwah in the Libyan Desert after his conquest of Egypt in 331. Arrian tells us that one of the reasons Alexander went to Siwah was to seek confirmation from the oracle – in this case from the oracle of Ammon himself that the Greeks syncretically regarded as Zeus – of the fact that his real father was Zeus and not Philip.[40] The oracle's confirmation of Alexander's divine birth made a profound and lasting impression on him, and by 328 Alexander's claim to be the son of Zeus-Ammon was openly spoken about at court.[41] The idea of a divine mortal may also have gained credibility in Alexander's mind when he was crowned pharaoh in Memphis. Egyptian pharaohs had been regarded as living gods for at least 3,000 years before Alexander's arrival.

Between 331 and 328, there was little talk of Alexander's divine birth as he instead stressed his heroic heritage from Achilles on his mother's side and Heracles on his father's. No doubt Alexander's conviction of his divine origin took deeper root in his mind, but he seems to have been careful not to stress the fact in public. Alexander surely knew that being the son of a god did not imply his own divinity or even confer heroic status. He also had to know that any attempt to affirm his divinity and require worship would provoke strong resistance from the Macedonians.[42] And yet, by 328 there was intense discussion at court regarding what to do about Alexander's belief in his own divinity.[43] It was in 327 that Alexander brought the matter to a head by attempting to establish the Persian custom of *proskynesis* for the Macedonians.

*Proskynesis* is the Greek word for the Persian custom of requiring the king's subjects to prostrate themselves when in the presence of the king. The Persian king was not regarded as divine, and performing the ceremony was not an act of religious worship.[44] It was, rather, an act of recognizing the sovereign's extreme superiority over his subjects. The custom was performed by any social inferior whenever a social superior was encountered. To Macedonians, however, the ceremony was abhorrent, and regarded as a servile barbarian custom, a violation of personal dignity, contrary to the Macedonian ideal of equality among warriors, and too close in form to religious worship offered to a living person. Alexander's attempt to impose the custom on Macedonians was met with predictable resistance, resentment, anger and ridicule. Why, then, did he do it?

After seven stressful years of war and violence, Alexander had come to believe that he was a god.[45] Perhaps his remarkable success in war had convinced him that he was permitted to achieve what was denied to other mortals. For a man to attempt to surpass the achievements of other beings who were thought to be gods could only be thought possible by a man who was already convinced that he had transcendent powers.[46] It is important to remember that extreme religiosity is closely associated with war trauma, and not an uncommon condition among soldiers suffering from prolonged stress. Extreme religiosity is a character disorder in which the stress of war creates problems so deeply seated that they become an integral part of the soldier's personality. Character disorders include stable obsessional states that represent a fundamental altering of the soldier's personality. All too commonly the symptoms accompany the soldier for the rest of his life.[47] Having believed himself the son of a god, it was but a short step for Alexander, under prolonged stress, to come to believe that he was a god.

Even so, why did Alexander attempt to establish *proskynesis* when he did? Why did he suddenly desire to be recognized and worshipped as a god? Recall that in the summer of 328, Alexander suffered a severe concussion at Cyropolis that caused lingering brain damage. One result of Alexander's injury was severe disinhibition that he continued to demonstrate in many ways for the rest of his life. It was only six months after his injury and the consequent reduction in his ability to control his emotions that Alexander revealed his deepest desire to be a god and be worshipped as one. It was then that he attempted to establish *proskynesis* among the Macedonians. His injury had made it impossible for him to control his most intense emotions. Alexander's now intense belief that he was a god burst forth because his dishinibition made it impossible to suppress it any longer. As with other emotions and drives that he could no longer control – anger, fear, paranoia, depression, dipsomania – Alexander could no longer control his desire to be recognized and worshipped as a god. And as in so many other things, Alexander required proof from others that he genuinely was divine.

That Alexander thought himself divine seems clear from his public behaviour after he returned from India. Phylarchus tells us of Alexander's grandiose receptions when he was treated with all the reverence due a god.[48] Arrian says that when the Greek envoys visited Alexander at Babylon, they treated him with all the reverence and demeanour attendant to religious worship, although they did not offer actual worship. The Greek envoys, 'wearing ceremonial wreaths, solemnly approached Alexander and placed golden chaplets on his head, as if their coming were a ritual in honour of a god.'[49] The ceremonial wreaths indicated that the envoys were *theoroi*, sacred envoys, and that their states acknowledged Alexander's divinity. Ephippus, quoted in full below, offers the most convincing evidence of Alexander dressing in the costumes of various Greek deities, requiring incense to be burnt around him, and being greeted with religious reverential silence due a god.[50]

> Alexander also wore the sacred vestments at his dinner parties, at one time putting on the purple robe of Ammon, and thin slippers and horns just like the god's, at another time the costume of Artemis, which he often wore even in his chariot, wearing the Persian garb and showing above the shoulders the bow and hunting spears of the goddess, while at still other times he was garbed in the costume of Hermes ... on social occasions he wore the winged sandals and broad-brimmed hat on his head, and carried the caduceus in his hand; yet often again, he bore the lion's skin and club in imitation of Heracles.[51]

Such behaviour was, of course, madness in the eyes of Greeks and Macedonians. It was a madness rooted in a mind weakened, then twisted, and finally broken by the burdens created by long exposure to death and violence and exacerbated by brain damage. In the end, Alexander wanted to become divine to escape the torment of his own mortality, to find a way to rid himself of the suffering many soldiers eventually come to feel. He had suffered enough, and wanted to quit this world. The price was his sanity, and Alexander willingly paid it. Peter Green brilliantly describes the role that divinity played in Alexander's mind during his final years:

> He became a god when he ceased wholly to trust his powers as a man, taking the divine shield of invincibility to combat his inner fear of failure; the divine gift of eternal youth as a talisman against the spectres of old age, sickness, and death: the perils of the flesh that reminded him of his own mortality. Alcoholism bred paranoia; his dreams became grandiose lunacies.[52]

## Megalomania

It is hardly necessary to note that a person who thinks he is a god is suffering from megalomania, a word derived from the Greek meaning 'great madness'. Megalomania is a psychopathological disorder characterized by fantasies of power, relevance, or omnipotence. Known also as narcissistic personality disorder, megalomania is accompanied by an inflated sense of self-esteem and an overestimation of one's powers and beliefs.[53] Alexander's megalomania was not only evident in his claim to divinity, but also in his grandiose plans for future campaigns: Philip was to receive a tomb equal in size to the Great Pyramid; great temples were to be constructed at Delos, Delphi, and other locations; the Susa weddings hinted at a grand delusion for the mass relocation of populations between Europe and Asia 'to bring the largest continents to common concord and familial amity by intermarriage';[54] a funeral and monument for Hephaestion that was to cost 10,000 talents; plans to conquer Arabia so that the inhabitants might have an opportunity to worship Alexander along with the only two other gods, Uranus and Dionysus, they worshipped. Arrian says Alexander 'felt it would not be beyond his merits to be regarded by the Arabs as a third god, in view of the fact that his achievements surpassed those of Dionysus'.[55]

Alexander was planning military campaigns that were equally delusional. He ordered the construction of 1,000 warships larger than triremes. A road was to be constructed along the entire North African coast as far as the Pillars of Hercules (Gibraltar), with harbours and shipyards at key intervals. The road, ships, and harbours were to support Alexander's campaign to conquer all non-Greek peoples in the Western Mediterranean, including Carthage, Sicily, and Spain.[56] Preparations for these constructions and the invasion were barely underway when Alexander died. There is no need to wonder what Alexander's senior officers thought of these grandiose expeditions. Within days of Alexander's death, Perdiccas, Alexander's chief of staff to whom he had entrusted his signet ring, called the Macedonian assembly into session which then voted to cancel all of Alexander's plans. Alexander's lunacies died with him.

It is likely that the officers and soldiers of the army never had much use for Alexander's insatiable pursuit of glory and conquest. When Isocrates first put forth the idea of a campaign against Persia when Philip was still alive, it was for the purpose of treating Asia only as a prize of war to be exploited for Macedonian benefit. Aristotle instructed Alexander to treat the people of Asia as barbarians and slaves to be exploited by their new Greek masters. By the time of Alexander's demise, the veterans of the Macedonian army had been at war for almost thirteen years, had been worn down, and only wanted an end to the ceaseless campaigns. They had fought hard for their ill-gotten gains, and now wanted to enjoy them. Tired of war, their hair turned gray, their bodies old and weak, many wanted only to return home with their wealth and live out their lives.

The motivation of the Macedonian army in following Alexander for as long as it did not rest in their support of their king's ambitions, and surely not in his delusion to establish some form of multi-ethnic empire. The Macedonian army was unlike any other army in Greece in that it was an army of full-time professionals, not the part-time citizen armies found in other Greek states. As with the mercenaries of the Peloponnesian Wars, military service was full-time employment, and in Macedonia this service came with retirement and death benefits for widows and children.[57] The soldiers of Macedonia followed their commanders for the same reasons the soldiers of Rome or the British Empire followed theirs: it was their work and, at times, it could be very lucrative indeed. As the army saw it, Alexander's exploits had little to do with glory or ideology. The march across Asia was one long *chevauchee* or plundering raid, much like the later English incursions into France for a century during the Hundred Years War.[58]

Alexander's officers, including the high command, shared the view that conquest was about personal enrichment and advancement, and they remained loyal to Alexander through to the end of the Persian conquest. When he decided to attack India, and when his dreams of glory and divinity began to get in the way of practicality, all but a few of the most loyal officers wanted out. It was no coincidence that the highest ranking officers sided with the troops during both mutinies. At some point it must have become clear to them that their own ambitions for power and wealth could no longer be achieved as long as Alexander was alive.

## A Death in Babylon

Alexander the Great died in Babylon on 10 June, 323 BC after an illness and fever that lasted for some two weeks.[59] Stories immediately began to circulate that the Macedonian king had been murdered, the victim of poison administered by someone close to him. Arrian, Curtius, Plutarch, and Diodorus all report the rumours that Alexander was poisoned, but only Justin, the earliest of the sources, claims Alexander was in fact murdered, naming Antipater's son, Iolaus, as the killer.[60] Modern physicians cannot definitively determine from the symptoms of Alexander's illness described in the sources what killed Alexander. Various attempts at a medical diagnosis have suggested that Alexander may have died from malaria exacerbated by alcohol abuse, acute alcohol withdrawal, strychnine poisoning, pancreatitis, leukaemia, porphyra, schistosomiasis, typhus, West Nile virus, alcoholic hepatitis, etc. The question of what or who killed Alexander remains unresolved.[61]

Having said that, it is not unreasonable to speculate that Alexander might indeed have been murdered by his officers. They alone had the means and opportunity to do so, and many of them the motivation. When Antipater was told that Parmenio had been murdered, he is supposed to have remarked, 'now no one is safe.' And indeed, no one was. Alexander's murders of old friends, comrades, officers, and others put everyone, including his senior officers, at risk. If Parmenio could be murdered, then anyone could be murdered. A drunken Alexander who thought himself divine was capable of killing any of them. By 323 Alexander was out of control, and everyone around him knew it.

Most of Alexander's officers had no use for Persians or their customs which they regarded as barbaric, and could not have cared less about Alexander's dream of military glory. The more Alexander adopted oriental habits and ceremonies, the more his officers came to resent him. Like Hermolaus, the page who tried to assassinate Alexander, the officers were appalled at Alexander's suspension of the ancient Macedonian right of trial by one's military peers. Alexander's orientalising and his bizarre behaviour made a mockery of the Macedonian ideal of a band of brother warriors who could speak openly and without fear. Even an offhand comment was now sufficient to place one under suspicion, and could cause one to be executed.

And now, Alexander was planning new campaigns of conquest that some may have come to regard as a grandiose plan to get them all killed. Alexander had done this before when he took a group of disgruntled soldiers, formed them into a separate battalion, and used them recklessly until they were all killed or wounded. When Alexander came to distrust Greek mercenaries, he forcibly 'settled' them in remote towns or garrisons, leaving them behind and unable to return to Greece. Professional soldiers are very realistic creatures. They knew that new campaigns ran the risk of their being killed, wounded, or left behind.[62] As long as Alexander lived, no one would be safe. Under these circumstances, murder may have been the only reasonable course.[63]

*Chapter 9*

# The Myth of Military Genius

Almost from the moment of his death, Alexander has been regarded as a military genius whose exploits on the battlefield were unprecedented. These exploits were recorded early on, and in ancient times Alexander had already become the great romantic warrior hero for kings and generals to emulate. The theme of Alexander's military brilliance survived the ages mostly unchallenged, and Alexander's battles are still studied in military colleges and academies as examples of combat leadership, and strategic and tactical brilliance. The assumption of military brilliance is, in my view, largely undeserved, and has led historians and military analysts to ignore the many shortcomings of Alexander's military performance. It also led to a neglect of the importance of Philip's accomplishments that made Alexander's achievements possible. It is no exaggeration to say that without Philip's military and political legacy, there would have been no Alexander the Great.

Alexander's opportunity for greatness began with the single truth that Philip was a great national king who created the first national territorial state in Europe, uniting disparate peoples under Macedonian leadership into a powerful national political entity. Philip enlarged, urbanized, and developed Macedonia's natural and human resources to a degree never seen before in Greece or the West. In doing so, he made Macedonia the wealthiest and most resource-rich state in Greece. With Macedonia as his national power base, Philip expanded his sphere of political and military dominance into the first great European land empire in history, uniting all of Greece into a single political entity with common political institutions and a single constitution. It was this imperial state that provided the material resources – ships, food, troops, reserve manpower, military equipment, and animals – that made Alexander's successful assault on the western half of the Persian Empire possible.[1]

The composition of the expeditionary force that Alexander took with him to Persia amply illustrates the extent of the resources provided by Philip's new imperial state. Alexander's army included 12,000 Macedonian infantry (phalanx and Guards Brigades), 7,000 Greek hoplites drawn from the League of Corinth's troops, 7,000 troops from the subject tribes, including light cavalry, *peltasts*, and javelin men, 1,000 archers and Agrianian mounted javelineers, and 5,000 mercenaries (heavy infantry). These are in addition to the 11,000 or so troops already in Ionia as the advance expeditionary force sent under the joint command of Attalus and Parmenio. Alexander also took with him 1,800 Macedonian cavalry, including the elite Companion cavalry, 1,800 Thessalian heavy cavalry, 900 Thracian and Paeonian scouts, 600 League cavalry, in addition to the 1,000 cavalry already in-country with the advance expedition.[2] Alexander's force amounted to 49,100 men. It was Philip's creation of the Macedonian empire that made raising such large numbers of troops and equipment possible.

Usually not mentioned, but surely present, in the invasion force were Philip's siege engineers and sappers responsible for Alexander's artillery, assault-gear for tunnelling and mining, and for the construction of roads and bridges. Also in train were the *bematistai*, or survey section that collected information about routes and camp grounds. Most important were Philip's experienced logistics officers. All these specialists had been introduced into the Macedonian army by Philip.

Raising and deploying the large invasion army was itself a great achievement. Sustaining its manpower in the field was another. Alexander's campaigns lasted for a decade and covered 10,000 miles of marching and fighting. His army would have been worn to helplessness without some system of manpower replacement. While Alexander made use of Persian and tribal troops, he did so only minimally and much later in his campaigns. Most of Alexander's replacements over the first four years of war when he had to fight the Persian army came from Macedonia, sent by Antipater who had been left behind as regent. Philip had introduced a system of nation-wide recruitment and training of Macedonian militia troops that made it possible to provide large numbers of trained and disciplined soldiers to Alexander on a regular basis, while still sustaining the manpower strength of Antipater's army to keep peace in the empire. No state other than Macedonia had such a large and comprehensive system of military recruitment and training, and no other could have sustained Alexander's army in the field for very long.

Hammond's figures suggest that Macedonian replacements alone counted for almost 15,000 infantry and cavalry over the life of Alexander's campaigns, most arriving within the first four years of the invasion.[3] This amounts to fully half the total Macedonian force in the field in 332.[4] Once Persia had been conquered, many of Alexander's replacements did not come from Macedonia, but from the Balkan tribes and the thriving market for Greek, Bactrian, and Indian, mercenaries.[5] Alexander's capture of the Persian treasury made it possible for him to afford large numbers of mercenaries. Brunt says, however, that between 326 and 323, Alexander received at least two large contingents of replacements that Arrian neglected to mention, some of which were surely Macedonians.[6] He notes that in 324 Alexander sent Craterus home with 10,000 Macedonian infantry and 1,500 cavalry, while sending 13,000 infantry and 2,000 cavalry to hold down Asia. This would have left Alexander with only 2,000 or 3,000 infantry and virtually no cavalry, clearly an impossible situation. Brunt concludes that Alexander had to receive considerable reinforcements.[7]

Before leaving the Punjab, Alexander received another large contingent of reinforcements amounting to 30,000 infantry and 6,000 cavalry from Thrace, Greece, and Babylon.[8] Although not Macedonians, the numbers speak to Antipater's ability to continue to recruit non-Macedonian imperial troops to sustain Alexander's field operations. Alexander could not have sustained his field operations without the continued support of Macedonian and imperial reinforcements that were the product of Philip's replacement system.

Wars occur within the political context that makes them possible. This context is often more important than the armies, troops, and equipment required. Alexander's campaign against Persia would not have been possible had Philip not first established a civic peace among the warring Greek states. More than anything, it was Philip's peace and its accompanying guarantee that the Greek states would observe their obligations to the League that made Alexander's attack on Persia possible. Without this guarantee, no Macedonian commander would have dared risk invading Persia while exposing himself to revolt and attack in his rear. Without the Athenian assurance to use its navy to oppose any Persian attempt to attack Greece by sea while Alexander was in the field, Alexander's expedition risked being cut off and destroyed piecemeal. The initial crossing into Asia also depended upon Philip's previous successes. Alexander crossed into Asia at the Hellespont. The crossing was possible because Philip had previously secured Thrace and the Chersonese in a year-long military campaign, creating the strategic platform from which Alexander could launch his invasion. Had Philip not accomplished this, no invasion of Persia was possible.

The strategic vision of taking a Greek army into Asia and conquering Persia was Philip's, not Alexander's. The idea had been around for at least a decade, espoused by men such as Isocrates as a way of stopping Greek civil strife by bringing the warring states together in the common effort against Persia, and then exploiting the country as a prize of war. Before Philip, the idea was less than fully formed, and the political conditions necessary to render an invasion possible were absent until Philip brought them into being. It was only after he had done so that a war against Persia became possible with some expectation of success. Philip gave the strategic idea operational possibility, and he planned the invasion in detail. Alexander carried out the invasion, but it was Philip who first transformed thought into action, and gave practical expression to the strategic vision itself.

It was Philip's military genius in devising and introducing new infantry and cavalry formations, expanding their tactical roles, and increasing exponentially their combat killing power, that created the military instrument that provided Alexander with the strong advantage in battle that made his victories possible. Robert Gaebel summed up this advantage in the following terms. 'Except for numbers, Alexander always had superior fighting ability at his disposal, so that a significant military asymmetry existed between his forces and those of his enemies. Most of this superiority resulted from the inherent qualities of the Macedonian army and was based on discipline, training, arms skill, professionalism, and cultural outlook, all of which had been enhanced by experience.'[9] Had Philip not invented a new Macedonian army, the odds are very good that there would have been no Alexander the Great.

It is no exaggeration to say that Philip was a military genius whose tactical and operational innovations revolutionized the Greek way of war, bringing into existence new and more powerful combat capabilities without which Philip's conquests in Greece and Alexander's in Asia would not have been possible. Philip's invention of a new form of infantry warfare constructed around a new combat formation, the pike-phalanx, armed with a new weapon, the *sarissa*, and capable of greater flexibility, stability, and manoeuvre than the hoplite phalanx, bequeathed Alexander his main combat arm for controlling the battlefield. The new phalanx could be employed in a number of new ways: in the defence to offset the numerical superiority of the Persian infantry, in the offence to strike at the Persian line with sufficient force to penetrate it, and as a platform of manoeuvre to anchor the battle line and freeze enemy dispositions while the Macedonian cavalry sought a weak spot through which to penetrate and turn inside the Persian lines. Philip's introduction of the long pike also afforded his infantry a great advantage in close combat over the Persian infantry which was armed mostly with short spear, shield, bow, and little armour, making it far less formidable than Macedonian heavy infantry.

Philip also revolutionized the killing capability of Greek cavalry. Until Philip, cavalry in Greece had been only a minor combat arm with little killing power, incapable of offensive action, limited in the pursuit, and unable to break infantry formations. Philip changed all this by replacing the short cavalry javelin with the long *xyston* lance and introducing the Thracian cavalry wedge to drive through infantry formations. He also taught the Macedonian cavalry to fight as units instead of individual combatants, and trained them in close combat and horsemanship to a level heretofore unseen in Greece.

Unlike traditional Greek cavalry, Philip's cavalry was tactically designed to close with the enemy, shatter its formations, and kill it where it stood. If the enemy took flight, Macedonian cavalry was expert in the lethal pursuit, something mostly absent in Greek warfare until then, hunting the enemy in small groups and striking it down with lance and sabre.

Philip's cavalry innovations transformed cavalry from an impotent combat arm into the Macedonian army's combat arm of decision. It was the killing power of the Macedonian cavalry in close combat that made Alexander's cavalry so effective against both Persian infantry and cavalry. Persian cavalry was employed mostly in the traditional manner, to ride close to the enemy and throw javelins, skirmishing, and closing here and there with the sabre. As such, it lacked ability for effective close combat against both disciplined infantry and aggressive cavalry. Again and again, Alexander used his cavalry to close the distance with the enemy and bring the killing power of his cavalry to bear upon his adversaries in close quarters. If Alexander had been equipped with traditional Greek cavalry, his combat arm of decision against the Persians would have been practically useless.

Another innovation that made Alexander's success possible was Philip's creation of an engineering and siege capability for the first time as an integral part of a Greek field army. Philip's siege engineers had almost two decades of field experience before Alexander took them to Asia, and were equipped with the new Macedonian torsion catapult that gave Alexander's army the capability to batter down the walls of cities. Alexander's chief engineer, Diades, had been trained by Polyeidos, Philip's chief engineer. The siege corps itself had been trained to a fine edge by Philip, who employed them in at least eleven sieges in his previous campaigns.[10]

The importance of a siege capability to Alexander's success cannot be overestimated. Having landed in Asia unopposed and defeated a Persian army at the Granicus River, Alexander had to secure his hold on the Asian coast. He had to quickly reduce the major coastal cities to avoid being caught from behind by the Persian army, as almost happened at Issus, and to deprive the Persian navy of bases from which to launch a sea-borne attack on Greece. It was Philip's veteran engineers and sappers that reduced Miletus, Hallicarnasus, Tyre, and Gaza in relatively short order.[11] Alexander also used his siege capability to great effect in Sogdiana and especially in India, where most city walls and fortifications were made of wood and wattle.[12] Without Philip's engineers, Alexander would have been forced to rely upon the usual Greek siege practice of isolation and starvation, and would not have gotten much beyond the coast, giving the Persian army plenty of time to reassemble.

Another major innovation upon which Alexander depended was Philip's commissariat corps. Philip introduced the science of logistics to Greek armies, allowing his armies to march long distances and sustain themselves in the field for months on end. By Alexander's time, Philip's logisticians had been at their work for two decades. Alexander's march up country lasted a decade and covered 10,000 miles. It was Philip's logistics officers that made this projection of force possible by finding the means to supply the army. The Persians were excellent logisticians themselves, and as Alexander moved inland he captured the extensive system of Persian supply depots holding food and military equipment. The Persian system of interior roads also aided Alexander, as did the Persian practice of requiring each satrap to collect supplies for the army on a semi-annual basis.[13] Once Alexander moved east through Bactria, Sogdiana, and India, however, he depended heavily upon his own Macedonian logistics officers who had been trained by Philip. Once in India, supplying the army became easier due to the astonishing fertility of the Indian river valleys and plains, that produced two harvests a year.[14] Here, the staple diet for the army was rice.

While Alexander is often given credit for being a good tactician, in fact his tactics were no different from those Philip had developed and used for the army.[15] There is no evidence at all of any sort of tactical innovation or employment in any of Alexander's campaigns or even individual battles. Even the famous story of using mountaineers to scale the Sogdian Rock was but a repeat of Philip's having used the same tactic to outflank a blocking force in Thessaly.[16] Alexander's famous night crossing of the Hydaspes River against Porus was another repeat of Philip's earlier night crossing of the Danube. Alexander's reputation as a tactical genius is largely overrated.

In Alexander's early battles against the Persian army, the Persian advantage in numbers presented the risk of single or double envelopment of Alexander's formations by Persian cavalry. Alexander countered this threat with a swift penetration of the enemy line, turning inward toward the enemy commander's position, and assaulting the interior ranks as he advanced. The key to a successful penetration of the Persian line was the ability of Alexander's cavalry to close with the enemy, engaging in violent close combat until it drove through the line and exploded behind it. It was Philip who first used his infantry as a platform of manoeuvre while unleashing his cavalry to achieve penetration of the enemy line. Philip first used this tactic in his battle with Bardylis, and then again at Chaeronea. The whole point of training and equipping the Macedonian heavy cavalry as it was trained was to give it the ability to penetrate an enemy infantry line, a tactical capability that Philip invented by adopting the Thracian wedge formation for his cavalry squadrons.

Alexander's infantry was always deployed in the centre-left of the line across from the location of the enemy commander, and used primarily as a platform of manoeuvre to hold the enemy infantry in check while the Companion cavalry, always deployed on the right under Alexander's personal command, manoeuvred until it found a weak spot in the enemy infantry line through which to attack. To weaken the ability of the enemy cavalry across from him to resist his cavalry assault, Alexander employed mounted skirmishers in front of his cavalry to engage the enemy and force it to throw its javelins and expend its energy in the defence. This done, Alexander then attacked with his fresh Macedonian cavalry.

A successful attack by Alexander's cavalry depended greatly upon the ability of Parmenio's reduced cavalry force to hold the other wing against an attack by numerically superior Persian cavalry, something Parmenio accomplished at the Granicus, Issus, and Gaugamela. Philotas, Parmenio's son and a fine cavalry commander in his own right, may have been correct when he told his mistress that it was he and his father more than Alexander that had won the battles! An analysis of Alexander's battle tactics reveals no innovations or even significant differences in his use of cavalry from that of Philip.

As Robert Gaebel has noted, Alexander always possessed a significantly more powerful and tactically sophisticated force than any of his opponents. Alexander's campaign was really three different campaigns, each one fought against an opponent with different military capabilities, none of which were a match for Alexander's. Alexander's victories over the Persians are often cited to support his claim to military brilliance. In truth, the Persian army was hollow, its excellent Median troops comprising only a minority of the fighting force, their infantry lightly armoured and equipped with bow and short spear. Most of the Persian cavalry was light cavalry, and even the famed Median cavalry was less well armed and armoured than the Macedonians. The rest of the Persian force was comprised of levied national and tribal forces that received only limited training, wore different uniforms, carried minor weapons, spoke a variety of languages, fought in different ways, were commanded by their own chiefs, and were highly unreliable. These circumstances made it impossible for Persian commanders to develop coordinated battle tactics. To insure that these native units did not break and run, Persian commanders were forced to occupy the centre of the line with their own reliable infantry and place their cavalry on the flanks and rear to create a tactical container within which the various national units were deployed. The Persian army was not a tactically integrated fighting force, and could not be deployed in many tactically different ways, nor relied upon to fight effectively as a whole.

Persian tactics were ill-designed to deal with an opponent possessing the combat power of the Macedonian army. The Persian way of war was centred around skirmishing, hit-and-run tactics, and using missile weapons (bows, thrown javelins, slings) to hit the enemy from a distance, while relying on the weight of numbers and light cavalry to carry the day.[17] The Persians usually formed up with the light infantry and archers acting as skirmishers in the front, trying to inflict as much damage with their missiles and javelins as possible. As the two lines clashed, the Persians would attempt to strike the flanks and rear with their cavalry and chariots to scatter the enemy, using their usually large numerical advantage to attack from several directions at once. Once enemy infantry began to scatter, cavalry could ride it down and finish it off with lance and javelin.[18]

The success of this tactical design depended upon the inability of the enemy infantry to withstand the initial Persian assault. Persian armies usually fought against rebellious nationalities on the eastern rim of the empire whose level of military skill, tactics, logistics, armament, training, and strength was far below that of the Persians. Under these circumstances, the Persian army's lack of tactical integration and, most important, its lack of heavy infantry did not matter very much, since its enemies also lacked these assets. Where this deficiency did matter, of course, was in Persia's battles with the Macedonian war machine developed by Philip and now commanded by Alexander.

The ability of disciplined Macedonian infantry to stand fast against Persian skirmishing attacks, to close with the enemy on command, and whose weapons outranged and could easily pierce Persian infantry armour, essentially gave command of the battlefield and its tempo to the Macedonians. With Macedonian heavy cavalry on the left holding fast even against superior numbers of Persian, mostly light, cavalry, Alexander's companion cavalry could easily penetrate the Persian infantry line almost at a point of his choosing. Macedonian cavalry also seems to have had little difficulty in attacking through Persian cavalry, which generally fought in an unorganized and individualized manner. These Persian weaknesses, disguised by centuries of Persian military success against equally flawed enemies, brought the empire to its knees before the unequalled combat power of Macedonian heavy infantry and cavalry.

The tale of Alexander's pursuit of Darius was one of the most widely told battle stories to demonstrate Alexander's use of strategic pursuit in his campaigns. But here again, we witness Alexander doing what Philip did first. Philip made strategic pursuit possible by creating a logistics system that made sustaining his forces in the field over long-distance forced marches a practical possibility. Philip not only used pursuit to destroy fleeing enemy armies, but for strategic political ends as well. He often conducted lethal pursuits with the political objective of destroying as many of the enemy's leadership corps and aristocracy as possible to make it easier for the survivors to come to terms with him. Alexander used it for the same purposes in hunting down Darius. Later he used pursuit to destroy the leadership of the insurgency that followed Darius' murder. The invention and effective use of strategic pursuit within the context of Greek warfare must be credited to Philip, however, and by Alexander's day was a stock element in the Macedonian commander's tactical repertoire.

Alexander faced a much different opponent in Bactria and Sogdiana when he attempted to put down the national insurgency that erupted after Darius' defeat. The insurgents ran Alexander ragged, inflicted heavy casualties, and tied down his army in a guerrilla war that lasted for three years (330–327). The area of operations ranged from Afghanistan to Bokhara, from Lake Seistan to the Hindu Kush, against the fiercest, most indomitable opposition Alexander had ever faced. In Afghanistan, Alexander was facing some of the most warlike tribes known to history, descendants of the Aryan invaders and warriors known for their horse-culture and cavalry fighting. These Aryan tribes – Ashvakas, Aspasians, Assakenoi, and Asvayanas – were tough highlanders and excellent horsemen like the Macedonians themselves.[19] Alexander lost more men in this campaign than in any other, against generals who proved his equal.[20]

Refusing to offer set-piece battles, the guerrillas fought a war of ambush, deception, and surprise with highly-mobile light cavalry units that were expert at these tactics.[21] While besieging Cyropolis, Alexander sent a force of 3,000 infantry and 800 Companion cavalry to block Spitamenes' route to Marakanda. Curtius tells us that Spitamenes trapped the Macedonians in a deadly ambush, killing 2,000 infantry and 300 cavalrymen.[22] Arrian says the casualties were even worse and only 'forty of the cavalry and 300 infantrymen escaped with their lives'.[23] He says the cavalrymen were all 'true-born Macedonians and Companions of the king', among them four general officers – Pharnuches, Andromachus, Menedemus, and Caranus.[24] The losses amount to almost 10 per cent of Alexander's field force! Alexander swore the few survivors to secrecy under penalty of death. In another case, fifty Companions were deceived by the hospitality of a tribe, and killed while they slept.[25] Unable to bring the enemy to battle, Alexander undertook a policy of systematic destruction of the civilian population.

Alexander is often given credit for his innovations in assembling units of mixed arms for specific missions. Arrian identifies twenty-seven examples of Alexander's combining forces of different arms for specific tactical missions.[26]

Most of Arrian's examples apply to the counter-insurgency operations that Alexander mounted in Afghanistan and the Swat Valley, where his opponents were highly mobile units armed with bow and javelin. While specialty units (archers, slingers, *peltasts*, javeliners, etc.) had been used by Greek armies for decades, albeit in minor roles, it was Philip who first incorporated them into a regular standing military force. Philip's wars in the mountains of western Macedonia and the Balkans forced him to deal with highly mobile tribal forces operating in difficult terrain. During the Thracian campaign, Philip used mixed forces with some regularity when he found himself short of regular infantry and had to request replacements from Macedonia. Specialty units – archers, *peltasts*, light cavalry, etc. – are recorded by Diodorus as being among the troops in the invasion force.[27]

There was never a national army fighting against Alexander in Afghanistan. The insurgency consisted of an assembly of local warlords banded together against a common foe. Most battles were small in scale and mostly inconclusive, except in their ability to inflict casualties on the invader. There was no large army for Alexander to lure into a decisive battle. Alexander had only one significant victory in open field operations, that against the Scythians. All others were against fixed positions, such as the Sogdian Rock and the Rock of Chorines, or against towns that were taken with great slaughter. Most of the casualties were civilians, not enemy combatants.

It was politics and not battlefield victories that finally ended the war in Afghanistan. The key leaders of the insurgency were all assassinated by political rivals. Eventually, the barons and their tribes grew weary of the war and, one by one, came to an accommodation with Alexander in which they mostly retained their lands and local authority as they had under the Persian king, an approach now being tried to bring the present war in Afghanistan (2013) to an end.

The cost of the war to Alexander's army was high. Forced marches through the highlands of eastern Afghanistan caused large numbers of soldiers to suffer frostbite, snow blindness, and chronic fatigue. The crossing of the Hindu Kush through the highest and most snow driven pass caused many additional deaths and injuries. On his march to the Oxus, Alexander drove his men across a burning waterless desert in which many died from heatstroke. The harsh conditions caused some Thessalian units and Philip's older veterans to mutiny, and demand to be demobilized. Alexander had little choice but to agree. Hundreds of additional troops died from dehydration following too much drinking. All these losses left Alexander short of first-rate troops, forcing him for the first time to recruit local 'barbarian' troops into the field army.[28]

Alexander's known manpower losses exceeded 7,000 men in this campaign alone, perhaps as much as one quarter of his field force, and more than he had lost in all the battles and sieges against Darius.[29] Within months of Alexander's departure for India, a regional governor and the *hyparch* assigned to the Assacenians were assassinated. Afghanistan remained in a state of sporadic civil war, as local barons and tribes manoeuvred for power. Alexander's campaign in Afghanistan was over, but it had been nasty business indeed, leaving Alexander with a reputation far more for brutality than for military brilliance.

As already noted earlier, Alexander's Indian campaign after his set-piece battle with Porus was more pointless slaughter than anything else, conducted more out of personal anger and a desire to punish his troops than to attain any military objective. Except for one or two battles when the tribes chose to fight, Alexander could easily have avoided most of his violent encounters with the Indians.

Alexander always had the advantage against his Indian opponents. Indian tribal infantry was light infantry, armed with bows and javelins, no match for Alexander's heavy infantry.[30] Indian infantry usually fought without body armour, or were equipped only with jackets of padded cotton.[31] Some infantry carried a two-handed broad sword and a small wicker or wooden shield, but without helmet or armour, were easy prey for Macedonian infantry and cavalry.[32] Nearchus tells us that among the Indians, 'to ride on a single horse is low', meaning that horse cavalry ranked below elephant riders, the four-horse chariot, and camels in social status.[33] What horse cavalry there was, was light cavalry, unarmoured, armed with two thrown javelins and sometimes the bow, and completely ineffective against Macedonian cavalry.[34] The same can be said for Indian elephant, chariot, and camel cavalry, all evident in small numbers and lightly armed with javelin and bow, and unable to match the Macedonian cavalry in speed and manoeuvrability. They were simply no match for Alexander's heavy Macedonian cavalry.

The construction of Indian towns and fortifications was extremely vulnerable to Alexander's siege and storm capabilities. Nearchus tells us that most Indian towns located on rivers or on the coast were constructed of wood because 'if they were built of brick, they could not last long because of the moisture due to the rain, and to the fact that the rivers overflow their banks and fill the plains with water'.[35] Only when the towns or forts are 'situated in commanding and lofty places' are they built of brick and clay, as was Sangala.[36] Alexander's route took him down the river valleys where few fortifications of this type were evident. We often hear of Indian forces retreating to their towns and forts to make a stand, only to have their fortifications easily overcome by Alexander's engineers or quickly stormed by the infantry. With the Indians trapped, terrible slaughter usually followed. There is little in the accounts of Alexander's victories in India that merits the claim of military brilliance.[37]

Great generals are not the only causes of their greatness. War is a co-operative enterprise by its nature, heavily dependent upon the talents and abilities of others orchestrated by the commander into a coherent whole of activity. The quality of leadership and experience is vitally important at all levels of command to the overall success of any army. Perhaps it is in the qualities of leadership, training, and experience of the Macedonian officer and non-commissioned officer corps that Alexander owes his greatest debt to Philip. Most of the important officers in Alexander's army had served with Philip at various levels of command over the years. They included Parmenio, the old war horse, who was Philip's best field commander, his sons, Philotas and Nicanor, commanding the horse and foot guards respectively, and Cleitus, the commander of the Royal Squadron. Even some of Alexander's peers had seen their first combat under Philip including, perhaps, Hephaestion, Alexander's closest friend, and later the commander of half the Companion cavalry, Craterus, commander of the left half of the phalanx, Seleucus, commander of the foot guards, Antigonus the One-Eyed, and Ptolemy, a fellow-student with Alexander under Aristotle's tutelage.[38]

Perhaps more important were the unnamed and unremembered battalion commanders, squadron commanders, file leaders, and section leaders, the small unit officer and non-commissioned officer corps upon which the combat effectiveness of an army depends most, that had served under Philip. The army staff system was comprised of officers that had also served Philip in previous wars. For a young officer with such limited experience as Alexander possessed, these officers and small unit combat leaders were critical to the army's operational success. Perhaps no general in history had ever received a better trained, experienced, and well-led army than Alexander did as his legacy from Philip.

Both Philip and Alexander were heads of state as well as field generals, a fact that radically changes the meaning of military greatness. In modern times, and even at times in antiquity, generals were most often not simultaneously heads of government. Accordingly, they are properly judged only by their achievements on the field of battle, and not held responsible for larger political concerns. In these circumstances, military performance may be regarded as an end in itself. But Alexander must be judged by a different standard, that is by the degree to which his military achievements worked to support his strategic objectives not only as a military man, but as a head of government. In these circumstances, military competence becomes not an end, but a means to additional ends for which the general is also responsible. The concerns of the general as general are the tactical and operational elements of war. The concerns of the general as statesman are the strategic objectives of the national state or people he leads.

For the general as strategist, war is but one means to achieve national objectives within the political and cultural context within which wars are fought for specified goals. Philip always properly saw war as a means to his strategic goals, and much preferred to achieve his objectives by other 'less kinetic' means, such as diplomacy. Even to as Homeric a warrior as Philip, the search for glory and heroism had but little place in his strategic thinking. Alexander, by contrast, was the prototypical Homeric warrior fighting for personal glory and reputation, a military adventurer almost entirely lacking in strategic vision. One is hard-pressed to discern in accounts of Alexander's adventures any strategic vision that might have reasonably been achieved by his many campaigns. When the Indian philosopher, Dandamis, met Alexander, he seems to have grasped Alexander's strategic mettle correctly when he asked, 'For what reason did Alexander make such a long journey hither?'[39]

Only in the Persian campaign can one discern a strategic objective, the conquest of Persia. Having achieved this, Alexander didn't seem to have any idea how to govern the country or for what purpose. The Bactrian and Sogdian campaigns were designed to suppress the insurgency, but again, to what strategic end is unclear. Alexander's efforts gained a temporary peace there, but the country fell back into civil war within a few months of his leaving for India. The Indian campaign makes no strategic sense at all, and none of our sources make an effort to explain just why Alexander undertook it, save for personal reputation and glory. Even this objective evaporated when the army mutinied, and Alexander was forced to turn back, subjecting his army to a number of pointless and lethal conflicts with Indian tribes. The crossing of the Gedrosian Desert was undertaken not for any strategic or tactical reasons, but to surpass the achievements of other generals. Nearchus tells us that 'Alexander chose it, we are told, because with the exception of Semiramis, returning from her conquests of India, no one had ever brought an army successfully through it … the Persian king, Cyrus the Great, supposedly had lost all but seven of his men when he crossed it. Alexander knew about these stories, and they had inspired him to emulate and hopefully surpass Cyrus and Semiramis'.[40] The crossing turned into a disaster. It is difficult to credit Alexander with being a brilliant strategist. At most, he can be said to have been a bold and reckless *conquistador* who conducted a decade long raid, leaving nothing of note behind him.

It might also be said that Alexander was not much of a king. Having inherited the government of the first truly national state in Western history, Alexander attempted nothing with it. He promptly turned over effective national authority to Antipater when he left for Asia, and Antipater governed and protected Macedonia until the end of his life. Alexander never returned to Macedonia nor, as far as we know, ordered any governmental action to be carried out by Antipater.

Nor did Alexander make much of an attempt to govern Persia, being content to leave most satraps in place, or to replace them with other loyal Persians more often than Macedonians. And he seems to have cared equally little for the survival of the Argead dynasty. He took no steps to secure the succession, barely fathering an heir before he died, and designating no clear successor on his deathbed. It was his conservative Macedonian officers who protected the dynastic line by insisting that Roxanne's child, though not fully Macedonian, retain the claim to the Argead throne. That Alexander cared nothing for governance of anything seems clear enough.

In Alexander's mind, war was the arena of fame and glory, an end in itself, his achievements the stuff of history and legend by which he would be remembered and, ultimately, fashioned into a god. Like his hero, Achilles, Alexander 'seems to have been possessed of some sort of restless, almost irrational desire for glory unchecked by a larger political sense', that is, by any strategic vision or calculation.[41] Without a sense of strategy or a national vision for his people, it is difficult to see how Alexander can be judged a great general or a great king. In the end, he was, at most, a savage *conquistador* who cared little for anything or anyone beyond himself.

# Notes

## Introduction

1. Carol G. Thomas, 'What You Seek Is Here: Alexander the Great', *Journal of the Historical Society*, 7 (March, 2007), p. 61.
2. Richard A. Gabriel, 'Can We Trust the Ancient Texts?', *Military History* (March–April, 2008), pp. 63–69.

## Chapter 1

1. A.J. Graham, 'The Historical Significance of Philip of Macedon', in Elin C. Danien (ed.), *The World of Philip and Alexander* (Philadelphia, PA: University Museum of Archaeology and Anthropology of the University of Pennsylvania, 1990), p. 6. There is evidence of some early Neolithic and early Bronze Age settlement in Macedonia as well, but it does not seem directly connected to the later events in Macedonia with which we are concerned.
2. The primary language groups of the Balkans were Thraco-Dacian, Illyrian, and Macedonian. Macedonian is closer to the Illyrian and Thracian groups in phonology than it is to Greek. Macedonians did not speak a dialect of Greek.
3. Ibid, 10. This origin story may be a myth propagated by King Alexander I of Macedonia, and the Temenid dynasty may be indigenous to Macedonia without any connection to the Argeads. See Eugene Borza, 'Origins of the Macedonian Royal House', *Hesperia*, Suppl. 19 (1982), pp. 7–13.
4. N.G.L. Hammond, *The Macedonian State: Origins, Institutions, and History* (Oxford, UK, Clarendon Press, 1989), p. 4.
5. J.R. Ellis, 'Population Transplants Under Philip II', *Macedonia* 9 (1969), p. 16; see by the same author, 'Macedonia Under Philip', in Haztopoulos and Loukipoulos (eds), pp. 164–165.
6. N.G.L. Hammond, *Philip of Macedon* (Baltimore, MD, Johns Hopkins University Press, 1994), p. 56.
7. Ibid, not including, of course, the non-circuit wall leading to Piraeus.
8. Nic Fields and Brian Delf, *Ancient Greek Fortifications, 500–300 BC* (London, Osprey Publishers, 2006), p. 10.
9. Ian Worthington, *Philip II of Macedonia*, pp. 226–227.
10. Hammond, *The Macedonian State*, pp. 5–6.
11. Ibid.
12. Quintius Curtius Rufus, *History of Alexander*, translated by John Yardley (London, Penguin Classics, 1984), 4.7.31.
13. Hammond, *The Macedonian State*, p. 49.

14. Worthington, *Philip II of Macedonia*, p. 34, says that Parmenio was a Paeonian by birth. This is incorrect.
15. Ellis, 'Population Transplants Under Philip II', pp. 14–17.
16. Lucius Flavius Arrianus (Arrian), *The Campaigns of Alexander* translated by Aubrey De Selincourt (London, Penguin Books, 1971), 7.9.4.
17. Hammond, *The Macedonian State*, p. 4. This work and N.G.L. Hammond and G.T. Griffith, *A History of Macedonia* 2 vols (Oxford, UK, Oxford University Press, 1979), are the definitive works on the subject of Macedonian history.
18. Graham, 'The Historical Significance of Philip of Macedon', p. 6.
19. J.R. Ellis, 'The Unification of Macedonia', in Miltiades B. Hatzopoulos and Louisa D. Loukopoulos (eds), *Philip of Macedon* (Athens, Ekdotike Athenon, 1980), p. 36.
20. Graham, 'The Historical Significance of Philip of Macedonia', p. 6.
21. The lower estimate is provided by Worthington, *Philip II of Macedonia*, p. 7; the higher estimate is taken from J.R. Ellis, 'Macedonia Under Philip', in Hatzopoulos and Loukipoulos (eds), p. 150.
22. Hammond, *The Macedonian State*, p. 93.
23. Ellis, 'The Unification of Macedonia', p. 36.
24. Arrian, 7.9.2.
25. Alan E. Samuel, 'Philip and Alexander as Kings: Macedonian Monarchy and Merovingian Parallels', *American Historical Review* 93, no. 5 (December, 1988), p. 1273.
26. The independent authority of the Assembly was evident when Philip was campaigning in Thrace and left Alexander behind in charge of the country. When a revolt broke out among the Maedi, Alexander had to secure the permission of the Assembly to mount a military expedition to put down the revolt.
27. Hammond, *The Macedonian State*, pp. 53–54.
28. Hammond, *Philip of Macedon*, p. 7.
29. Hammond, *The Macedonian State*, p. 56.
30. Ibid, see also N.G.L. Hammond, 'Royal Pages, Personal Pages, and Boys Trained in the Macedonian Manner During the Period of the Temenid Monarchy', *Historia* 39 (1990), pp. 261–290.
31. Hammond, *Philip of Macedon*, 41. Apparently the cadet had appeared for battle without his armour!
32. Robert E. Gaebel, *Cavalry Operations in the Ancient Greek World* (Norman, OK, University of Oklahoma Press, 2002), p. 158.
33. Paul Cartledge, *Alexander the Great* (New York, Vintage Books, 2005), p. 50.
34. Ellis, 'Macedonia Under Philip', in Hatzopoulos and Loukopoulos (eds), *Philip of Macedon*, p. 146.
35. Hammond, *The Macedonian State*, p. 69.
36. Peter Green, *Alexander of Macedon: A Historical Biography* (Berkeley, University of California Press, 1991), p. 2.
37. Polyaenus, *Stratagems of War*, vol. 1 (Chicago, Ares Publishers, 1994), 4.2.6.
38. E.A. Fredricksmeyer, 'Alexander and Philip: Emulation and Resentment', *Classical Journal* 85, no. 4 (April–May, 1990), p. 304.
39. Green, *Alexander of Macedon: A Historical Biography* p. 6.

40. George Cawkwell, *Philip of Macedon* (London, Faber and Faber, 1978), p. 51.
41. Eugene Borza, 'The Symposium at Alexander's Court', *Archaia Makedonia* 3 (September, 1977), pp. 45–55. Alexander attended these symposia regularly as a youth, and they were a characteristic element in his court later on. It was at one of these gatherings that Alexander first saw the beautiful Roxane, a dancer in a native company providing entertainment to the symposium.
42. Manolis Andronikos, 'The Royal Tombs At Aegae (Vergina)', in Hatzopoulous and Loukopoulos, pp. 152–153.
43. Hammond, *Philip of Macedon*, p. 178
44. Hammond *The Macedonian State: Origins, Institutions, and History*, p. 33.
45. Elizabeth Carney, 'The Politics of Polygamy: Olympias, Alexander, and the Murder of Philip', *Historia* 41, no. 2 (1992), p. 170.
46. Richard A. Gabriel and Karen S. Metz, *The History of Military Medicine* vol. 1 (Westport, CT, Greenwood Press, 1992), p. 28.
47. William S. Barnett, 'Only the Bad Died Young in the Ancient Middle East', *Journal of International Aging and Human Development*, 21, no. 2 (1985), pp. 155–160.
48. Carney, 'The Politics of Polygamy: Olympias, Alexander, and the Murder of Philip', p. 171.
49. Marcus Junianus Justin, *Epitome of the Philippic History of Pompeius Trogus*, translated by John Shelby Watson (London, Henry G. Bohn Press, 1853), 9.8.3.

**Chapter 2**

1. Cawkwell, *Philip of Macedon*, p. 27; see also Thomas, 'What you seek is here: Alexander the Great', p. 73; Green, *Alexander of Macedon: A Historical Biography*, p. 11 citing Aristotle's *Politics*.
2. Thomas, 'What You Seek is Here', p. 73.
3. Richard McKeon, *The Basic Works of Aristotle* (New York, Random House, 1941), p. 1306.
4. Green, *Alexander the Great: A Historical Biography*, p. 61.
5. Ibid, 62.
6. Peter Tsouras, *Alexander: Invincible King of Macedonia* (Dulles, VA, Potomac Books, 1997), pp. 15–16.
7. E.A. Fredricksmeyer, 'Introductory Essay', in Heckel and Trittle (eds), *Alexander the Great: A New History* (Malden, MA, Wiley-Blackwell, 2009), p. 3.
8. Daniel Mendelsohn, 'Battle Lines', *New Yorker* (7 November 2011), p. 76.
9. Ibid, 78.
10. Ibid.
11. Elizabeth Carney, 'Elite Education and High Culture in Macedonia', in Heckel and Trittle (eds), *Alexander the Great: A New History*, pp. 56–59.
12. Ibid, 57.
13. Ibid, 58, citing Hammond, *Philip of Macedonia*, pp. 41–42.
14. Thomas, 'What You Seek Is Here', p. 78.
15. Arrian, 3.6; the former exiles were 'raised by Alexander to important offices'.

16. Plutarch, *The Parallel Lives*, translation by Bernadette Perin, 5.2. (Loeb Classical Library, 1919).
17. Diodorus of Sicily, *Histories* (Harvard, MA, Harvard University Press, 1963), vol. VIII translated by C. Bradford Welles, 16.86. pp. 1–4; Richard A. Gabriel, *Philip of Macedonia: Greater Than Alexander* (Dulles, VA, Potomac Press, 2010), p. 218.
18. Ibid, 16.86.4
19. Gabriel, *Philip II of Macedonia*, p. 219.
20. Green, *Alexander of Macedon*, pp. 92–93.
21. Diodorus, 17. pp. 3–5.
22. Green, p. 91, who argues that Philip may have decided to repudiate both Olympias and Alexander because of rumours of a plot against him by his wife and son.
23. Jonathan H Musgrave, A.J. Prag, and R. Neave, 'The Skull from Tomb II at Vergina: King Philip II of Macedon', *Journal of Hellenic Studies* 104 (1984), pp. 63–78 for the autopsy of Philip's remains and the calculation of his physical characteristics.
24. Gabriel, *Philip II of Macedonia*, p. 25.
25. Ibid.
26. Ibid, 26.
27. Ibid, 4.
28. Daniel Ogden, 'Alexander's Sex Life', in Heckel and Trittle (eds), p. 213, citing Theopompus, *Die Fragmente der griechischen Historiker* (FgrH) (Berlin and Leiden), fragment 115 F22a.
29. Green, *Alexander of Macedon*, p. 55. Even in modern armies, officer training involves the development of a 'command voice' as a necessary element in establishing an officer's presence as an authority figure and, one might add, his manhood. It is likely that in ancient armies, a commander's physical presence and his voice may have been even more important.
30. Plutarch, 4.1.
31. Green, *Alexander of Macedon*, p. 55.
32. The story is from Livy's account of the Carthaginian wars as cited in Richard A. Gabriel, *Hannibal: The Military Biography of Rome's Greatest Enemy* (Dulles, VA, Potomac Books, 2011), p. 12.
33. On the general subject of homosexuality in ancient Greece and antiquity, see Kenneth Dover, *Greek Homosexuality* (Harvard, MA, Harvard University Press, 1978); Ogden, 'Alexander's Sex Life', in Heckel and Trittle (eds), pp. 203–217; James Davidson, 'Bonkers About Boys', *London Review of Books* (1 November 2013), pp. 7–10; and Bruce Gerig, 'Greek Homosexuality', pp. 1–10 (online at: epistle.us/hbarticles/greeks2.html).
34. Ogden, 'Alexander's Sex Life', p. 216.
35. Theopompus, *FgrH* 115 F225 as cited in Ogden, 'Alexander's Sex Life', p. 213. The reference here is to homosexual soldiers in Macedonia, not Greece.
36. Ogden, 209.
37. Plutarch, 21.7.
38. Gerig, *Greek Homosexuality*, p. 5.
39. James Davidson, *The Greeks and Greek Love* (London, Weidenfeld, 2007), p. 371.
40. Plutarch, 22.1–3.

41. Ogden, 'Alexander's Sex Life', p. 210.
42. Ibid, 207 for the military-diplomatic reasons for Alexander's marriages.
43. Arrian, 7.14.
44. Plutarch, 72.4.
45. Justin, 9.8.3. Interestingly, Ptolemy may have been one of Philip's sons. Curtius 9.22 tells us that 'He (Ptolemy) was a blood relative of Alexander and some believed he was Philip's son. It was known for certain that he was the child of a concubine of Philip's'. This concubine was Arsinoe, who belonged to the royal Macedonian family.
46. Justin 11.2.3. tells us that after Philip's death, Alexander 'took care likewise to have Karanos, his brother begot of a step-mother, his rival for the kingdom, slain.'
47. For insecurity as a factor in Alexander's early life, see J.R. Hamilton, 'Alexander's Early Life', *Greece and Rome*, second series, vol. 12, no. 2 (October, 1965), pp. 117–124.
48. Gerig, 'Greek Homosexuality', p. 5 citing the famous letter sent by Diogenes (*Epistles* 24) which was circulated by Eumenes after Alexander died. The critique of Alexander's behaviour deserves to be taken seriously if only because if anyone knew what Alexander was doing, it was likely to be Eumenes, Alexander's intelligence chief.
49. A.B. Bosworth, *Conquest and Empire: The Reign of Alexander the Great* (Cambridge, UK, Cambridge University Press, 1988), p. 29. Bosworth estimates the size of the expedition at only 15,000 Macedonian troops. Alexander conducted raids against the Getae, Agrianians, Triballi, and the Illyrians.
50. Green, *Alexander of Macedon*, p. 125.
51. For a contrary analysis of Alexander's Illyrian campaign, see N.G.L. Hammond, 'Alexander's Campaign in Illyria', *Journal of Hellenic Studies* 94 (1974), pp. 66–87.
52. Bosworth, *Conquest and Empire*, p. 30.
53. The army carried out only routine manoeuvres, including in one instance close order combat drill, and there is no evidence of Alexander's tactical brilliance. In a number of instances, Alexander seems to have erred in his executions as, for example, when he failed to take into account the Danube's current and had to abandon its crossing, the failure to coordinate with the arrival schedule of the ships from Byzantium, and getting trapped on the far side of the Danube, having to use his catapults as covering artillery to extricate his troops.
54. Gabriel, *Philip II of Macedonia*, p. 2.
55. The Macedonians were the best horse breeders in Greece, with most nobles, including the king, owning horse breeding farms. It is simply beyond belief that these men knew so little about training horses that Alexander, at the age of 8, would have to instruct them in how to do it. Even Alexander's naming the horse Bucephalas or 'ox-headed' seems false. The name is simply the common Macedonian usage for large horses, often of the Thessalian breed. To name a horse Bucephalas is akin to naming the animal 'big horsey', a name an 8-year-old child might well give a huge animal. See Lynn R. Li Donnici, *The Epidaurian Miracle Inscriptions* (Atlanta, GA, Scholars Press, 1995), p. 113.
56. Green, *Alexander of Macedon*, p. 5.

57. Tsouras, *Alexander: Invincible King of Macedonia*, pp. 15–16; see also J.M. O'Brien, 'Alexander and Dionysius: The Invisible Enemy', *Annals of Scholarship* 1 (1980), p. 92.
58. Green, *Alexander of Macedon*, p. 56.
59. Ibid.
60. This incident is interesting in that it seems to imply that as early as when Alexander was a young man, the concern that he was not of pure Macedonian blood had already arisen in some court circles.
61. Green, *Alexander of Macedon*, p. 68.
62. Ibid.
63. Ibid, citing Plutarch, 10.1.
64. Plutarch, 5.4.
65. Justin, 11.5.1–2
66. Hamilton, 'Alexander's Early Life', p. 124.
67. Hammond, 'Alexander's Personality', in Ian Worthington (ed.), *Alexander the Great: A Reader*, p. 299.
68. Richard A. Gabriel, 'Alexander the Monster', *Military History Quarterly* (summer, 2013), pp. 11–14.

**Chapter 3**

1. Christine F. Salazar, *The Treatment of War Wounds in Graeco-Roman Antiquity* (Boston, Brill, 2000), p. 184.
2. On the subject of Alexander's death, see Eugene Borza, 'Malaria in Alexander's Army', *Ancient History Bulletin* 1.2 (1987), pp. 36–38; David W. Oldach, Robert E. Richmond, Eugene N. Borza, and R. Michael Benitez, 'A Mysterious Death', *New England Journal of Medicine* 338 (Boston, 11 June, 1998), pp. 1764–1770; Donald Engels, 'A Note on Alexander's Death', *Classical Philology* 73 (July, 1978), pp. 224–228; and A.B. Bosworth, 'The Death of Alexander the Great: Rumour and Propaganda', *Classical Quarterly* 21 (May, 1971), pp. 112–136.
3. Information regarding the purely medical aspects of Alexander's wounds is sparse. The best source in English is Salazar, *The Treatment of Wounds in Graeco-Roman Antiquity*, chapter 8; see also J.J. Vollet, *De Characters Particuliers et du Traitment de la Blessure d'Alexandre le Grand* (1987); F. Lammert, *Alexanders Verwundung in der Stadt der Maller und die Damalige Heilkunde* (1960); and M. Bertolotti, *La Critica Medica Nella Storia Alessandro Magno* (1933).
4. Arrian, 7.10.
5. Xenophon, *On The Art of Horsemanship*, translated by G.W. Bowersock (Cambridge, MA, Harvard University Press, 1968), 11.6–10.
6. I am indebted to my friend and colleague, Christopher Matthew, of the Australian Catholic University, for the information about the thickness of the linothorax.
7. For the experiment concerning the ability of the linothorax to resist penetration, see Rossella Lorenzi, 'Laminated Linen Protected Alexander the Great', paper delivered at the annual conference of the *Archaeological Institute of America* (Anaheim, California, 10 January, 2010). See also Gregory S. Aldrete, Scott Bartell, and Alicia Alorete,

*Reconstructing Ancient Linen Body Armour* (Baltimore, MD, Johns Hopkins University Press, 2013).

8. Christopher Matthew, 'Testing Herodotus', *Ancient Warfare* (May, 2011), pp. 41–46; see also P.H. Blyth, *The Effectiveness of Greek Armour Against Arrows in the Persian Wars (490–479 BC): An Interdisciplinary Inquiry* (Unpublished thesis, Reading, U.K. 1977). Although Nearchus (*Indica*, 353) tells us that Persian arrows could 'penetrate anything, shield or breastplate, or any armour, however strong', this is not true. It is the curvature of the bow measured from its belly to the tips, not its length, which determines the strength of its pull. Persian bows were in fact much weaker than shorter, curved, or recurved bows used by Bactrians, Scynthians, and Sogdians.
9. Plutarch says Alexander's helmet was made of iron. Salazar, *Treatment of War Wounds*, p. 166.
10. Richard A. Gabriel and Karen S. Metz, *From Sumer To Rome: The Military Capabilities of Ancient Armies* (Westport, CT, Greenwood Press, 1991), pp. 57–59.
11. N.G.L. Hammond, 'Casualties and Reinforcements of Citizen Soldiers in Greece and Macedonia', *Journal of Hellenic Studies* 109 (1989), p. 60.
12. N.G.L. Hammond, *Alexander the Great: King, Commander, and Statesman* (Princeton, NJ, Princeton University Press, 1980), p. 31 says that Philip may have invented the *xyston* for use by his cavalry. It is true that Philip standardized the use of the weapon for his cavalry, but in all likelihood the spear itself was used for centuries for hunting on horseback, as a number of hunting scenes from tombs suggest.
13. Gaebel, *Cavalry Operations in the Ancient World*, p. 164.
14. Arrian, 1.5.8.
15. The gaudy helmet with rams' horns and vertical white feathers sometimes shown in later artists' works first appears on Egyptian coins sometime after Alexander left Egypt. It is by no means certain that it was a combat helmet or that Alexander wore it in battle. Most likely, it was a ceremonial helmet, the rams' horns being the symbol of the Egyptian god Ra.
16. Gabriel and Metz, *From Sumer To Rome*, p. 87.
17. Richard A. Gabriel, *Man and Wound in the Ancient World: A History of Military Medicine from Sumer to the Fall of Constantinople* (Dulles, VA, Potomac Books, 2012), p. 143.
18. Fielding H. Garrison, *Notes on the History of Military Medicine* (Washginton, D.C., Association of Military Surgeons, 1922), p. 37.
19. Fielding H. Garrison, *An Introduction to the History of Military Medicine* (London, W.B. Saunders, 1967), p. 85.
20. *Iliad*, 4.218.
21. On wound sucking, see Robert B. Wagner and Benjamin Slivko, 'History of Non-penetrating Chest Trauma and Its Treatment', *Maryland Medical Journal* 37 (April, 1988), pp. 297–304.
22. Garrison, *Introduction to the History of Military Medicine*, p. 82.
23. Garrison, *Introduction to the History of Military Medicine*, p. 94.
24. Erwin H. Ackerknecht, *A Short History of Medicine* (Baltimore, MD, Johns Hopkins University Press, 1982), p. 58.

25. Chester G. Starr, *A History of the Ancient World* (New York, Oxford University Press, 1974), p. 430.
26. This was the only period in Greek history when dissection was legal. Ptolemy II, king of Egypt, ordered that permission for dissection be granted. When he died, however, that permission was rescinded. Ackerknecht, *Short History of Medicine*, p. 65. Regarding sensory versus motor nerves, see Garrison, *Introduction to the History of Medicine*, p. 103. For major innovations in Greek medicine during this period and their innovators, see Ackerknecht, pp. 68–71.
27. Xenophon, *Anabasis*, 5.3.
28. Ibid, 4.5.
29. Ibid, 3.4.
30. Arrian, 2.7.1; 4.16.6; 5.29.3
31. Ibid, 8.15.11.
32. Donald Engels, *Alexander the Great and the Logistics of the Macedonian Army* (Berkeley, CA, University of California Press, 1978), pp. 16–17.
33. Gabriel, *Man and Wound in the Ancient World*, p. 151.
34. Ibid.
35. Ibid.
36. Guido Majno, *The Healing Hand* (Cambridge, MA, Harvard University Press, 1975), p. 154.
37. Ibid, 152.
38. Salazar, *The Treatment of War Wounds*, p. 23.
39. For the effect of these medical practices on the Roman casualty survival rate, see Gabriel and Metz, *From Sumer To Rome*, Chapter 7.
40. The most famous Roman physician of the time was Galen of Pergamon (130–201 AD), who wrote no fewer than a hundred medical treatises. His surviving works fill twenty-two volumes. A great surgeon and dissector (he once dissected an elephant!), Galen incorporated the Greek doctrine of laudable pus into his written works, but rejected it as false. Galen's works survived into the Middle Ages, but were often mistranslated, so that the rejected doctrine of laudable pus paradoxically became accepted medical practice until the nineteenth century. Ackerknecht, *Short History of Medicine*, pp. 72–74. On Galen, see George Sarton, *Galen of Pergamon* (Lawrence, KS, University of Kansas Press, 1954).
41. Majno, *Healing Hand*, p. 176.
42. Majno, *Healing Hand*, pp. 87–88.
43. R. Davies, 'Some Roman Military Medicine', *Medical History* 14 (January, 1970), p. 105.
44. Gabriel, *Man and Wound in the Ancient World*, p. 155.
45. Arrian, 1.14.6–7.
46. Diodorus 17.20. 6–21.
47. Arrian, 1.16.
48. Curtius, 8.1.20.
49. Diodorus 17.21.2.
50. Gabriel and Metz, *From Sumer To Rome*, p. 63.

51. Curtius, 3.2.10.
52. Arrian, 2.12.
53. Hammond, 'Casualties and Reinforcements of Citizen Soldiers in Greece and Macedonia', p. 60.
54. Curtius, 4.17.
55. Ibid.
56. Curtius, 4.19–20.
57. Arrian, 2.27.
58. These are figures for surviving examples of Roman catapult bolts. I am assuming that the Persian models were roughly similar.
59. Curtius, 4.17.
60. Curtius, 4.21–24.
61. Arrian, 3.29–30.
62. Salazar, *The Treatment of War Wounds*, p. 198.
63. Curtius, 6.3.
64. Gabriel, *Philip of Macedonia*, pp. 11–12.
65. Curtius, 6.10.
66. The danger of wound infection and disease in Afghanistan was clearly evident in the Soviet experience there. Of the 620,000 Soviet soldiers that served in Afghanistan, 469,685 were hospitalized for wounds or disease. Fully 75.7 per cent of the Soviet force was hospitalized, 11.4 per cent for wounds and 415,932 or 88.5 per cent for disease. The diseases that affected the Soviet force were hepatitis, plague, malaria, cholera, diphtheria, meningitis, infectious dysentery, amoebic dysentery, rheumatism, heat stroke, pneumonia, typhus, and para-typhus, most of which were probably extant during Alexander's time. The failure of the sources to mention any examples of infection or even the inflammation of wounds in India or Afghanistan during Alexander's campaigns there is suspicious. See Richard A. Gabriel, 'Bugs, Bullets, and Bones: Death Disease, Casualties, and Military Medicine in the Soviet War in Afghanistan', *Military History* (forthcoming, 2014).
67. Curtius, 7.22.
68. John Lascaratos, 'The Wounding of Alexander the Great in Cyropolis: The First Reported Case of the Syndrome of Transient Cortical Blindness', *History of Ophthalmology* 42 (November–December, 1997), p. 286.
69. Salazar, *The Treatment of War Wounds*, p. 199, citing Plutarch, *Moralia*, translated by P. Clement, VIII (London, 1969), 341 B.
70. Arrian, 4.4.
71. Curtius, 7.5–6.
72. Curtius, 7.19.
73. Ibid, 8.3.
74. We may take Curtius' account as reliable. Hammond notes that this section of Curtius' work draws heavily upon Aristobulus who was a staff officer with Alexander and is generally considered reliable. See N.G.L. Hammond, *Three Historians of Alexander the Great: The So-Called Vulgate Authors* (Cambridge, UK, Cambridge

University Press, 1983), whose work makes a bold attempt to assess the reliability of the sources.

75. Lascaratos, 'The Wounding of Alexander the Great in Cyropolis', p. 284–285.
76. Until recently, the traditional medical view of the symptoms of concussion was that they were largely self-resolving. Only with the recent investigations in the United States of the deaths and suicides of National Football League players have physicians begun to appreciate the long-term physiological, emotional, and behavioural consequences of severe and/or repeated concussions which have included violent rage, depression, and suicide.
77. Arrian, 4.2–3.
78. No less a Greek medical authority than Hippocrates recommended wine as a way of treating fever. We have two examples of Macedonian medical practice where the patient was regularly given wine instead of water while suffering from an illness. Both Hephaestion and Alexander regularly consumed wine to slake their thirst while trying to recover from fever. Moreover, the shortage of supplies of safe drinking water in Afghanistan and India, a condition that obtains to this day, probably forced the Macedonians to drink wine instead of water on a regular basis to quench their thirst.
79. I am indebted to my friend, John Cowan, former Chair of the Physiology Department of the Faculty of Medicine at the University of Ottawa for much of the medical information in this section.
80. O'Brien, 'The Engima of Alexander: The Alcohol Factor', *Annals of Scholarship* (1980), p. 32.
81. Arrian, 4.14.
82. Ibid, 4.26.
83. Curtius, 8.28.
84. Arrian, 6.10; Curtius, 9.5.9–11.
85. Ibid.
86. Curtius, 9.5.1–2.
87. Arrian, 6.13.
88. The average thickness of body tissue below the breast line ranges from approximately 1–1½ inches from top to bottom. Above the breast, average thickness is 3 inches. Alexander is described in the sources as 'muscular', and it is possible that the thickness of his upper breast was greater, perhaps almost 4 inches.
89. See previous note 66.

**Chapter 4**

1. Thucydides, *History*, 3.82.4–5
2. Peter Green, *Alexander the Great and the Hellenistic Age* (London, Modern Library, 2008), p. 142.
3. Lawrence A. Trittle, 'Alexander and the Killing of Cleitus the Black', in Waldemar Heckel (ed.), *Crossroads of History: The Age of Alexander the Great* (Clarement, CA, Regina Books, 2002), p. 134.
4. Richard A. Gabriel, *Man and Wound in the Ancient World: A History of Military Medicine from Sumer to the Fall of Constantinople*, p. 154.

5. Ibid.
6. Some scholars have argued, however, that Homer portrays Odysseus as suffering from psychiatric collapse. *Odyssey*, 8.83.
7. Herodotus, 7.230, 232, for Aristodemus and Pantites respectively. Xenophon in the *Constitution of the Spartans* 9.3–6 tells of the difficulties faced by men in Sparta who failed to perform adequately in battle, including the difficulties their sisters faced in finding husbands.
8. Herodotus, 9.71 tells us that a year later at the battle of Plataea Aristodemus 'rushed forward with the fury of a madman in his desire to be killed before his comrade's eyes'. This was not an attempt to retrieve his lost honour, but out of his sense of guilt at having survived the earlier battle at Thermopylae. See Lawrence A. Trittle, *From Melos to My Lai: War and Survival* (New York, Routledge, 2000), pp. 75–76
9. *The Complete Plays of Sophocles: Ajax*, translated by Sir Richard Claverhouse Jebb (London, Bantam, 1982), p. 9011.
10. Herodotus, 9.63.
11. Xenophon, *The Anabasis*, Book 3, Chapter 1. 'I am sure that not numbers or strength bring victory in war; but whichever army goes into battle stronger in its soul.'
12. On the Aesclepian temples as psychiatric treatment, see D. Kouretas, 'The Oracle of Trophonius: A Kind of Shock Treatment Associated with Sensory Deprivation in Greece', *British Journal of Psychiatry* 113, no. 505 (1979), pp. 1441–1446; Jon Romano, 'Temples, Asylums, or Hospitals?' *Journal of the National Association of Private Psychiatric Hospitals* 9, no. 4 (Summer, 1978), pp. 5–12; M.G. Papageorgiu, 'Incubation as a Form of Psychotherapy in the Care of Patients in Ancient Greece', *Psychotherapy* 26 (1975), pp. 35–38.
13. For an analysis of the case studies found on the *stelae* at Epidaurus, see Lynn Li Donnici, *The Epidaurian Miracle Inscriptions: Text, Translation, and Commentary* (Atlanta, GA, Scholars Press, 1995).
14. Ibid, p. 115, 109 respectively.
15. Richard A. Gabriel, 'The Roman Military Medical Corps', *Military History* (January, 2011), pp. 39–44.
16. Richard A. Gabriel, *No More Heroes: Madness and Psychiatry in War* (New York, Hill and Wang, 1987), pp. 109–113, for a description of the Russian contributions to military psychiatry.
17. Richard A. Gabriel, *Between Flesh and Steel: A History of Military Medicine from the Middle Ages to the War in Afghanistan* (Dulles, VA, Potomac Books, 2013), pp. 176–179.
18. Richard A. Gabriel, 'War, Madness and Military Psychiatry', *Military History* (forthcoming, 2014).
19. Roy L. Swank and Walter E. Marchand, 'Combat Neuroses: The Development of Combat Exhaustion', *Archives of Neurology and Psychiatry*, vol. 55 (1946), p. 244.
20. Jules Wasserman, *Principles of Dynamic Psychiatry* (Philadelphia, PA, W.B. Saunders Company, 1961), pp. 180–182.
21. Gabriel, 'War, Madness, and Military Psychiatry', p. 46.
22. Emanuel Miller, *Neuroses in War* (New York, Macmillan, 1942), p. 87.

23. David Marlowe, *Cohesion, Anticipated Breakdown, and Endurance in Battle* (Washington, D.C., Walter Reed Army Institute of Research Report, 1979), p. 31
24. Gabriel, *No More Heroes*, p. 79; Swank and Marchand, p. 244.
25. Gregory Belenky, *Israeli Battle Shock Casualties: 1973 to 1982* (Washington, D.C., Walter Reed Army Institute of Research Report, 1983), p. 12.
26. Gabriel, *No More Heroes*, p. 84.
27. Swank and Marchand, 'Combat Neuroses', p. 238.
28. Ibid, 240.
29. Ibid, 240–241.
30. Eli Ginsberg, *The Lost Divisions* (New York, Columbia University Press, 1950), pp. 91–92 notes that the American divisions in the Second World War were psychiatrically screened no fewer than five times before being sent into combat without lowering the psychiatric casualty rate. Some 970,000 inductees were rejected for military service for emotional reasons, another 504,000 were separated from service after being inducted and sent to training bases, and thousands of others were separated when they developed psychiatric symptoms when their unit was notified that it would be shipped to Europe.
31. Gabriel, *No More Heroes*, Chapter 2, for examples of soldiers suffering the same psychiatric symptoms in antiquity that they do in modern times.
32. Miller, *Neuroses in War*, p. 17.
33. Ibid, 229.
34. Belenky, 10; Table 2 Symptom Clusters in Various Wars.
35. Miller, 17.
36. Ibid, 17.
37. Ibid, 229.
38. Ibid, 229.
39. *Iliad*, 17:757
40. Gabriel, 'War, Madness, and Military Psychiatry', p. 44.
41. Max Hastings, *Military Anecdotes* (New York, Oxford University Press, 1985), p. 38.
42. Miller, 232.
43. Li Donnici, *The Epidaurian Miracle Inscriptions*, p. 107.
44. Gwynne Dyer, *War* (New York, Crown Publishers, 1985), p. 22.
45. David Grossman, *On Killing: The Psychological Cost of Learning to Kill in War and Society* (Boston, Little Brown, 2009), p. 144 citing the work of S.L.A. Marshal, *Men Against Fire* (Gloucester, MA, Peter Smith, 1978).
46. Hastings, *Military Anecdotes*, p. 64.
47. Swank and Marchand, 'Combat Neuroses', p. 238.
48. Ibid, 237.
49. Philip Sabin, 'The Mechanics of Battle in the Second Punic War', in Tim Cornell, Boris Rankov, and Philip Sabin (eds), *The Second Punic War: A Reappraisal* (London, Institute for Classical Studies, University of London, 1966), p. 66.
50. Philip Sabin, 'The Face of Roman Battle', *Journal of Roman Studies* 90 (2000), p. 17.
51. The concept of combat pulses is taken from Adrian Goldsworthy, *The Roman Army At War* (Oxford, UK, Clarendon Press, 1996), p. 222. It squares nicely with Livy's

description of the fighting at Zama in Book 30.34 where he refers to 'repeated charges' and steady advances and withdrawals.

52. Sabin, 'The Face of Roman Battle', p. 14.
53. Richard A. Gabriel, *Soldiers' Lives Through History: The Ancient World* (Westport, CT, Greenwood Press, 2007), p. 134.
54. Ibid.
55. Grossman, *On Killing*, Section III, pp. 99–140, for an analysis of killing distance and its traumatic effect on the psychology of the killer.
56. Jonathan Shay, *Achilles in Vietnam* (New York, Scriber, 1994), p. 134.
57. Gabriel, *Soldier's Lives Through History*, pp. 139–144, for an analysis of the diseases and infections that plagued ancient armies. The common infections were tetanus infection, gangrene, and septicaemia; major diseases were malaria, dysentery, typhoid fever, typhus, and smallpox.
58. Donald W. Engels, *Alexander the Great and the Logistics of the Macedonian Army*, p. 54.
59. Gabriel, *Soldiers' Lives Through History*, pp. 149–150.
60. Gabriel, 'War, Madness, and Military Psychiatry', p. 47.
61. Ibid.

**Chapter 5**

1. Nassir Ghaemi, *A First-Rate Madness* (New York, Penguin, 2011). The analysis focuses upon the following personalities: General William T. Sherman, Ted Turner, Winston Churchill, Abraham Lincoln, Mahatma Gandhi, Martin Luther King, President John Kennedy, Adolf Hitler, President George W. Bush, President Richard Nixon, and Prime Minister Tony Blair.
2. Ibid, 16–17.
3. Ibid, 26–28.
4. Ibid, 17.
5. Ibid, 28.
6. Ibid, 28–31. For example, Sherman suffered from depression, and twice feared that he would commit suicide. He had episodes of paranoia, convinced he was surrounded by spies, and talked incessantly, could not bear to be interrupted or disagreed with, and often exploded in anger. He drank heavily, and slept little, and thought on more than one occasion that he was going insane. Sherman's superior, General Halleck, ordered a medical examination for him, and the examining physician found Sherman 'unfit for command' because of his nervousness. Sherman's grandiose plan to invade and destroy the south was his own concoction that other generals thought 'crazy'. He wrote to his brother, 'I should have committed suicide were it not for my children.'
7. For an account of Philip's personality and life, see Richard A. Gabriel, *Philip of Macedonia: Greater Than Alexander* (Dulles, Virginia, Potomac Books, 2010).
8. J.R. Hamilton, 'Alexander's Early Life', pp. 117–124. See also J.M. O'Brien, 'Alexander and Dionysus: The Invisible Enemy', *Annals of Scholarship* 1 (1980), p. 86 for a portrait of Olympias' personality.
9. Hamilton, 'Alexander's Early Life', pp. 117–124 who explores the effects of both motivations on Alexander's life.

10. Plutarch, 5.4–6
11. Hamilton, 'Alexander's Early Life', p. 121.
12. See Trittle, 'Alexander and the Killing of Cleitus the Black', in *Crossroads of History*, pp. 127–146, for an account of Cleitus' murder as a result of Alexander's post-traumatic reaction to battle stress.
13. Examples included Parmenio warning Alexander against a frontal attack at the Granicus, an attack that failed; Alexander disagreed with Parmenio when Parmenio recommended a surprise night attack at Gaugamela; and the famous rejection by Alexander of Darius' offer of half the Persian Empire that Parmenio recommended he accept. Callisthenes, Alexander's historian, suggests several other disagreements between the two.
14. Shay, *Achilles in Vietnam*, p. 31.
15. Robert Fagles (trans), *Iliad* (London, Penguin, 1998), 1:221.
16. *Iliad*, 18:111.
17. Ibid, 18:35.
18. *Iliad*, 24:6
19. Shay, *Achilles in Vietnam*, p. 26.
20. *Iliad*, 22:421.
21. Shay, *Achilles in Vietnam*, p. 88.
22. Shay, *Achilles in Vietnam*, p. 98.
23. Matthew Gonzales, 'The Ethical World of the Homeric Warrior', lecture at St Anselm College Humanities Programme, 30 April 2013. Professor Gonzales kindly provided me with a copy of his notes.
24. Plutarch, 42.2–4.
25. Arrian, 7.28.1.
26. Shay, *Achilles in Vietnam*, p. 80.
27. *Iliad*, 23.29.
28. Plutarch, 72.4
29. Shay, *Achilles in Vietnam*, p. 80.
30. The two best books on the subject of war stress and post-traumatic stress disorder are Shay, *Achilles in Vietnam*, op. cit., and Trittle, *From Melos to My Lai* (New York, Routledge, 2000).
31. Shay, *Achilles in Vietnam*, xx.
32. Ibid.
33. Ibid.
34. Ibid, 178.
35. Hamilton, 'Alexander's Early Life', pp. 121–124.
36. Shay, *Achilles in Vietnam*, xx.
37. For a detailed analysis of Alexander's drinking that may have made him an alcoholic, see John Maxwell O'Brien, *Alexander the Great: The Invisible Enemy* (New York, Routledge, 1992).
38. Herodotus, *Histories*, 9.71.
39. Trittle, *Melos to My Lai*, p. 60, outlines Xenophon's portrait of Clearchus.

40. Anabasis, 1.5. Xenophon's quotes are from the translation by W.H.D. Rouse, Xenophon. *Anabasis* (Ann Arbor, University of Michigan Press, 1958).
41. Trittle, *Melos to My Lai*, p. 71.
42. Swank and Marchand, 'Combat Neurosis: The Development of Combat Exhaustion', p. 230.

**Chapter 6**

1. Victor Davis Hanson, 'Alexander', *Military History Quarterly* (summer, 1998), p. 12.
2. Gabriel, *Philip of Macedonia*, xi–xiv.
3. Ibid, see pp. 154–155 for the destruction of Olynthos and pp. 202–203 for the massacre of the Scythian males.
4. Worthington, *Philip of Macedon*, p. 27; also J.R. Ellis, 'The Stepbrothers of Philip II', *Historia* 22 (1973), pp. 350–354, for the events surrounding the deaths of Philip's stepbrothers.
5. Ibid.
6. Hanson, 'Alexander', p. 17. For a detailed analysis of this purge of officials, see E. Badian, 'Alexander the Great and the Loneliness of Power', in E. Badian, *Studies in Greek and Roman History* (New York, Barnes and Noble, 1964), pp. 192–205.
7. Curtius, 10.42.
8. Justin, 8.4.7 as cited by Worthington, *Philip of Macedonia*, p. 195.
9. Diodorus, 13.2–6.
10. Ibid, 14.1–4.
11. Aubrey De Selincourt, translator, *Arrian: The Campaigns of Alexander* (London, Penguin Books, 1958), p. 62, note 30.
12. Diodorus, 9.3–6.
13. Diodorus, 9.3–6.
14. The accounts of the battle of the Granicus River are contradictory, and the debate as to what really happened continues. Those interested in participating in the debate should read, N.G.L. Hammond, 'The Battle of the Granicus River', *Journal of Hellenic Studies* 100 (1980), pp. 73–88; Clive Foss, 'The Battle of the Granicus: A New Look', *Ancient Macedonia* (August, 1977), pp. 495–502; E. Badian, 'The Battle of the Granicus', *Ancient Macedonia* (August, 1977), pp. 271–293.
15. Arrian, 1.16.
16. Victor Davis Hanson, 'Alexander the Killer', *Great Commanders* (Fall, 2002), p. 57.
17. Plutarch, 151.
18. Hanson, 'Alexander the Killer', p. 57.
19. Plutarch, 151.
20. Hanson, 'Alexander the Killer', p. 57.
21. Arrian, 2.16.
22. Ibid, 2.24.
23. Arrian, 2.24–25.
24. Diodorus, 17.46.3–6.
25. Ian Worthington, 'How Great Was Alexander the Great?', *Ancient History Bulletin* 13 (1999), p. 46.

26. Hanson, 'Alexander', p. 14.
27. Curtius, 4.6.30.
28. Ibid, 4.6.27–28.
29. Ibid, 4.6.29.
30. De Selincourt, p. 147, note 58 suggests that the story of Betis being dragged around the city need not be credited, but offers no reason why not.
31. Hanson, 'Alexander', p. 18.
32. Plutarch, 37.4–6 says that Alexander butchered the Persian prisoners at Susa: 'In this country, then, as it turned out, there was a great slaughter of the prisoners taken; for Alexander himself writes that he gave orders to have the inhabitants butchered, thinking that this would be to his advantage.' Neither Curtius nor Arrian make mention of this event, and I have chosen not to include it in the list of atrocities.
33. Diodorus, 69.8.70.
34. Curtius, 6.6.6–9.
35. Diodorus, 5.7.4.
36. Arrian, 3.19.
37. Curtius, 5.7.2.
38. Ibid, 5.7.1.
39. Ibid, 6.11.
40. Diodorus, 17.76.1–6.
41. Curtius, 6.19.
42. Diodorus, 17.76.6–7.
43. Curtius, 7.32–33.
44. Ibid.
45. H.W. Parke, 'The Massacre of the Branchidae', *Journal of Hellenic Studies* 105 (1985), pp. 59–68, for a good examination of the incident.
46. Shay, *Achilles in Vietnam*, p. 92. Even Achilles speaks of the 'rush' of battle and killing as pleasurable, saying it is 'sweeter than slow-dripping honey'. *Iliad*, 18.122.
47. Arrian, 3.30.
48. Ibid.
49. Arrian, 4.7. Holt notes that disfigurement was a Persian custom. 'According to Persian custom, the rightful King of Kings, should be a handsome man ... Usurpers, therefore, were brutally disfigured before they were killed, in order to render them thoroughly unfit for the throne they had coveted.' in Frank L. Holt, *Into the Land of Bones: Alexander the Great in Afghanistan* (Berkeley, University of California Press, 2005), p. 43. Interestingly, disfigurement later became a practice among Christian Byzantines. Disfigured people could not gain the throne.
50. Curtius, 7.40.
51. 'The Ten-Horned Beast: Alexander The Great' (online at: http://www.livius.org/aj-al/alexander/alexander12.html).
52. Ibid.
53. Arrian, 4.3.
54. Curtius, 7.16.
55. Curtius, 7.21.

56. Arrian, 4.4.
57. Ibid.
58. Green, *Alexander the Great: A Historical Biography*, p. 338.
59. Curtius 7.9.20–21. See also Holt, *Into the Land of Bones*, p. 58.
60. Arrian, 4.7.
61. Holt, *Into the Land of Bones*, p. 104.
62. Ibid, 107.
63. For an account of the Soviet war in Afghanistan, see Richard A. Gabriel, 'Bugs, Bullets, and Bones: Death, Disease, Casualties and Military Medicine in the Soviet War in Afghanistan', *Military History*, 2014 (forthcoming).
64. Diodorus, 17.84.
65. Arrian, 4.27 says Alexander 'butchered them all'.
66. Arrian, 4.27.
67. Curtius, 8.10.4.
68. Ibid, 8.10.6.
69. Ibid, 5.24. Arrian (5.24.5–8) says 1,200 troops were wounded including several officers.
70. Ibid, 5.25.
71. Curtius, 9.4.
72. Ibid, 9.6.
73. Diodorus, 17.96.5.96.
74. Curtius, 6.4.
75. Ibid, 6.7.
76. De Selincourt, 310, note 13 quoting J.F.C. Fuller, *The Generalship of Alexander the Great* (New York, Da Capo Press, 1960).
77. Curtius, 6.8.
78. Arrian, 6.11.
79. Curtius, 9.19.
80. Cartledge, *Alexander the Great*, p. 209.
81. Diodorus, 17.102.6.103.
82. Selincourt, 324, note 24 citing Curtius, 9.8.15 and Diodorus, 17.102.6.103.
83. http://www.livius.org/aj-al/alexander/alexander12.html.
84. Diodorus, 17.104.3–7.
85. Hanson, 'Alexander', p. 15, citing Arrian.
86. Arrian, 6.21–22.
87. Ibid.
88. Arrian, 7.14.
89. Ibid., 7.15.
90. Plutarch, 72.4 says Alexander 'put the whole nation to the sword from the youth upwards'.
91. Arrian, 7.14; Plutarch, 72.1
92. Plutarch, 72.4
93. Arrian, 6.13.

**Chapter 7**

1. Shay, *Achilles in Vietnam*, xx.
2. Jona Lendering, 'Cleitarchus', in *Alexander the Great* (http://www.livius.org/cg-cm/cleitarchus/cleitarchus.html.
3. Other sources for Arrian are Ptolemy's lost history and Nearchus' *Indica*.
4. Some modern authors have attributed these 'seizures' to malaria.
5. The idea of pothos is also associated with death, and the word is used to describe the Delphinium flowers that were often placed on tombs. It is likely that the idea to be conveyed by pothos is a longing for an unattainable goal.
6. Two authors who explore the idea of Alexander's paranoia are J.R. Hamilton, 'Alexander and His So-Called Father', *Classical Quarterly* 3, no. 2 (October 1953), pp. 151–157 and E. Badian, 'Alexander the Great and the Loneliness of Power', in E. Badian (ed.), *Studies in Greek and Roman History* (New York, Barnes and Noble, 1964), pp. 192–205.
7. F. Jacoby, *Fragmente der griechisschen Historiker* (Leiden, Brill, 1923), vol. 2, p. 438; see also p. 126, F 5.
8. Ibid.
9. Bosworth, *Conquest and Empire*, p. 24; see also Anthony F. Spawforth, 'The Pamphleteer Ephippus, King Alexander and the Persian Royal Hunt', *Historia* 6 (2012), pp. 169–213.
10. Trittle, *From Melos to My Lai*, p. 56.
11. Ibid, 58, citing Shay.
12. J.R. Hamilton, 'Alexander and His So-Called Father', p. 151 and E. Badian, 'Alexander the Great and the Loneliness of Power', p. 203.
13. *Diagnostic and Statistical Manual of Mental Disorders*, American Psychiatric Association (Fourth Text Revision, 2000), pp. 690–693.
14. World Health Organization ICD-10 (jonline at: /en.wikipedia.org/wiki/Paranoid_personality_disorder).
15. E. Badian, 'Conspiracies', in Ian Worthington (ed.), *Alexander the Great: A Reader* (London, Routledge, 2003), pp. 277–295. Offers an excellent overview and analysis of the conspiracies Alexander believed were made against him.
16. Waldemar Heckel, 'The Conspiracy Against Philotas', *Phoenix* 31, no. 1 (Spring, 1977), p. 16.
17. E. Badian, 'The Death of Parmenio', *Transactions and Proceedings of the American Philological Association*, 91 (1960), p. 335.
18. Ibid, 326.
19. Ibid, 327.
20. Curtius, 7.27.
21. Justin, 12.5.
22. Ibid.
23. Curtius, 6.20.
24. Justin, 12.5.
25. Curtius, 6.7.

26. Heckel, 'The Conspiracy Against Philotas', pp. 21–22. See also E. Badian, 'The Death of Parmenio', p. 328, 334.
27. E. Badian, 'Conspiracies', p. 286.
28. Curtius, 8.43.
29. Arrian, 4.8.
30. Ibid, 4.13.
31. Ibid, 4.14.
32. Curtius, 8.14.
33. Arrian, 4.12.
34. See Arrian, 5.25–28 for an account of their grievances.
35. There is some debate as to whether Coenus died of disease or was killed by Alexander. I am following Holt here who argues there is no evidence that Coenus met his end by violence. See Frank L. Holt, 'Alexander the Great Today: In the Interest of Historical Accuracy', *Ancient History Bulletin* 13, no. 3 (1999), p. 112.
36. E. Badian, 'Alexander the Great and the Loneliness of Power', p. 200.
37. Bosworth, *Conquest and Empire*, pp. 139–142.
38. Arrian, 6.24 citing Nearchus.
39. Ibid.
40. Waldemar Heckel, *The Wars of Alexander the Great* (London, Routledge, 2002), p. 68.
41. Arrian, 6. 25–28 for a description of the march. De Selincourt's translation of Arrian who gives these figures for the strength of Alexander's army at the beginning of the march on p. 336, note 46.
42. Bosworth, *Conquest and Empire*, p. 145.
43. Plutarch, 66.4.
44. Curtius, 10.11; Arrian, 6.27.
45. E. Badian, 'Harpalus', *Journal of Hellenic Studies* 81 (1961), pp. 17–19.
46. Harpalus left Babylon in February, 324 BC.
47. Arrian, 7.24; Plutarch, 73.7.
48. Arrian, 7.4.
49. Alexander's solution to the problem of unemployed mercenaries was to issue a decree ordering the Greek states to readmit all soldiers who were exiled back into their societies.
50. Arrian, 7.8.
51. Curtius, 10.41.
52. Curtius, 10.39–42.
53. Arrian, 7.9.
54. Arrian, 7.12.
55. Curtius, 10.8.
56. For an analysis of the reinforcements sent to Alexander and the casualties incurred in his campaigns see Hammond, 'Casualties and Reinforcements of Citizen Soldiers in Greece and Macedonia', pp. 56–68; see also Worthington, 'How Great Was Alexander', in Worthington (ed.), *Alexander the Great: A Reader*, pp. 316–317, who argues with Bosworth that at least 30 per cent of Alexander's troops may have been killed in battle and another similar number wounded. If other factors such as disease and death

by natural causes are included, it seems inescapable that by the time of the Opis mutiny, the great Macedonian army had been worn to a nub and was by any standard of the day, combat ineffective.

57. Plutarch, 74.1.
58. While there is some debate, the most likely candidate is Demetrios.
59. Plutarch, 73.1. Arrian, 7.22–24.
60. Ibid, 75.1–2.
61. Ibid, 196.
62. E. Badian, 'Alexander the Great and the Loneliness of Power', pp. 202–204 and Hamilton, 'Alexander and His So-Called Father', p. 151, fn. 20 argue that at the end of his life Alexander was insane.
63. An excellent and comprehensive treatment of suicide in ancient Greece can be found in Elise P. Garrison, 'Attitudes Toward Suicide in Ancient Greece', *Transactions of the American Philological Association* 121 (1991), pp. 1–34.
64. Garrison, 'Attitudes Toward Suicide in Ancient Greece', p. 4.
65. Gabriel, 'American Military Psychiatry', p. 43.
66. In his response to Alexander, Cleitus gives us a glimpse into the nature and violence of the insurgency in Sogdiana when he says the province 'is far from being pacified, and cannot even be reduced to subjection. I am being sent against wild animals with bloodthirsty natures'. Curtius, 8.35.
67. Ibid, 8.38.
68. Ibid, 8.41
69. Trittle, 'Alexander and the Killing of Cleitus the Black', p. 137.
70. An interesting insight into how seriously Alexander took his claim that he was the son of a god.
71. Curtius, 8.52.
72. Ibid, 8.4.
73. Justin, 12.16.
74. Ibid, 12.6.
75. Curtius, 8.13.
76. Curtius, 8.12.
77. Justin, 11.6.
78. E. Badian, 'Alexander the Great and the Loneliness of Power', p. 200; Arrian 5.29 says that it was 'the only defeat he [Alexander] had ever suffered'.
79. Plutarch, 5.5.
80. Arrian, 6.9.
81. Curtius, 9.5.
82. Diodorus, 7.99
83. Arrian, 6.10.
84. Jacoby, *FgrH* 126, F 5.
85. Arrian, 7.14.
86. Ibid.
87. Ibid, 7.15.

**Chapter 8**

1. Plutarch, *Moralia*, p. 623.
2. Arrian, 4.8.2.
3. Curtius, 5.7.1.
4. Justin, 9.8.15.
5. T. Africa, *Critical Issues in History: The Ancient World* (Boston, 1967), p. 41; Green, *Alexander of Macedon*, p. 443.
6. A. McKinley, 'Ancient Experience With Intoxicating Drinks: Non-Attic Greek States', *Quarterly Journal of Studies on Alcohol*, 10 (1949), pp. 311–312.
7. Ibid.
8. Ephippus in Athenaeus, *The Deipnosophists*, translated by C. Gulick, IV (London, 1930), 10, p. 435.
9. The idea that a god can 'come into' or 'dwell within' a human being or an inanimate object is very old, and is first found in Egypt around 2800 BC. Modern Catholics believe that the Monstrance, an inanimate rendition of the sun and its rays placed on the altar, also contains the host, i.e., the presence of god. See my work on this subject in Richard A. Gabriel, *Gods of Our Fathers: The Memory of Egypt in Judaism and Christianity* (Westport, CT, Greenwood Press, 2002), pp. 35–50.
10. Euripides, *The Bacchae*, translated by W. Arrowsmith as quoted in D. Grene and R. Lattimore (eds), *Greek Tragedies* (Chicago, University of Chicago Press, 1966), pp. 279–286.
11. J.R. Hamilton, 'Alexander's Early Life', p. 117.
12. Plutarch, 2.9.
13. Ibid, 7.5.
14. Diodorus, 16.87.1.
15. C.F. Leventhal, *Drugs, Behaviour, and Modern Society* (Boston, Allyn Bacon, 1999), pp. 210–211.
16. E.O. Johnson *et. al.*, 'Extension of a Topology of Alcohol Dependence Based on Relative Genetic and Environmental Loading', *Alcoholism: Clinical and Experimental Research* 22 (1998), p. 1421.
17. Leventhal, pp. 210–211.
18. James Graham, *The Secret History of Alcoholism* (Virginia, Aculeus Press, 1994), p. 13.
19. Ephippus, *FgrH* 126 F. 3.
20. E.N. Borza, 'The Symposium at Alexander's Court', *Ancient Macedonia* 3 (1983).
21. Trittle, 'Alexander and the Killing of Cleitus the Black', p. 138; see also J. Herman, *Trauma and Recovery* (New York, Barnes and Noble, 1997), p. 44.
22. Diodorus, 17.16.3–4.
23. Plutarch, 17.9.
24. Curtius, 3.12.2.
25. Ibid, 5.7.3–5.
26. Ibid, 6.2.1–5.
27. For a list of the symposia see John O'Brien, *Alexander the Great: The Invisible Enemy*, p. 259.
28. Arrian, 5.2.7.

29. J.R. Hamilton, 'Alexander and His "So-Called" Father', p. 151.
30. Aelian, 3.23.
31. Graham, 156.
32. Arrian, 2.3.7.
33. Lowell Edmunds, 'The Religiosity of Alexander', in Joseph Roisman (ed), *Alexander the Great: Answers and Modern Perspectives* (Lexington, MA, D.C. Heath, 1995), p. 174.
34. N.G.L. Hammond, 'Alexander's Personality', in Ian Worthington, *Alexander the Great: A Reader* (London, Routledge, 2003), p. 300 for a list of the portents that Alexander witnessed. Alexander may have had good reason to believe that the gods favoured him, for at each crucial juncture in his life the portents proved true in that his good fortune held. Alexander might well have agreed with old Oedipus in that 'in all the signs the gods themselves have given me, they never played my false'.
35. E. Badian, 'The Deification of Alexander the Great', in Roisman (ed.), *Alexander the Great* p. 190. See also Bosworth, *Conquest and Empire*, p. 278.
36. Peter Green, *Alexander the Great and the Hellenistic Age* (London, Orion books, 2008), p. 60.
37. E. Badian, 'The Deification of Alexander the Great', p. 191.
38. E. Badian, 'Alexander the Great Between Two Thrones and Heaven: Variations on an Old Theme', in Alastair Small (ed), *Subject and Ruler: The Cult of the Ruling Power in Classical Antiquity*, *Journal of Roman Archaeology* 17 (13–15 April), 1994, pp. 11–26.
39. Plutarch, 3.3; see also Bosworth, 282.
40. Arrian, 3.3.2.
41. Bosworth, 283.
42. J.P.V.D. Balsdon, 'The Divinity of Alexander', *Historia* 1, no. 3 (1950), p. 378 notes that the senior officer corps was worried about Alexander's megalomania.
43. Bosworth, 282.
44. Ibid, 375.
45. Bosworth, 286.
46. P. Brunt, 'The Aims of Alexander', *Greece and Rome* 12, no. 2 (October, 1965), p. 209.
47. Swank and Marchand, 'Combat Neuroses', p. 230 for an examination of religiosity in combat psychiatric cases.
48. Jacoby, *FgrH* 81, F. 4.
49. Arrian, 7.23.2.
50. Jacoby, *FgrH* 126, F. 5.
51. Ibid.
52. Green, *Alexander of Macedon*, p. 453.
53. I.B. Weiner and W.E. Craighead, *The Corsini Encyclopedia of Psychology: Volume 3* (2010), p. 977.
54. Diodorus, 18.4.4.
55. Arrian, 7.20; see also Green, *Alexander the Great and the Hellenistic Age*, p. 24.
56. Arrian, 7.19 for Alexander's plans; see also Green, *Alexander the Great and the Hellenistic Age*, p. 24.
57. Gabriel, *Philip II of Macedonia: Greater Than Alexander*, pp. 83–85.

58. For the *chevauchee* see Richard A. Gabriel, *Empires At War* vol 3 (Westport, CT, Greenwood Press, 2005), p. chapter 28.
59. Arrian, 19.8.
60. Justin, 15.
61. Holt, *Into the Land of Bones*, p. 151.
62. Bosworth estimates that over the life of Alexander's campaigns, 30 per cent of the army was killed in action. This does not count the wounded, those who died of disease, those left behind when sick, or those forcibly settled in colonies. Alexander's army had been virtually annihilated during its long campaign. See Worthington, 'How Great Was Alexander?', *Ancient History Bulletin* (1999), p. 2.
63. For a balanced treatment of the possibility of Alexander's murder see A.B. Bosworth, 'The Death of Alexander the Great: Rumour and Propaganda', *Classical Quarterly* 21, no. 1 (May, 1971), pp. 112–136.

**Chapter 9**

1. For an analysis of Philip's achievements, see Gabriel, *Philip of Macedon*.
2. Diodorus, 17. 3–5; Green, *Alexander the Great*, p. 158.
3. Hammond, 'Casualties and Reinforcements of Citizen Soldiers in Greece and Macedonia', p. 68.
4. Ibid.
5. Ibid.
6. P.A. Brunt, *Nearchus' Indica* (Cambridge, MA, Harvard University Press, 1983), pp. 489–490.
7. Ibid.
8. Green, *Alexander the Great: A Historical Biography*, p. 413.
9. Gaebel, *Cavalry Operations in the Ancient World*, p. 213.
10. For an account of Philip's innovations in Macedonian siege capability see E.W. Marsden, 'Macedonian Military Machinery and Its Designers Under Philip and Alexander', *Ancient Macedonia* (1968), pp. 211–223.
11. An analysis of Alexander's six sieges can be found in *Ancient Warfare*, iv, no. 2 (2012), pp. 17–21.
12. Brunt, *Indica*, p. 335.
13. Gabriel, 'The Persian Army and Alexander the Great', in *Empires at War*, pp. 313–314.
14. Brunt, *Indica*, p. 453.
15. For Alexander's tactics see A.R. Burn, 'Alexander the Great', *Greece and Rome* 12, no. 2 (October, 1965), pp. 146–154. See also Gaebel, pp. 183–193.
16. With his advance blocked in Thessaly, Philip had his soldiers cut steps into a mountain cliff, crossed the mountain, and took the enemy by surprise. Gabriel, *Philip of Macedonia*, pp. 117–121.
17. Christopher Matthew and W.W. How, 'Arms, Tactics, and Strategy in the Persian Wars', *Journal of Hellenic Studies* 43.2 (2013), pp. 117–132.
18. Jim Lacey, 'The Persian Fallacy', *Military History* (July, 2012), pp. 50–51.
19. Buddha Prakash, *History of the Punjab*, Punjabi University Patiala Publications Bureau (1997), p. 225.

20. Green, *Alexander the Great*, p. 338.
21. Valerii Nikonorov, *The Armies of Bactria, 700 BC–450 AD* (Stockpot: PA, Montvery Publications, 1997) for the tactics of the Bactrian combatants that Alexander faced.
22. Curtius, 7.7.39.
23. Arrian, 4.6.
24. Holt, *Into the Land of Bones: Alexander the Great in Afghanistan*, p. 57.
25. Curtuis, 6.17.
26. Arrian, 1.5.10; see also Gaebel p. 194, for other citations in Arrian on the same subject.
27. Diodorus, 17.17.3–5.
28. Green, *Alexander the Great*, p. 353.
29. Holt, *Into the Land of Bones*, p. 107.
30. Nearchus, *Indica*, 16. 1–9.
31. Duncan Head, *Armies of the Macedonian and Punic Wars, 359 BC to 146 BC* (Sutton, UK, Wargames Research Group (1982), p. 137.
32. Nearchus, *Indica*, 9.17.
33. Ibid.
34. Head, 139.
35. Nearchus, *Indica*, 10.2–9.
36. Ibid.
37. A.K. Narin, 'Alexander and India', *Greece and Rome* vol. 12, no. 2 (1965), pp. 155–165.
38. Burn, 'The Generalship of Alexander', *Greece and Rome* vol. 12, no. 2, pp. 142–143, for Alexander's debt to his officers.
39. Guy MacLean Rogers, *Alexander: The Ambiguity of Greatness* (New York, Random House, 2004), p. 222.
40. Ibid.
41. Cawkwell, *Philip of Macedon*, p. 164.

# Bibliography

**Works Cited**

Ackerknecht, Erwin H, *A Short History of Medicine* (Baltimore, MD, Johns Hopkins University Press, 1982).

Africa, T, *Critical Issues in History: The Ancient World* (Boston, 1967).

Aldrete, Gregory S., Scott Bartell, and Alicia Alorete, *Reconstructing Ancient Linen Body Armour: Unraveling the Linothorax Mystery* (Baltimore, MD, Johns Hopkins University Press, 2013).

Andronikos, Anolis, 'The Royal Tombs at Agae (Vergina)', in *Philip of Macedon* edited by Hatzopoulous and Loukopoulos (Athens Ekdotike Athenon, 1980), pp. 188–231.

Badian, Ernst, 'Conspiracies', in Ian Worthington (ed.), *Alexander the Great: A Reader* (London, Routledge, 2003), pp. 277–295.

Badian, Ernst, 'Alexander the Great Between Two Thrones and Heaven: Variations on an Old Theme' in Alastair Small (ed.) 'Subject and Ruler: The Cult of Ruling Power in Classical Antiquity' *Journal of Roman Archaeology*, 17 (13–15 April 1994), pp. 11–26.

Badian, Ernst, 'The Battle of the Granicus', *Ancient Macedonia* (August, 1977), pp. 271–293.

Badian, Ernst, 'Alexander the Great and the Loneliness of Power', in E. Badian (ed.), *Studies in Greek and Roman History* (New York, Barnes and Noble 1964), pp. 192–205.

Badian, Ernst, 'Harpalus', *Journal of Hellenic Studies*, 81 (1961), pp. 16–43

Badian, Ernst, 'The Death of Parmenio', *Transactions and Proceedings of the Americal Philological Association*, 91 (1960), pp. 324–338.

Badian, Ernst, 'The Deification of Alexander the Great', in Roisman, *Alexander the Great: Answers and Modern Perspectives*, pp. 188–201.

Balsdon, 'The Divinity of Alexander', 1, no. 3, pp. 363–388.

Barnett, William S, 'Only the Bad Died Young in the Ancient Middle East', *Journal of Development* 21, no. 2 (1985), pp. 155–160.

Belenky, Gregory, *Israeli Battle Shock Casualties: 1973 to 1982* (Washington, D. C., Walter Reed Army Institute of Research Report, 1983).

Bertolotti, M, *La Critica Medica Nell Storia Alessandro Magno* (1933).

Borza, Eugene, 'Malaria in Alexander's Army', *Ancient History Bulletin* 1.2 (1987), pp. 36–38.

Borza, Eugene, 'The Symposium at Alexander's Court', *Ancient Macedonia* 3 (1983), pp. 45–55.

Borza, Eugene, 'Origins of the Royal Macedonian House', *Hesperia* 19 (1982), pp. 7–13.

Borza, Eugene, 'The Symposium at Alexander's Court', *Archaia Macedonia* 3 (September, 1977), pp. 45–55.

Bosworth, A. B, *Conquest and Empire: The Reign of Alexander the Great* (Cambridge, UK, Cambridge University Press, 1988).

Bosworth, A. B, 'The Death of Alexander the Great: Rumour and Propaganda', *Classical Quarterly* 1 (May, 1971), pp. 112–136.

Bowersock, G. W (trans), Xenophon, *On The Art of Horsemanship* (Cambridge, MA, Harvard University Press, 1968).

Blyth, P. H, *The Effectiveness of Greek Armour Against Arrows in the Persian Wars (490–479 B.C.): An Interdisciplinary Inquiry* (Unpublished thesis, Reading, UK, 1977).

Bradford Welles, C. (trans), Diodorus of Sicily, *Histories* (Harvard, MA, Harvard University Press, 1963).

Brunt, Peter, *Nearchus' Indica* (Cambridge, MA, Harvard University Press, 1983).

Brunt, Peter, 'The Aims of Alexander', *Greece and Rome* 12, no. 2 (October, 1965), pp. 205–215.

Burn, A. R, 'Alexander the Great', *Greece and Rome* 12, no. 2 (October, 1965), pp. 146–154.

Burn, A. R, 'The Generalship of Alexander', *Greece and Rome* 12, no. 2 (1965), pp. 140–147.

Cartledge, Paul, *Alexander the Great* (New York, Vintage Books, 2005).

Carney, Elizabeth, 'Elite Education and High Culture in Macedonia', in Waldemar Heckel and Lawrence A. Trittle (eds), *Alexander the Great: A New History* (Malden, MA, Wiley-Blackwell, 2009), pp. 55–60.

Carney, Elizabeth, 'The Politics of Polygamy: Olympias, Alexander, and the Murder of Philip', *Historia* 41, No. 2 (1992) pp. 169–189.

Cawkwell, George, *Philip of Macedon* (London, Faber and Faber, 1978).

Claverhouse Jebb, Richard (trans), *The Complete Plays of Sophocles: Ajax* (London, Bantam, 1982).

Clement, P (trans), Plutarch, *Moralia* (VIII London, 1969).

Davidson, James, 'Bonkers About Boys', *London review of Books* (1 November, 2013), pp. 7–10.

Davidson, James, *The Greeks and Greek Love* (London, Weidenfeld, 2007).

Davies, Roy, 'Some Roman Military Medicine', *Medical History* 14 (January, 1970), pp. 101–106.

*Diagnostic and Statistical Manual of Mental Disorders* (American Psychiatric Association, Fourth Edition Revision, 2000).

Dover, Kenneth, *Greek Homosexuality* (Cambridge, MA, Harvard University Press, 1978).

Dyer, Wynne, *War* (New York, Crown Publishers, 1985).

Edmunds, Lowell, 'The Religiosity of Alexander', in Joseph Roisman (ed.), *Alexander the Great: Answers and Modern Perspectives* (Lexington, MA, D.C. Heath, 1995), pp. 172–188.

Ellis, John R, 'The Unification of Macedonia', in Miltiades B. Hatzopoulos and Louisa D. Loukopoulos (eds), *Philip of Macedon* (Athens, Ekdotike Athenon, 1980), pp. 36–47.

Ellis, John R, 'Macedonian Under Philip', in *Philip of Macedon*, edited by Hatzopoulos and Loukopoulos, pp. 146–165.

Ellis, John R, 'The Stepbrothers of Philip II', *Historia* 22 (1973), pp. 348–356.

Ellis, John R, 'Population Transplants Under Philip II', *Makedonika* 9 (1969), pp 9–16.

Engels, Donald, 'A Note on Alexander's Death', *Classical Philology* 73 (July, 1978), pp. 224–228.

Engels, Donald, *Alexander the Great and the Logistics of the Macedonian Army* (Berkeley, CA, University of California Press, 1978).

Fagles, Robert (trans), *Iliad* (London, Penguin, 1998).

Fields, Nic and Brian Delf, *Ancient Greek Fortifications, 500–300 BC* (London, Osprey Publishers, 2006).

Foss, Clive, 'The Battle of the Granicus: A New Look', *Ancient Macedonia* (August, 1977), pp. 495–502.

Fredricksmeyer, E. A, 'Alexander and Philip: Emulation and Resentment', *Classical Journal* 85, no. 4 (April–May, 1990), pp. 300–315.

Fuller, J.F.C, *The Generalship of Alexander the Great* (New York, Da Capo Press, 1960).

Gabriel, Richard A, 'War, Madness, and Military Psychiatry', *Military History* (forthcoming, 2014), pp. 45–49.

Gabriel, Richard A, 'Bugs, Bullets and Bones: Death, Disease, Casualties, and Military Medicine in the Soviet War in Afghanistan', *Military History* (forthcoming, 2014).

Gabriel, Richard A, *Between Flesh and Steel: A History of Military Medicine from the Middle Ages to the War in Afghanistan* (Dulles, VA, Potomac Books, 2013).

Gabriel, Richard A, 'Alexander the Monster', *Military History Quarterly* (summer, 2013), pp. 11–14.

Gabriel, Richard A, *Man and Wound in the Ancient World: A History of Military Medicine from Sumer to the Fall of Constantinople* (Dulles, VA, Potomac Books, 2012).

Gabriel, Richard A, 'The Roman Military Medical Corps' *Military History* (January, 2011), pp. 39–44.

Gabriel, Richard A, *Hannibal: The Military Biography of Rome's Greatest Enemy* (Dulles, VA, Potomac Books, 2011).

Gabriel, Richard A, *Philip of Macedonia: Greater Than Alexander* (Dulles, VA, Potomac Books, 2010).

Gabriel, Richard A, 'Can We Trust the Ancient Texts?', *Military History* (March–April, 2008), pp. 63–69.

Gabriel, Richard A, *Soldiers' Lives Through History: The Ancient World* (Westport, CT, Greenwood Press, 2007).

Gabriel, Richard A, *Empires At War* 3 (Westport, CT, Greenwood Press, 2005).

Gabriel, Richard A, 'The Persian Army and Alexander the Great', in *Empires At War*, pp. 306–368.

Gabriel, Richard A, *Gods of Our Fathers: The Memory of Egypt in Judaism and Christianity* (Westport, CT, Greenwood Press, 2002).

Gabriel, Richard A. and Karen S. Metz, *The History of Military Medicine* vol. 1 (Westport, CT, Greenwood Press, 1992).

Gabriel, Richard A. and Karen S. Metz, *From Sumer To Rome: The Military Capabilities of Ancient Armies* (Westport, CT, Greenwood Press, 1991).

Gabriel, Richard A, *No More Heroes: Madness and Psychiatry in War* (New York, Hill and Wang, 1987).

Gaebel, Robert E, *Cavalry Operations in the Ancient Greek World* (Norman, OK, University of Oklahoma Press, 2002).

Garrison, Elise P, 'Attitudes Toward Suicide in Ancient Greece', *Transactions of the American Philological Association* 121 (1991), pp. 1–34.

Garrison, Fielding H, *An Introduction to the History of Military Medicine* (London, W.B. Saunders, 1967).

Garrison, Fielding H, *Notes on the History of Military Medicine* (Washington, D.C., Association of Military Surgeons, 1922).

Gerig, Bruce, 'Greek Homosexuality', internet epistle 1–10 (epistle.us/hbarticles/greeks.html, 2013).

Ginsberg, Eli, *The Lost Divisions* (New York, Columbia University Press, 1950).

Gulick, C. B (trans), Athenaeus (London, Loeb Classical Library, William Heinemann Ltd., 1930).

Goldsworthy, Adrian, *The Roman Army at War* (Oxford, UK, Clarendon Press, 1996).

Graham, A. J, 'The Historical Significance of Philip of Macedon', in Elin C. Danien (ed.), *The World of Philip and Alexander* (Philadelphia, University of Pennsylvania Museum of Archaeology and Anthropology, 1990), pp. 1–14.
Graham, James, *The Secret History of Alcoholism* (Virginia, Aculeus Press, 1994).
Green, Peter, *Alexander the Great and the Hellenistic Age* (London, Orion Books, 2008).
Green, Peter, *Alexander of Macedon: A Historical Biography* (Berkeley, University of California Press, 1991).
Green, Peter, *Alexander of Macedon* (Harmondsworth, 1974).
Grossman, David, *On Killing: The Psychological Cost of Learning to Kill in War and Society* (Boston, Little Brown, 2009).
Hamilton, J. R, 'Alexander's Early Life', *Greece and Rome* vol. 12, no. 2 (October, 1965), pp. 117–124.
Hamilton, J. R, 'Alexander and His So-Called Father', *Classical Quarterly* 3 (1953), pp. 151–157.
Hammond, N.G.L, 'Royal Pages, Personal Pages, and Boys Trained in the Macedonian Manner During the Period of the Temenid Monarchy', *Historia* 39 (1990), pp. 261–290.
Hammond, N.G.L, *The Macedonian State: Origins, Institutions, and History* (Oxford UK, Clarendon Press, 1989).
Hammond, N.G.L, 'Casualties and Reinforcements of Citizen Soldiers in Greece and Macedonia', *Journal of Hellenic Studies* 109 (1989), pp. 56–68.
Hammond, N.G.L, *Three Historians of Alexander the Great: The So-Called Vulgate Authors* (Cambridge, UK, Cambridge University Press, 1983).
Hammond, N.G.L, 'The Battle of the Granicus River', *Journal of Hellenic Studies* 100 (1980), pp. 73–88.
Hammond, N.G.L, *Alexander the Great: King, Commander, and Statesman* (Princeton, NJ, Princeton University Press, 1980).
Hammond, N.G.L. and G.T. Griffith, *A History of Macedonia* 2 vols (Oxford, UK, Oxford University Press, 1979).
Hammond, N.G.L, 'Alexander's Campaign in Illyria', *Journal of Hellenic Studies* 94 (1974), pp. 66–87.
Hammond, N.G.L, 'Alexander's Personality', in Ian Worthington (ed.), *Alexander the Great: A Reader*, pp. 299–302.
Hanson, Victor Davis, 'Alexander the Killer', *Great Commanders* (fall, 2002), pp. 55–60.
Hanson, Victor Davis, 'Alexander', *Military History Quarterly* (summer, 1998), pp. 10–14.
Hastings, Max, *Military Anecdotes* (New York, Oxford University Press, 1985).
Hatzopouloss, Miltiades B. and Louisa D. Loukopoulos (eds), *Philip of Macedon* (Athens, Ekdotike Athenon, 1980).
Head, Duncan, *Armies of the Macedonian and Punic Wars, 359 BC to 146 BC* (Sutton, UK, Wargames Research Group, 1982).
Heckel, Waldemar, *The Wars of Alexander the Great* (London, Routledge, 2002).
Heckel, Waldemar, 'The Conspiracy Against Philotas', *Phoenix* 31, no. 1 (spring, 1977), pp. 14–22.
Herman, J, *Trauma and Recovery* (New York, Global Books, 1997).
Holt, Frank L, 'Alexander the Great Today: In the Interest of Historical Accuracy', *Ancient History Bulletin* 13, no. 2 (1999), pp.111–117.
Holt, Frank L, *Into the Land of Bones: Alexander the Great in Afghanistan* (Berkeley, University of California Press, 2005).
Jacoby, F, *Die Fragmente der griechischen Historiker* (FgrH) (Berlin and Leiden, 1923).

Kouretas, D, 'The Oracle of Trophonius: A Kind of Shock Treatment Associated with Sensory Deprivation in Greece', *British Journal of Psychiatry* 113, no. 505 (1979), pp. 1441–1446.

Krentz, Peter and E.L. Wheeler (ed., trans), Polyaenus, *Stratagems of War* vol. 1 (Chicago, Ares Publishers, 1994).

Lacy, James, 'The Persian Fallacy', *Military History* (July, 2012), pp. 50–54.

Lambert, F, 'Alexanders Verwundung in der Stadt der Maller und die Damalige Heilkunde' (1960).

Lascaratos, John, 'The Wounding of Alexander the Great in Cyropolis: The First Reported Case of the Syndrome of Cortical Blindness', *History of Ophthalmology* 42 (November–December, 1997), pp. 285–286.

Leventhal, C. F, *Drugs, Behaviour, and Modern Society* (Boston, Allyn Bacon, 1999).

Lendering, Jona, 'Cleitarchus', in Alexander the Great, http://www.livius.org/cg-cm/cleitarchus/cleitarchus.html.

Li Donnici, Lynn R, *The Epidaurian Miracle Inscriptions: Texts, Translations, and Commentary* (Atlanta, GA, Scholars Press, 1995).

Lorenzi, Rossella, 'Laminated Linen Protected Alexander the Great', paper at *Annual Conference of the Archaeological Institute of America* (Anaheim, CA, 10 January 2010).

Macaulay, G. C (trans), Herodotus, *The Histories* (New York, Barnes and Noble, 2004).

Musgrave, Jonathan H., A.J. Prag, and R. Neave, 'The Skull from Tomb II at Vergina: Kings Philip II of Macedon', *Journal of Hellenic Studies* 104 (1984), pp. 63–78.

Matthew, Christopher and W.W. How, 'Arms, Tactics, and Strategy in the Persian Wars', *Journal of Hellenic Studies* 43, no. 2 (2013), pp. 117–132.

Marsden, E. W, 'Macedonian Military Machinery and Its Designers Under Philip and Alexander', *Ancient Macedonia* (1968), pp. 211–223.

Marlowe, David, *Cohesion, Anticipated Breakdown, and Endurance in Battle* (Washington, DC, Walter Reed Army Institute of Research Report, 1979).

McKinley, A, 'Ancient Experience With Intoxicating Drinks: Non-Attic States', *Quarterly Journal of Studies On Alcohol* 10 (1949), pp. 309–316.

Manjo, Guido, *The Healing Hand* (Cambridge, MA, Harvard University Press, 1975).

Marshal, S.L.A, *Men Against Fire* (Gloucester, MA, Peter Smith, 1978).

Matthew, Christopher, 'Testing Herodotus', *Ancient Warfare* (May, 2011), pp. 41–46.

McKeon, Richard, *The Basic Works of Aristotle* (New York, Random House, 1941).

Mendelsohn, Daniel, 'Battle Lines', *New Yorker* (November, 7, 2011), pp. 75–76.

Miller, Emanuel, *Neuroses in War* (New York, Macmillan, 1942).

Nikonorov, Valerii, *The Armies of Bactria: 700 BC–450 AD* (Stockport, PA, Montvery Publications, 1997).

Narin, A. K, 'Alexander and India', *Greece and Rome* 12, no.2 (1965), pp. 155–156.

O'Brien, John M, *Alexander the Great: The Invisible Enemy* (London, Routledge, 1992).

O'Brien, John M, 'The Enigma of Alexander: The Alcohol Factor', *Annals of Scholarship* 1 (1980), pp. 31–46.

O'Brien, John M, 'Alexander and Dionysus: The Invisible Enemy', *Annals of Scholarship* 1 (1980), pp. 31–46.

Ogden, Daniel, 'Alexander's Sex Life', in Heckel and Trittle (eds), pp. 203–217.

Oldach, David W, Robert E. Richmond, Eugene N. Borza, and R. Michael Benitez, 'A Mysterious Death', *New England Journal of Medicine* 338 (Boston, 11 June 1998), pp. 1764–1770.

Papageorgiu, M. G, 'Incubation as a Form of Psychotherapy in the Care of Patients in Ancient Greece', *Psychotherapy* 26 (1975), pp. 35–38.

Parke, H. W, 'The Massacre of the Branchidae', *Journal of Hellenic Studies* 105 (1985), pp. 59–68.

Perin, Bernadette (trans), Plutarch, *The Parallel Lives* (Loeb Classical Library, 1919).

Prakash, Buddha, *History of the Punjab* (Punjabi University Patiala Publications Bureau, 1997),

Rogers, Guy MacLean, *Alexander: The Ambiguity of Greatness* (New York, Random House, 2004),

Rolleston, J. D, 'Alcoholism in Classical Antiquity', *British Journal of Inebriety* 24 (1927), pp. 101–120,

Romano, Jon, 'Temples, Asylums, or Hospitals?', *Journal of the National 'association of Private Psychiatric Hospitals* 9, no. 4 (summer, 1978), pp. 5–12.

Rouse, W.H.D. (trans), Xenophon, *Anabasis* (Ann Arbor, University of Michigan Press, 1958).

Sabin, Philip, 'The Face of Roman Battle', *Journal of Roman Studies* 90 (2000), pp. 15–29.

Sabin, Philip, 'The Mechanics of Battle in the Second Punic War', in Tim Cornell, Boris Rankov, and Philip Sabin (eds), *The Second Punic War: A Reappraisal* (London, Institute for Classical Studies, University of London 1966), pp. 34–72.

Samuel, Alan E, 'Philip and Alexander as Kings: Macedonian Monarchy and Merovingian Parallels', *American Historical Review* 93, no. 5 (December, 1988), pp. 1270–1286.

Salazar, Christine F, *The Treatment of War Wounds in Graeco-Roman Antiquity* (Boston, Brill, 2000).

Sarton, George, *Galen of Pergamon* (Lawrence, KS, University of Kansas Press, 1954).

Selincourt, Aubrey De (trans), Lucius Flavius Arrianus, *The Campaigns of Alexander* (London, Penguin Books, 1971).

Shay, Jonathan, *Achilles in Vietnam* (New York, Scriber, 1994).

Spawforth, Anthony F, 'The Pamphleteer Eohippus, King Alexander and the Persian Royal Hunt', *Historia* 6 (2012), pp. 169–213.

Starr, Chester G, *A History of the Ancient World* (New York, Oxford University Press, 1974).

Swank, Roy L. and Walter E. Marchand, 'Combat Neuroses: The Development of Combat Exhaustion', *Archives of Neurology and Psychiatry* 55 (1946), pp. 232–254.

Thomas, Carol, 'What You Seek Is Here: Alexander the Great', *Journal of the Historical Society* 7 (March, 2007), pp. 61–83.

Trittle, Lawrence A, 'Alexander and the Killing of Cleitus the Black', in Heckel (ed.), *Crossroads of History: Alexander the Great* (2002), pp. 127–146.

Trittle, Lawrence A, *From Melos to My Lai* (New York, Routledge, 2000).

Tsouras, Peter, *Alexander: Invincible King of Macedonia* (Dulles, VA, Potomac Books, 1997).

Vollet, J. J, 'De Characters Particuliers et du Traitment de la Blessure d'Alexandre le Grande' (1987).

Wagner, Robert B. and Benjamin Slivko, 'History of Nonpenetrating Chest Trauma and Its Treatment', *Maryland Medical Journal* 37 (April, 1988), pp. 297–304.

Wasserman, Jules, *Principles of Dynamic Psychiatry* (Philadelphia, W.B. Saunders, 1961).

Watson, John Shelby (trans), Marcus Junianus Justin, *Epitome of the Philippic History of Pompeius Trogus* (London, Henry G. Bohn Press, 1853).

Weiner, I.B. and W.E. Craig, *The Corsini Encyclopedia of Psychology* (2010).

Worthington, Ian, *Philip of Macedon* (New Haven, Yale University Press, 2008).

Worthington, Ian, 'How Great Was Alexander the Great?', *Ancient History Bulletin* 13 (1999), pp. 44–49.

Yardley, John (trans), Quintius Curtius Rufus, *History of Alexander* (London, Penguin Classics, 1984).

# Index